A CHRISTIAN'S STUDY OF THE BIBLE

(The Hebrew Scriptures and the Christian Scriptures - including an explanation of the 400 years between)

Library of Congress © 2016 Patricia J. Setter
ISBN-13: 978-1533217912
Title I.D.: 6267592

COPYRIGHTS AND ACKNOWLEGEMENTS:

As stated above, I chose to use the KJV Open Bible (1978) for my study. That bible has since been revised and pronouns referring to God are now gender-neutral (after all, God is not human, but is Spirit!). It is my hope that the reader will understand that words such as "mankind" are meant to include all of humankind.

Permission was obtained from Pastor Tania Haber to include her sermon entitled "The Ten Commandments – Tying together the Hebrew Scriptures and the Christian Scriptures." (pgs. 155-160)

No permission was needed to use the anonymous introduction to the Christian Scriptures. (pg. 161)

All illustrations were purchased from istock.com.

PREFACE

This bible study and summary is a work of love. . .

A number of years ago, out of a lack of knowledge of the bible or its history, I made a decision to read both the Old Testament (Hebrew Scriptures) and the New Testament (Christian Scriptures) through one time. Or so I told myself. That first read-through left me puzzled. For the most part, I did not understand what I was reading – or how the parts (or books) of the bible fit together.

With a determination to make sense of the bible, I read it through another time. Slowly, historical pictures began to take shape. And I found other versions of the bible to help in my understanding.

Another read-through – and I decided to approach this as one would approach a classroom assignment: I began to take notes – many notes.

Handwritten notes became notes in a document on the computer. I began to see the panorama of God's intentions towards mankind – His determination to guide people towards Him – and towards life everlasting.

While this bible study includes all the books of the bible, please note that it is a summary and not the entire bible. Where possible, I attempted to tie together significant events from book to book. Then, in order to create a bridge between the Hebrew Scriptures and the Christian Scriptures, I added what I hope is helpful information about the years between the scriptures. That time period of about 400 years was an extremely active political time and events that took place during that period shaped the political atmosphere into which was born our Lord and Savior Jesus Christ.

It is hoped that this study and summary will give new meaning to your readings of the Word of God – and encourage you to delve into the full scriptures. Perhaps there you will find the Spirit of God and His grace – His unmerited favor.

DEDICATION

To all my beloved family members and friends and especially my dear husband Richard.

Patricia J. Setter
6/2016

INTRODUCTION

The Bible is the book of redemption for fallen mankind.

We are redeemed from the penalty of sin - and from Satan's power and evil - **by the price Jesus paid for us on the cross.**

The **Bible is** superior to all other books, because it is **divinely inspired by God**.

The Holy Spirit is the real author of the Bible.

The Bible was produced over a period **of some 15 centuries** by a variety of authors. The books of the Hebrew Scriptures (the Old Testament) were not in written form for centuries. The words of the prophets were passed down from generation to generation, until they were written down, collected together and translated (many times), finally reaching the form in which we have them today.

The Old Testament was originally written in three different **languages: Hebrew, Aramaic and Greek.**

The New Testament was written in Greek (the universal language of Christ's time).

These notes and quotes are only a "taste" of the Bible. They are not meant - in any way - to take the place of Bible reading or Bible study.

It is hoped that perhaps something within these notes about - and selected quotations from - the Bible may encourage the reader to dip into the Word of God given to us in the Bible - and there find God's love and grace.

TABLE OF CONTENTS

39 Hebrew Scriptures
(The Old Testament)

Title	Pg.
Introduction to the 39 Books of the Hebrew Scriptures (the Old Testament)	1
The First Book of Moses Commonly Called Genesis	3
The Second Book of Moses Commonly Called Exodus	15
The Third Book of Moses Commonly Called Leviticus	25
The Fourth Book of Moses Commonly Called Numbers	27
The Fifth Book of Moses Commonly Called Deuteronomy	31
The Book of Joshua	33
The Book of Judges	37
The Book of Ruth	39
Introduction to the Books of Samuel and Kings	41
The First Book of Samuel	43
The Second Book of Samuel	47
The First Book of the Kings	51
The Second Book of the Kings	57
The First Book of the Chronicles	63
The Second Book of the Chronicles	67
The Book of Ezra	75
The Book of Nehemiah	79
The Book of Esther	83
The Book of Job	87
The Psalms	89
The Proverbs	95
The Book of Ecclesiastes	101
The Song of Solomon	103
The Book of Isaiah	105
The Book of Jeremiah	109
The Lamentations of Jeremiah	115
The Book of Ezekiel	117

TABLE OF CONTENTS (continued)

39 Hebrew Scriptures
(The Old Testament)
(continued)

Title	Pg.
The Book of Daniel	119
The Book of Hosea	121
The Book of Joel	123
The Book of Amos	125
The Book of Obadiah	127
The Book of Jonah	129
The Book of Micah	131
The Book of Nahum	133
The Book of Habakkuk	135
The Book of Zephaniah	137
The Book of Haggai	139
The Book of Zechariah	141
The Book of Malachi	143

27 Christian Scriptures
(The New Testament)

Title	Pg.
The time between the Hebrew Scriptures (the Old Testament) and the Christian Scriptures (the New Testament)	145
The Ten Commandments – Tying together the Hebrew Scriptures and the Christian Scriptures (a Sermon by Pastor Tania Haber)	155
Introduction to the 27 Books of the Christian Scriptures (the New Testament)	161
The political climate of Judea at the time of Jesus' birth	163
The New Testament begins with the Four Gospels ("good news"): Matthew, Mark, Luke and John	167

TABLE OF CONTENTS (continued)

27 Christian Scriptures
(The New Testament)
(continued)

Title	Pg.
The Gospel According to Matthew	169
The Gospel According to Mark	181
The Gospel According to Luke	191
The Gospel According to John	213
The Acts of the Apostles	229
Introduction to the Epistles	251
The Epistle of Paul to the Romans	253
The First Epistle of Paul to the Corinthians	257
The Second Epistle of Paul to the Corinthians	259
The Epistle of Paul to the Galatians	261
The Epistle of Paul to the Ephesians	263
The Epistle of Paul to the Philippians	265
The Epistle of Paul to the Colossians	267
The First Epistle of Paul to the Thessalonians	269
The Second Epistle of Paul to the Thessalonians	271
The First Epistle of Paul to Timothy	273
The Second Epistle of Paul to Timothy	275
The Epistle of Paul to Titus	277
The Epistle of Paul to Philemon	277
The Epistle of Paul to the Hebrews	279
The Epistle of James	283
The First Epistle of Peter	285
The Second Epistle of Peter	287
The First Epistle of John	289
The Second Epistle of John	291
The Third Epistle of John	291
The Epistle of Jude	293
The Revelation to John (The Apocalypse)	295
Resources	303

INTRODUCTION TO THE 39 BOOKS OF THE HEBREW SCRIPTURES (THE OLD TESTAMENT)

Although creation has been - through the years and continues to be today – the **subject of heated debate**, the fields of science and astronomy are now acknowledging evidence which supports the theory of creation as set forth in the bible.

While a "day" as we know it (24 hours in length), has, no doubt, a different meaning for God, it is now becoming an accepted belief that the world, and all that is in it, did not "evolve" in and of itself (i.e., Darwin's Theory), but came about over a **very long period of time**, as is so simply stated in Genesis. **The hand of God** (referred to by some scientists as Intelligent Design) **brought the world into being**. Hence, God is the creator and mastermind of what we know as evolution.

It is my personal belief that the distinct break between ancient hominids (no longer in existence) and "mankind" as we know it to be, came about when God imbued the first humans with immortal souls made in His likeness.

It is believed that **Moses** is the **author of** the **first five books of the bible: Genesis, Exodus, Leviticus, Numbers and Deuteronomy -** or 1/6th of the Old Testament (also known as the Hebrew scriptures).

These five foundational **books of the Old Testament** are oftentimes **referred to as the "Pentateuch"** ("five scrolls") and they comprise "The Law," which is also **known as the Torah.**

With the exception of Genesis, the other four books of the Pentateuch tell us about God's revelation to Israel and Moses' 40 years of leadership, as he brings God's people on their sojourn out of Egypt into Canaan.

The **"Tetrateuch"** is the word which describes the **first four books of the Old Testament**. These four books establish Israel as a nation.

The **"Septuagint"** is the Old Testament as translated from Hebrew into Greek since, as the centuries went on, the Greek influence became very strong and many Jews were no longer able to read Hebrew.

In reading the Hebrew Scriptures, it helps to know that, in ancient times, the group – or community – was more important than the individual. This was so in order that the group be held together, be preserved, grow and prosper. When the group did well, so did persons within the group.

Ancient peoples believed in God or **gods.** The ancient nomadic peoples believed their gods traveled with them as they wandered.

THE FIRST BOOK OF MOSES COMMONLY CALLED GENESIS

The Book of Genesis, which **means "origin," "source," or "begetting"** sets forth God's establishment of His family and the giving of divine revelation to mankind.

Genesis is the accounting of all creation and the origin of sin.

Genesis begins with God creating the world in an orderly fashion.

"In the beginning God created the heavens and the earth. And the earth was formless and void, and darkness was over the surface of the deep; and the Spirit of God was moving over the surface of the waters." (1:1-2)

God then created light and separated the light from the dark. God called the light day and the darkness night. God went on with creation of earth and sky and He saw to it that the earth was fertile and produced vegetation of all kinds. He created the seasons, the sun, moon and all the other stars and bodies in the sky. God then made the waters and the earth teem with life.

"And God created man in His own image, in the image of God He created him; male and female. . .And blessed them; and God said to them, 'Be fruitful and multiply. . .'" (1:27-28)

"And God saw all that He had made, and behold, it was very good. And there was evening and there was morning, the sixth day. . . And by the seventh day God completed His work which He had done; and He rested on the seventh day from all His work. . .Then God blessed the seventh day and sanctified it, because in it He rested from all His work which He had done." (1:31 and 2:1-3)

"Then the Lord God formed man of dust from the ground, and breathed into his nostrils the breath of life; and man became a living being." (2:7) "Then the Lord God took the man and put him into the Garden of Eden to cultivate it and keep it. And the Lord God commanded the man, saying, 'From any tree of the garden you may eat freely; but from the tree of the knowledge of good and evil you shall not eat, for in the day that you eat from it you shall surely die." (2:15-17)

"God creating Adam" by Michelangelo – the Sistine Chapel

"Then the Lord God said, "It is not good for the man to be alone; I will make him a helper suitable for him.'. . .So the Lord God caused a deep sleep to fall upon the man, and he slept; and then He took one of his ribs, and closed up the flesh at that place. And the Lord God fashioned into a woman the rib which He had taken from the man, and brought her to the man. And the man said, 'This is now bone of my bones, and flesh of my flesh; she shall be called Woman, because she was taken out of Man." (2:18-23)

After a time, the serpent, being crafty, convinced the woman to eat from the forbidden tree in Eden, by saying, *"You surely shall not die! For God knows that in the day you eat from it your eyes will be opened, and you will be like God, knowing good and evil." (3: 4-5)*

". . .she took from its fruit and ate; and she gave also to her husband with her, and he ate. Then the eyes of both of them were opened, and they knew that they were naked; and they sewed fig leaves together and made themselves loin coverings."(6:7)

4.

When Adam and Eve went against God's commandment, they sinned ("original sin") and God, as He had promised, punished them by removing them from the Garden of Eden. Their sin, and God's punishment, established that they and all their descendants would live lives of hardship, sorrow and pain, ending in death.

When Adam and Eve were no longer permitted to live in the Garden of Eden, they and all their descendants (all of humankind) not only became subject to death, but also were required to work (to keep body and soul together), to know good and evil, to have to choose between good and evil, to experience hardships and to suffer. In short, all the trials and tribulations of life as we know it on earth.

Genesis follows with the story of Adam and Eve's sons, Cain and Abel. Out of jealousy, Cain, a farmer, kills Abel, a herdsman.

God, in His unhappiness with Cain, forces Cain to spend the rest of his life wandering the earth, never again to farm as he once had.

Adam and Eve had another son, Seth, who became the ancestor of all peoples on earth. Seth had many descendants - and many generations of Seth's descendants lived their lives and died. One of Seth's descendants was a man of God named Noah.

By the time Noah is born, the majority of the people of earth are so sinful and so lacking in redemptive attributes that God considers wiping out all of mankind. God knows, however, that Noah is a good man, and so God directs Noah to build an ark.

In Genesis, we follow Noah through the building of the ark as directly inspired by God; the gathering of Noah's family and all the animals to be taken into the ark; the 40 days of rain which results in enormous flooding and the deaths of all earth's creatures, except for Noah, his family and the other inhabitants of the ark. Safe in the ark, they endure a long wait for a sign of dry land.

When dry land finally appears, the ark at last comes to rest at the top of a mountain (believed to be in the Ararat Mountains, a high mountain range in eastern Armenia). God promises Noah that He will never again send a flood to destroy mankind. The visible sign of His promise is the rainbow.

> God also said, *"While the earth remains, seed time and harvest, and cold and heat, and summer and winter, and day and night shall not cease." (8:22)*

Noah's three sons, Shem, Ham and Japheth, their wives and children, along with the animals who were safe within the ark, are all dispersed upon the earth, which becomes populated once again.

All people on earth are descendants of Noah's three sons. Ham's descendants became the Canaanites (Syria and Palestine) and they worshipped a pantheon of pagan gods, chief of which was Baal. Shem's descendants became the Shemites or Semites (it is from this descriptor that "anti-Semitism" derives). Shem's descendants are the peoples of the ancient Near East, specifically the Israelites. Japheth's descendants populated the rest of the world.

Again, generations pass, and we learn about another good man named Abram (who is a direct descendent of Shem) and his wife Sarai. This couple lives in a place called Ur of the Chaldeans (later to be known as Babylon – today's Iraq – located north of the Persian Gulf). God tells Abram to pack up and go to Canaan (the land around today's Israel). He promises to make Abram the father of a great nation.

Abram takes with him Sarai, his servants, his cattle and all that he owns, along with his nephew Lot and all that he owns. Eventually, the two families part company, since both have so many cattle, servants and possessions, the land can't sustain them living so close to each another.

Abram settles in the desert and Lot and his family settle in the sinful city of Sodom (located in the Jordan valley). Sodom and its sister city Gomorrah are so full of evil that God wishes to wipe out these two cities completely.

Abram, however, asks God to spare Sodom and he enters into negotiations with God regarding the number of good people it will take to spare this evil city. At last God agrees to spare the city if 10 good people can be found. God then sends His avenging angels to visit Sodom. Once in Sodom, the two angels are invited by Lot and his family (the only good people in the city) to stay the night.

The townspeople of Sodom are so evil that they bang on Lot's door, demanding that the two visitors be turned out so that they can be used as sexual objects by all of the townspeople.

Lot offers his two daughters to Sodom's sinners rather than the two "visitors." Because Lot has shown himself and his family to be good people, the avenging angels instruct Lot to immediately take his family and flee the city, warning that they are not to look back.

As the cities of Sodom and Gomorrah are being destroyed (by volcanic ash) Lot's wife looks back to see what is happening, and is turned into a pillar of salt. As Lot and his two daughters go on with their lives, Lot's daughters, who are without husbands, plot to get their father drunk on successive evenings and each goes in and sleeps with him. Both daughters become pregnant by Lot. Their offspring are Moabites and Ammonites.

Genesis again turns to Abram and Sarai who have no children. Sarai is now too old to become pregnant and she urges Abram to take a slave woman named Hagar. Abram does so, and has a son by her. He names this son Ishmael, who, as he matures, is described as a wild man.

At God's direction, and as a sign that Abram and his offspring belong to God, circumcision is instituted. Hebrew males are traditionally circumcised at eight days of age; Arab males (Ishmael's offspring) at 13 years of age.

God then visits Abram in a dream and establishes a covenant with him. God promises that Abram and Sarai will have a son of their own. God informs Abram that his name is now Abraham and Sarai's name is now Sarah. God then tells Abraham that he will be the father of many nations, with offspring too numerous to count.

> *"I am God Almighty; walk before me, and be blameless. And I will establish My covenant between Me and you, and I will multiply you exceedingly." (17:1-2)*

When Abraham tells Sarah that she will become a mother, she laughs in disbelief that she will bear a child at her advanced age (90). But she does become pregnant and bears a son whom they name Isaac. Sarah now wants no competition from Hagar and Ishmael. She orders them to be gone.

God promises Abraham that Ishmael, too, will have many descendants. Ishmael's descendants are the Arab peoples and they, like Jews and Christians, consider Abraham their father.

When Abraham and Sarah's son, Isaac becomes a young man, God asks Abraham to make a sacrifice of Isaac to show his faithfulness to Him. Abraham, in complete obedience to God, takes Isaac to the top of a mountain, binds him and prepares to kill him. When it is obvious that Abraham intends to be faithful to God's direction, an angel stops Abraham from killing Isaac *(a foretelling of the sacrifice which God the Father made centuries later – when His only son was sacrificed to save sinful mankind)*.

When Isaac becomes older, he is sent to Northern Syria to find a wife from a branch of Abraham's family. Isaac meets and marries Rebekah (the daughter of Abraham's nephew, Bethuel).

Rebekah and Isaac have twin sons, Esau and Jacob. Although Esau is born first, Jacob is Rebekah's favorite. Esau is hairy and red and becomes a rugged outdoorsman. Jacob is much less hairy and is a quieter person.

As young adults, Jacob persuades Esau to sell him his birthright for food (at a time when Esau is very hungry). Jacob also obtains his father's blessing (intended for the first-born). Through trickery, in order to deceive their father Isaac, Jacob dresses himself like Esau by wearing the skin of an animal so that Isaac, who is now blind, will, by touch, be led to believe that Jacob is really Esau, the first-born.

Isaac is deceived into giving Jacob the blessing of the first-born meant for Esau. Later, Esau learns that he has had this special blessing taken from him. And, once a blessing is given it cannot be taken back, thus Esau is no longer in the honored position of having his father's blessing.

Even though Esau begs his father for a blessing, Isaac cannot give it to him, and sadly tells his favorite son that he is now to look to Jacob as his master. Understandably, Esau is angry with Jacob and vows to kill him.

Fearful for Jacob's life, Rebekah sends him away to her brother Laban in Syria for safekeeping. Isaac blesses Jacob again and instructs him to take a wife from among Laban's daughters.

Esau also leaves home and marries two Hittite women whom his father dislikes. He also marries Ishmael's daughter (Abraham and Hagar's granddaughter).

One night, while on the way to Laban's home in Syria, Jacob dreams of angels going up and down a ladder to heaven, and hears the Lord tell him that he will have many descendants. (Jacob named the spot where this happened "Bethel").

Is it possible that Jacob's dream was a foretelling of the Messiah – Jesus Christ – being the ultimate connection between God and mankind?

In John 1:51, Jesus, in speaking to Nathanael, referred to this as well, when he said, *"Truly, truly, I say to you, you shall see the heavens opened and the angels of God ascending and descending on the Son of Man."*

When Jacob reaches Syria and nears Laban's property, he finds and falls in love with Rachel, Laban's second daughter. Jacob agrees to work for Laban for seven years with the promise that at the end of seven years he can marry Rachel.

But, at the end of the seven years, Laban tricks Jacob into marrying his oldest daughter, Leah. Jacob is understandably upset. He keeps Leah as his first wife and beseeches Laban to let him marry Rachel. Laban promises Jacob that, at the end of one week's time he can marry Rachel but he extracts a promise from Jacob of another seven years of labor in exchange.

More years go by. Jacob and his several wives eventually have 12 sons and one daughter. Children born to Leah: sons Reuben, Simeon, Levi, Judah, Issachar and Zebulun and daughter Dinah. Sons born to Rachel's maid, Bilhah: Dan and Naphtali. Sons born to Leah's maid, Zilpah: Gad and Asher. After being barren for many years, Rachel gives birth to two sons: Joseph and Benjamin.

Eventually, Jacob leaves Laban's territory. He takes his entire family - servants, cattle and all - and moves to Shecham in Canaan. An interesting scene is played out when Laban comes after Jacob, Leah and Rachel, believing that Jacob had stolen his daughters, his flocks and some of his household idols. Jacob and Laban reach a peaceful parting and make a covenant at a place they call "Mizpah" meaning "May the Lord watch between you and me when we are absent one from the other."

Continuing on the way to Canaan, Jacob wrestles one night - all night long - with a stranger during which time his hip is injured. He comes to understand that he has been wrestling with an Angel of God - and the angel changes his name to Israel which, the angel tells him, means, "You have striven with God and with men and have prevailed."

As the group travels along, Jacob learns that Esau wishes to meet with him. Jacob is frightened and does what he can to protect his family. However, when the two brothers meet, Esau embraces him and they both weep. Their feud is over; they are now friends as well as brothers.

As Jacob's children become young adults, his only daughter, Dinah, is raped by a man of Shechem. Her brothers seek revenge by tricking all the men in Shechem to agree to circumcision, promising that after they are circumcised, the man who raped Dinah can marry her. The men of Shechem submit to circumcision and, while still in a weakened state, all are killed by Dinah's brothers.

Now we turn to Joseph (the elder of Jacob and Rachel's two sons). Joseph was next-to-the youngest of all of Jacob's sons (Benjamin being the youngest) and was Jacob's favorite. Joseph's older brothers are jealous of him because of this and also because he seems to possess special talents such as predicting the meaning of dreams. In their jealousy, the older brothers plot to kill Joseph. They throw him into a pit where they expect he will die. Unbeknownst to all but one of the brothers, Joseph is rescued by traveling Midianite merchants who sell him as a slave in Egypt.

Believing Joseph to be dead, the brothers bring back to their father, Joseph's coat of many colors (given to him by Jacob) smeared with the blood of an animal, so as to convince Jacob that Joseph is dead. Jacob is desolate in his grief over the loss of his favorite son.

Meanwhile, Joseph, who is now in Egypt, first spends time in jail, after having been falsely accused of raping the wife of Potiphar (the king's official who is in charge of the palace guard). While in jail, he gains favor with the king (pharaoh) when he correctly interprets the king's dreams as being about seven years of plenty followed by seven years of famine. The pharaoh rewards Joseph by not only putting him in charge of the entire country but also in charge of seeing to it that there are provisions stored up for the lean years to come.

After seven years of plenty, the lean years do come. The resulting famine extends even into the land of Canaan where Jacob and his other 11 sons still live. Desperate to feed his family, Jacob sends 10 of his sons to Egypt to buy food. He does not permit Benjamin to go, fearing that the boy might come to harm. When Jacob's older sons reach Egypt, they come into the presence of their brother Joseph, but do not know who he is. Joseph, however, realizes that these men are his brothers, but does not reveal his identity to them. Instead, he coerces his brothers into returning to their home and bringing their youngest brother, and eventually their father, back to Egypt to see him. It is only when Benjamin - and then Jacob - come to Egypt that Joseph reveals his true identity to his family.

Out of gratitude for all that Joseph has done for Egypt and its people during the years of famine, the pharaoh invites Joseph's entire extended family to come live in Egypt and to take possession of the best land for themselves and their flocks in the land of Goshen.

At the time of their move to Egypt, Jacob is 130 years old. Once settled in Egypt, the family prospers and multiplies. Joseph marries Asenath, the daughter of an Egyptian priest and has two sons - Manasseh and Ephraim. Before Israel (Jacob) dies at age 147, he blesses Joseph's sons but makes the younger son, Ephraim, greater than the older, Manasseh.

Jacob's (Israel's) 12 sons become the 12 tribes of Israel. Jacob's fourth son with Leah is Judah. Judah has three sons – Er, Onan and Shelah. Judah finds a wife for Er named Tamara. However, Er commits some sort of evil in the sight of the Lord and dies.

Judah directs his son Onan to *"go into your brother's wife and perform your duty as a brother-in-law,"* so that there will be offspring in Er's name. Onan, knowing the children that he might father with Tamar will not be his in name, spills his seed on the ground when he goes into his sister-in-law. Because this was displeasing to the Lord, Onan also lost his life. *(38:1-8)* Judah tells his daughter-in-law to wait for Shelah to grow up, and, in time, Shelah does. But Judah is afraid Shelah will also die if he goes into Tamar, so he does not send Shelah to Tamar.

Tamar resorts to tricking her father-in-law into thinking she is a temple prostitute and he (not knowing that it is his daughter-in-law) goes into her. Still not knowing who she is, he promises to give her a kid from his flock of goats and as a pledge that he will send her the young goat, he gives her his seal, his cord and his staff. After he leaves, Tamar changes back into her widow's clothing. When Judah sends a servant to pay the temple prostitute with the kid, she cannot be found. Later, it is reported to Judah that his daughter-in-law is pregnant, because *"she played the harlot."* Judah threatens to have her burned to death. Tamar then says to Judah, *"I am with child by the man to whom these things belong,"* showing Judah the seal, cord and staff which he gave her. Judah declares, *"'She is more righteous than I, inasmuch as I did not give her to my son Shelah.' And he did not have relations with her again."* *(38:24-26)*

Tamar is pregnant with twins. During the birthing process, one child's hand emerges and the midwife ties a scarlet thread on the hand (signifying the first child to emerge). However, the other child actually emerges first and the midwife declares, *"'What a breach you have made for yourself!'"* So he was named Perez. *(38:29)* The brother with the scarlet thread on his hand was then born and named Zerah.

Perez becomes the direct ancestor of King David and, ultimately, Jesus.

Genesis - this majestic first book of the Hebrew scriptures - ends with the story of Joseph, his rise to power in Egypt, and the establishment of his brothers and their families in Egypt. Jacob, Abraham, Sarah, Isaac and Rebekah are buried in Machpelah Cave (in the land of Canaan).

THE SECOND BOOK OF MOSES COMMONLY CALLED EXODUS

Exodus is a very important book because it deals with the birth of the Jewish nation.

This is the story of Moses bringing the Israelites out of slavery in Egypt and beginning the search for the Promised Land. The exodus is led by Moses and his brother Aaron.

God's name in Hebrew is YHWH (pronounced "Yahweh") and is considered to be so sacred a name that the Jewish people neither speak nor write it.

Another name for God is Adonai ("My great Lord"). The name Jehovah is a composite of YHWH and Adonai. The name Yahweh is interpreted to mean, "I will be what I will be" or "I am that I am."

Exodus ("departure" or "going out") is the central event of the Hebrew Scriptures – the Old Testament - and is viewed as Yahweh's mighty act of deliverance on behalf of His people. It is the focus for the Hebrew religion.

Note that in the New Testament, John's Gospel uses the phrase "I am" many times in relating Jesus Christ's relationship to mankind.

The Exodus theme can be said to be a precursor of themes in the Christian Scriptures – the New Testament in these ways:

- **The Israelites spent 40 years in the wilderness** before crossing the Jordan and entering the Promised Land. **Jesus spent 40 days in the wilderness** before He began His public ministry.

- **Moses received the 10 Commandments on the Mount. Jesus gave the Sermon on the Mount.**

- **There were 12 tribes of Israel. Jesus called twelve disciples.**

- **The Passover meal** of Exodus is paralleled by **the Lord's Last Supper.**

- **The passing of Israel through the Red Sea is recalled by Christian baptism.**

- **Moses lifted up the serpent in the wilderness as a means of healing for the Hebrew people. Jesus was lifted up in shame and suffering in his crucifixion** as the expansion of the original Book of the Covenant which Moses read in the hearing of his people.

Exodus begins with more than four hundred years having passed in Egypt, and now all of Jacob's (Israel's) sons have died. Their many descendants are still living in Egypt and the Hebrews have become so numerous that the Egyptians are concerned. The pharaoh who favored Joseph has long since died and the present pharaoh is Seti. The political atmosphere is very restrictive for the Israelites, and they are made slaves of the Egyptians. Out of fear of the Hebrew people, pharaoh decrees that all newborn Hebrew boys be killed.

When a certain baby boy is born to a couple from the Tribe of Levi, his mother, in order to save his life, makes a basket of reeds and puts the baby in the basket and places the basket in the Nile River. She has the baby's older sister Miriam watch to see what happens.

Pharaoh's daughter finds this beautiful baby boy, takes pity on him and names him Moses. (The name "Moses" is Egyptian, even though we may think of it as being a Jewish name.) Miriam offers her mother's services, and so Moses is raised in his own family for several years and then taken to the pharaoh's daughter. Moses is then raised as an Egyptian prince. Growing up, he sees the Egyptians' cruelty to the Israelites. He stops an Egyptian who is beating a Jewish workman, and in the process, he kills the Egyptian.

Moses' Hebrew lineage is revealed and his life threatened by the Egyptians. He flees Egypt and finds refuge with a Midian priest named Jethro and his family ("Jethro" means "His Excellency." Jethro is first referred to as "Ruel" meaning "a friend of God"). Moses marries Jethro's daughter, Zipporah.

Moses tends flocks for his father-in-law, until one day God speaks to him from a burning bush.

It is common in Old Testament writings, for fire to be used as a symbol of the presence of God and is technically called a "theophany," or an appearance of God, which usually happened when God is present in a particular place at a particular time for a particular reason.

In Acts of the Apostles, the Holy Spirit, in the form of "tongues of fire" (a theophany) came to Jesus' disciples on two separate occasions.

When Moses asks God what His name is, so that he can relate this to the people of Israel, God reveals, *"I am who I am."*

God tells Moses that he is to go talk to pharaoh and convince him to let the captive Israelite tribes go free. Moses tries to avoid God's command, pleading he is a poor speaker. God tells him to take his brother Aaron along. God assures Moses by telling him that he is to perform miracles to impress pharaoh - and that there will be plagues on both the Egyptians and their lands until God's people, the Israelites, are set free.

And so, Moses and Aaron visit pharaoh Ramses (Seti's son), to ask that he release the Hebrew people from bondage. Ramses refuses to let the Israelite people go. Moses and Aaron return time and time again to ask for the release of their people. Each time Ramses refuses. And each time he refuses, a plague comes to Egypt. First, the Nile River is turned into blood; then there are plagues of frogs, gnats, flies, dead animals, sores, hailstones, locusts and darkness over the land. Finally, the last plague is the worst - the firstborn in every Egyptian family, including the animals, dies.

During this last, most horrible plague, the Israelites are spared, since, at God's direction, they smear the blood of a lamb on their door posts so that God's avenging angel will know to **pass over** their homes.

This great event marks the first Passover. God directs the Israelites to prepare unleavened bread for their flight out of Egypt. This, too, becomes a significant part of the celebration of Passover (the "Feast of Unleavened Bread").

Jews continue to celebrate Passover and give thanks to God for freeing them from slavery.

Passover was the precursor of God's son, Jesus Christ, becoming the Pascal lamb when He died on the cross and rose again to free believing mankind from sin and eternal death.

The blood of the lamb is a symbol for Christ's sacrifice of his life for the redemption of all mankind.

Following the last plague, in which the firstborn of all the Egyptians died and the Jewish people are spared, Pharaoh is finally moved to release the Jews and so the massive Exodus out of Egypt begins.

Exodus tells us that about 600,000 men on foot, aside from children was the number of Israelites who left Egypt with Moses.

Moses leads his people out of Egypt and he parts the Red Sea (The Sea of Reeds) for safe crossing. After the Israelites are safely across, the pursuing Pharaoh and all his army are killed by the waters which rush to cover them in the middle of the sea.

Moses and the sons of Israel rejoice and sing a song in gratitude to the Lord.

> *"I will sing to the Lord for He is highly exalted; the horse and its rider He has hurled into the sea. The Lord is my strength and song, And He has become my salvation; this is my God, and I will praise Him; My father's God, and I will extol Him; The Lord is a warrior; The Lord is His name."(15:1-3)*

As the Hebrew people leave Egypt, God goes before them in a pillar of cloud by day and a pillar of fire by night, to guide them as they travel. But soon the people begin to grumble that Moses should have left them in Egypt rather than bringing them to the wilderness to starve.

So Moses again appeals to God who then provides quail at night and manna (thin sweet bread on the dew) in the morning. The people are to gather only as much as they can eat that day. If they gather more in an effort to stockpile it, the manna becomes wormy. The lesson is to trust the Lord.

On the sixth day of each week, they were to gather twice the amount of manna so that there would be enough for the Sabbath, since the Lord did not provide manna and meat on the Sabbath. Whatever they collected on the sixth day did not spoil, but was good for the Sabbath.

The Lord provides manna daily for the Israelites for 40 years (along with their clothes never wearing out!).

The importance of bread is clearly established in the unleavened Passover bread and the manna. These foretell of God's giving us his only Son as our Bread of Life.

Moving on, they camp at Masseh and Meribah, but there is no water and the people grumble again. So Moses begs God to help and God tells Moses to wield the rod he had used to separate the Red Sea - to strike a rock and it would produce water. Moses, at God's direction, strikes a rock and obtains water. The Israelites are attacked by Amalekites. Joshua leads the counterattack and, as long as Moses has his arms raised, the Israelites are victorious. Aaron and Hur support Moses's arms until the battle is won.

Up to this point, Moses is the only decision-maker (lawmaker, judge and jury, so to speak) for the Hebrew people in any dispute they have with one another. Moses's father-in-law advises Moses that he can't possibly hear and decide all these disputes himself – there are too many, and he won't be able to endure. And so Moses appoints judges to handle ordinary cases. He chooses competent leaders from every tribe and appoints one for every group of 10, 50, 100 and 1000.

In the third month after leaving Egypt, the Israelites come into the wilderness of Sinai. Moses is summoned by God to go alone to meet with God on Mt. Sinai (also known as Mt. Horab). He is gone for 40 days.

When Moses comes down from the mountain, he brings with him the 10 commandments written on tablets of stone. During his absence, however, the people lost hope in God and are worshipping a golden calf which Aaron has made. Moses loses his temper and smashes the stone tablets on which God had written the 10 commandments.

Later, Moses again meets the Lord on Mt. Sinai for another 40 days. Moses asks to see God's face, but God tells him that no man can see His face and live, so God hides Moses between two rocks and then God passes by Moses, so that Moses can see His back. God also gives Moses a second set of tablets. When Moses returns from the mountain, the skin of his face shines so brightly that the people are afraid; thus Moses must put a veil over his face.

The 10 Commandments touch upon man's relationship with God
and neighbor:

> *"Then God spoke all these words, saying:*
>
> *'I am the Lord your God, who brought you out of the land of Egypt,
> out of the house of slavery. You shall have no other gods before me.*
>
> *'You shall not make for yourself an idol, or any likeness of what is
> in heaven above or on the earth beneath or in the water under the
> earth. You shall not worship them or serve them; for I, the Lord
> your God, am a jealous God, visiting the iniquity of the fathers on
> the children, on the third and the fourth generations of those who
> hate Me, but showing lovingkindness to thousands, to those who
> love Me and keep My commandments.*

'You shall not take the name of the Lord your God in vain, for the Lord will not leave him unpunished who takes His name in vain.

'Remember the Sabbath day, to keep it holy. Six days you shall labor and do all your work, but the seventh day is a Sabbath of the Lord your God; in it you shall not do any work, you or your son or your daughter, your male or your female servant or your cattle or your sojourner who stays with you. For in six days the Lord made the heavens and the earth, the sea and all that is in them, and rested on the seventh day; therefore the Lord blessed the Sabbath day and made it holy.

'Honor your father and your mother, that your days may be prolonged in the land which the Lord your God gives you.

'You shall not murder.

'You shall not commit adultery.

'You shall not steal.

'You shall not bear false witness against your neighbor.

'You shall not covet your neighbor's house.

'You shall not covet your neighbor's wife or his male servant or his female servant, or his ox or his donkey or anything that belongs to your neighbor.'" (20:1-17)

Along with the 10 Commandments, God also gave Moses laws and instructions for issues such as murder, violent crimes, property crimes, laws for everyday life, the Sabbath, three annual festivals (Passover, the Festival of Shelters and the Festival of Harvests), the sacred tent, the tabernacle and its curtains, the sacred chest, the table for the sacred bread, the lampstand, curtains, and coverings for the sacred tent, the framework for the sacred tent, the curtains inside the sacred tent, the altar for offering sacrifices, the court yard, the oil, the clothing for the priests, ordaining priests, daily and special sacrifices, and so on and so forth.

Exodus ends with the completion of the sacred tent and all its accessories, just as the Lord had directed Moses. The Lord then traveled with the Israelites in a cloud covering the tent by day, and in a fire by night. When the cloud moved, the Israelites moved, when the cloud stood still, the Israelites did not move forward.

This is another example of a "theophany" - where fire is used as a symbol of God's presence – such as was earlier the case with Moses and the burning bush.

THE THIRD BOOK OF MOSES COMMONLY CALLED LEVITICUS

Leviticus is the continuation of the Exodus from Egypt and deals with the regulations given by God to Moses for proper worship and sacrifice along with the holy functions of the Hebrew priests. **Leviticus describes man's basis for fellowship with God – a Holiness Code – a plan for God's chosen people** to approach Him in a holy and reverent manner.

Leviticus brings us three concepts:

1) **Holiness.** The key idea of Leviticus is "Holiness." God said, "Be holy for I am holy."
2) **Sacrifice.** Sacrifice simply means a gift – and a gift to God is an expression of love and gratitude).
3) **Atonement.** *At-one-ment.* The forgiving or pardoning of sin.

Yom Kippur is the Day of Atonement for Jews, when the High Priest entered into the Holy of Holies.

The description of the great Day of Atonement was also used by early Christians to explain the meaning of the death of Christ for sinners, since Christians believe that Christ is the High Priest who entered "once for all" the heavenly Holy of Holies, having offered His own blood for the redemption of mankind's sins.

The concept of Christ's atonement for our sins is explained by the Apostle Paul in his letter to the Romans, where he said:
"But now apart from the law the righteousness of God has been manifested, being witnessed by the Law and the Prophets, even the righteousness of God through faith in Jesus Christ for all those who believe; for there is no distinction; for all [of mankind] have sinned and fall short of the glory of God, being justified as a gift by His grace through the redemption which is in Christ Jesus; whom God displayed publicly as a propitiation in His blood through faith. This was to demonstrate His righteousness, because in the forbearance of God He had passed over the sins previously committed;. . ." (Romans 3:21–25)

> **Note: The term, "scapegoat" comes from Chapter 16** in which the vicarious sacrifice of a goat is used as a sin offering. A scapegoat is one who takes on the wrongs of another, who bears another's iniquities. Jesus became the scapegoat for mankind's sinfulness.

The family of Levi (one of the 12 tribes of Israel), was designated as the Israelites' priests and charged with the responsibility for recording the regulations given by God for proper worship in the rites of the Tabernacle.

Near the end of Leviticus, God makes this promise to those who would obey him:

> *"Moreover, I will make My dwelling among you, and My Soul will not reject you. I will walk among you and I will be your God and you will be My people. I am the Lord your God who brought you out of Egypt, so that you should not be their slaves. . ." 26:11-13*

> It is interesting to note that in **Revelation, 21:1-7**, John's vision of heaven includes the **same promise of God to His people who persevere** in their belief in – and obedience to – God.

THE FOURTH BOOK OF MOSES COMMONLY CALLED NUMBERS

An ancient title for this book of Hebrew scripture is, "In the Wilderness."

Numbers continues the history of the people of Israel. It begins with the arrival of the Israelites in the wilderness of Sinai. Numbers relates the experiences in the wilderness as well as the law and regulations which God - through Moses - gave the people.

This chapter in the Old Testament tells about the forty years when the Israelites lived in the desert on their journey from Mount Sinai to Canaan.

The sequence of events was: from Sinai, the Israelites went north to the Paran Wilderness. Their forward guard - or spies - brought back an unfavorable report which started a rebellion and the people refused to enter the land. They suffered defeat at pagan hands and were turned back to continue wandering in the wilderness.

This book is named Numbers because it begins with Moses counting the Israelites to determine the number of people in each of Israel's twelve tribes. They counted, *"every male from 20 years old and upward, whoever is able to go out to war in Israel. . ."* (1:2-3) The exception to this numbering was the Tribe of Levi, since they were the Israelites' priests. The initial number arrived at was 603,550.

As the Lord outlined (through Moses) the priestly duties of the Levites, Aaron's son Eleazar, was named the chief of the leaders of Levi and oversaw the duties of those who worked in the sanctuary. The Tribe of Levi was then numbered and that number was 22,000.

The Book of Numbers can be divided into 3 parts:

In the first part, Moses counts the people, sets up Israel's camp and assigns the Levites their duties. This part ends with everyone celebrating Passover and offering sacrifices to the Lord.

The second part includes events which happen while the Israelites are on their way to Moab, a nation living east of the Jordan River. (Moabites were descendants of Lot and his elder daughter.) The Israelites travel to the plains of Moab, east of the Jordan, and defeat and occupy all of Trans-Jordan north of the river Arnon. Here they fall into sin with the Moabite and Midianite women and worship their gods. They are punished with a deadly disease. The Israelites are counted again.

During their wandering in the wilderness, the people grew tired of the food (manna and quail) which God was providing for them, and they began again to complain bitterly. They were punished by a plague of deadly snakes and many people died. The people then begged Moses to intercede with God to end this affliction.

God told Moses to make a bronze snake and lift it up on a pole and to tell the people that, should they be bitten by a snake, they need only look at the bronze snake and they could be sure of survival.

> **John 3: 14-21 (New Testament)** tells us that this Old Testament story is a metaphor for the ultimate sacrifice which God called upon his Son to make: that to save mankind from eternal death, God's Son would be lifted up, and that those who turned to Him in belief would be saved from eternal death.

The third part of Numbers begins with the Israelites conquering the land just east of the Jordan River.

As the Israelites proceed to the land which God had promised them, they ask safe passage through lands ruled by other nations. Even though the Israelites ask only for safe passage, promising to not even drink water from any wells while passing through, several of the nations refuse to let them pass.

One nation – the Moab nation and its king Balak – calls upon Balaam, a prophet, diviner or seer (son of Beor), to curse the Israelites in order to defeat and destroy them. But God speaks to Balaam and informs him that the Israelites are not to be cursed but are blessed by God. Much to the anger of King Balak, Balaam blesses the Israelites. The Israelites then become too friendly with the Moabite people and *"began to play the harlot with the daughters of Moab." (25:1)*

28.

Because of their disobedience to the Lord, the Israelites are struck by a plague in which many of them die. God instructs Moses to slay all the leaders of the people in broad daylight in order to turn away the Lord's anger. Phineas, the son of Eleazar (and grandson of Aaron – Moses' brother), takes a spear and kills an Israelite man and a Midianite woman (who are engaged in a relationship) and the plague on the sons of Israel is checked, although 24,000 people had already died.

Moses, with the help of his brother Aaron, leads the people. Their sister, Miriam is an important figure in the exodus from Egypt, as well. One of the sidelights of this time in history is that Miriam and Aaron become jealous of Moses, and Miriam is punished with leprosy.

The Israelites again complain, saying that they should have stayed in Egypt. Two and a half tribes (the Tribes of Reuben, Gad and ½ of Manasseh) stake out their lands as being east of the Jordan River. Moses permits this, providing they fight the Midianites. They proceed to fight, kill, plunder, burn villages and take slaves.

Miriam dies and is buried in the Zin Desert near the town of Kadesh.

The Israelites had come to the wilderness of Zin but there was no water, and so the people complained to Moses. When Moses appealed to the Lord, he was told by the Lord, to,

> *"Take the rod; and you and your brother Aaron assemble the congregation and speak to the rock before their eyes, and it will yield water for them out of the rock. . .Then Moses lifted up his hand and struck the rock twice with his rod; and water came forth abundantly, and the congregation and their beasts drank. But the Lord said to Moses and Aaron, 'Because you have not believed Me, to treat Me as holy in the sight of the sons of Israel, therefore you shall not bring this assembly into the land which I have given them.'"* *(20:8-12)*

Although Moses successfully brought water out of the rock for the congregation at Meribah, he disobeyed the Lord when he struck the rock rather than speaking to the rock. "The Lord spoke to Moses and Aaron at Mount Hor by the border of the Land of Edom, *saying, "Aaron shall be gathered to his people; for he shall not enter the land which I have given to the sons of Israel, because you rebelled against My command at the waters of Meribah.'. . .Aaron died there. . .all the house of Israel wept for Aaron thirty days." (20:23-29)*

Israel, as a new generation, is numbered again.

A blessing that has come down through the ages is found in Numbers 6:22-27:

> *"Then the Lord spoke to Moses, saying, 'Speak to Aaron and to his sons, saying, 'Thus you shall bless the sons of Israel. You shall say to them: the Lord bless you and keep you; the Lord make His face shine on you, and be gracious to you; the Lord lift up His countenance on you, and give you peace.' So they shall invoke My name on the sons of Israel and I then will bless them."6:22-27*

This is the end of the summary of the Tetrateuch – the first four books of the Hebrew scriptures.

THE FIFTH BOOK OF MOSES COMMONLY CALLED DEUTERONOMY

Deuteronomy is the Old Testament book most often quoted by Jesus and the Apostles with more than 80 references to this book in the New Testament.

The central theme of Deuteronomy is the renewal of the Covenant between God (Yahweh) and His people. And the theological message is that if the people are faithful to Yahweh, they prosper. If they are not faithful to Yahweh, they are punished.

Deuteronomy means "second law" in Greek. Moses gives God's Ten Commandments to the Israelites for the second time *(Chapter 5)*.

Deuteronomy contains the farewell, ceremonial address of Moses to the Israelites in the Plains of Moab. In this talk, Moses tells the story of their exodus from Egypt, their trials and tribulations, his meeting God on Mt. Sinai and the giving of the 10 Commandments. He reiterates that God chose these people for His own and that they will prosper if they obey God's commandments and hold Him as their only god. But should they fall into idol worship, like the countries they come in contact with, then God will leave them to their evil ways.

> *"And He humbled you and let you be hungry, and fed you with manna which you did not know, nor did your fathers know, that He might make you understand that man does not live by bread alone but man lives by everything that proceeds out of the mouth of the Lord." (8:3-4)*

When the rebellious exodus generation had perished in the wilderness and Moses' own death was imminent, it was necessary to renew the Covenant to the second generation.

The Israelites were reminded of what God had done to rescue them out of Egyptian slavery.

The goodness of God was extolled as the people were reminded of the wonderful land which God had opened before them.

Israel was challenged to be the *"people for His own possession"* of the Lord, an instrument in His purpose of redemption for the nations.

A central place of worship was designated - the tabernacle in the wilderness - and eventually the temple in Jerusalem.

Originally established at Sinai, the Covenant is renewed on the Plains of Moab as the children of Israel prepare to enter the Promised Land. For 40 years they wandered in the wilderness, and they learned that the firm promises of God still stand - both in times of blessing when they obey Him, and in times of judgment, when they sin against Him and disobey His law.

Moses sings a song for his people. *(32, 33)* In his song and in his words to his people, he gives warnings and pleadings to the people to keep the divine Law underlined by the certainty of divine punishment for disobedience. Finally there is a promise of the blessings and "rest" which would attend their faithful observance of the covenant relationship with God.

> *"Since then, no prophet has risen in Israel like Moses, whom the Lord knew face to face, for all the signs and wonders which the Lord sent him to perform in the land of Egypt against Pharaoh, all his servants, and all his land."(34:10-11)*

Deuteronomy ends with the death of Moses (now 120 years old) on Mt. Nebo. Although the Lord showed Moses the *"land of milk and honey,"* He told Moses he would not live to go there, because Moses had displeased the Lord at Meribah. *(See Numbers 20:2-12)*

This is the end of the summary of the five foundational books of the Hebrew scriptures (the "Torah"), also known as the Pentateuch.

THE BOOK OF JOSHUA

Joshua is the first book of the prophets and this book continues the history of Israel begun in the Pentateuch and demonstrates God's faithfulness to His covenants by settling the tribes in their promised homeland.

Joshua led Israel into Canaan about 1406 B.C. during the Late Bronze Age (1550 - 1200 B.C.).

Joshua is the Hebrew word for "Jesus" and means "The Lord is salvation."

By the time of Joshua and the Judges, Canaanite religious observances had degenerated to licentiousness and brutality - fertility practices unearthed at Beth-shan and Megiddo. The immoral character of the Canaanite deities led their devotees into the most demoralizing rites of the ancient Near East.

The Book of Joshua and the Book of Judges give differing accounts of the conquest of the land: Joshua depicts it as swift and decisive; Judges shows a more gradual taking over of the territories.

Although named for Joshua, he could not have been the author of the entire book, since his death is told herein.

This book opens with God speaking to Joshua:

> *"Moses My servant is dead; now therefore arise, cross this Jordan, you and all this people, to the land which I am giving to them, to the sons of Israel. . . From the wilderness and this Lebanon, even as far as the great river, the river Euphrates, all the land of the Hittites, and as far as the Great Sea toward the setting of the sun, will be your territory." (1:2-4)*

The book of Joshua has two parts: first, the Lord helps Israel capture many of the cities and towns of Canaan. For example in overtaking Jericho, the Lord made the city walls collapse when, at his direction, the priests and people march once around the city on six successive days, blowing their horns. On the seventh day, they march around the city seven times, blowing their horns. *"And they utterly destroyed everything in the city." (6:20-21)*

In leading the Israelites into the Promised Land, Joshua defeats the various kings and cities and takes the land for the Israelites.

During the capture of the City of Jericho, because of her kindness towards Israel, a harlot named Rahab and her family were spared and she came to live out her days with the Israelites.

This came about when Joshua sent spies ahead to scout out the city of Jericho. The spies came to the home of Rahab and stayed there. Somehow the king of Jericho suspected that Rahab was sheltering spies from Israel and he demanded that she bring them out. Instead, Rahab hid the men in stalks of flax on her roof. When it was safe, she let the men down from her roof by a rope and asked them to spare her and her family. The Israelite men told her that if she would tie a scarlet thread on a cord at the window as a sign that her family was safe inside her home, the Israelites would spare her home.

Rahab plays an eternally-important role in Christian history, since later she married Salmon and became the mother of Boaz, from whom the lineage of Jesse, David and eventually Jesus, derives. In the Book of Ruth, the love story of Boaz and Ruth unfolds.

Joshua listened to all that the scouts had to tell him when they returned to camp. He commanded the people, *"When you see the ark of the covenant of the Lord your God with the Levitical priests carrying it, then you shall set out from your place and go after it." (3:3)*

Joshua then instructed the priests to take the Ark of the Covenant and cross on ahead of the people. The Lord then said to Joshua that he would, *"exalt you in the sight of all Israel and they will know that just as I have been with Moses, I will be with you." (3:7)*

The Lord directed that when the priests who were carrying the Ark of the Covenant came to the Jordan River, they were to stand still in the Jordan.

> The Lord said, *"And it shall come about when the soles of the feet of the priests who carry the Ark of the Lord, the Lord of all the earth, shall rest in the waters of the Jordan, the waters of the Jordan shall be cut off, and the waters which are flowing down from above shall stand in one heap." (3:13)*

And so it was that the priests who carried the Ark of the Covenant were instruments of the Lord, Who again (as He had for Moses) afforded safe passage across a body of water for His people Israel. And so Joshua was revered by the people Israel just as Moses had been revered.

There are other battles depicted in Joshua - the battle at Gibeon where the Lord made huge hailstones fall from the sky and crush the enemy soldiers. Then He made the sun stand still so that the Israelites had a longer period of daylight to catch and kill as many of the enemy soldiers as possible before nightfall. But, in the battle at Ai, Israel was defeated because one person (Achan) disobeyed God's commandment and took some of the spoils of battle for himself.

The second part of Joshua describes how each tribe receives its land. A telling part of this book is in Chapter 17, verses 12-13: *"But the sons of Manasseh could not take possession of these cities, because the Canaanites persisted in living in that land. And it came about when the sons of Israel became strong, they put the Canaanites to forced labor, but they did not drive them out completely."*

Chapter 17 of the Book of Joshua contains the first record of women inheriting.

In Joshua's farewell address to his people, he recounted the Lord's entrance into their lives through Abraham *(Chapter 23)* and their enslavement in Egypt to how God is bringing them out of Egypt and asking that the Israelites reject all other gods, *". . .you are to cling to the Lord your God, as you have done to this day." (23:8)*

At the end of the book, Joshua retells the history of the people of God from Abraham through Moses up to the present time. In his review of the Israelites' history, he states, *". . . as for me and my house, we will serve the Lord." (24:15)*

Joshua dies and is buried, along with Joseph and Eleazar in the hill country of Ephraim.

THE BOOK OF JUDGES

It is not known who authored Judges, although it is believed possible that the prophet Samuel wrote this book.

The title comes from the civil magistrates or heads of state, who were appointed to help Moses establish order among his people.

Judges illustrates a time of anarchy and trouble when there was no king over the land and people did what they wanted to do. *"In those days there was no king in Israel; everyone did what was right in his own eyes." (21: 25)*

Judges covers about 200 years following the entry of Israel into Canaan. The use of iron was becoming common. This strong metal revolutionized agriculture and warfare.

In Judges, the scriptures step back in time to explain the establishment of laws and rules for the Hebrew people. The central message of Judges is that the hand of God is in all that happens.

For a long time, Moses had tried to personally make decisions, rules and judgments for the people he had led out of Egypt. At the urging of Jethro, his father-in-law, Moses set up a system so that these responsibilities could be handled by others (civil magistrates or heads of state) who would be in charge of groups of people varying from 10 to 100 to 1,000.

Israel's failure to consolidate the land and keep their religion and cultural life strong was the cause of tragedy which followed. Idolatry crept in, vicious oppressors rose up to torment the people, hunger and famine were their constant companions.

Yet, God always raised up a "man of the hour." Whenever the suffering was worst and the people cried out in despair, God called forth a "judge," a deliverer, to throw off the yoke of the oppressor. Sometimes these were good and noble men like Gideon and Samuel, but sometimes they were erratic and unstable men, like Samson.

Judges stresses the theme that God raises up the weak to confound the strong, and that no weapons can destroy a people that puts its faith in God.

The final lesson is that civilized life is impossible when every man has "his own way." It is an expression of original sin which goes all the way back to the Garden of Eden. Only by obedience to the Law and love of God can man ever find the happiness for which God made him.

The Israelites go to war with the Canaanites. The Israelites defeat the Canaanites, but fail to drive them out of the land. Instead, they live there together and the Israelites take on some of the pagan ways of the Canaanites.

THE BOOK OF RUTH

> **Ruth is a story of love and devotion** involving a family from the Tribe of Judah (from Bethlehem) - a father, mother (Naomi) and two sons - who sojourn to Moab.

While in Moab, the father dies and the sons marry Moab women, Orpah and Ruth (descendants of Lot and one of his daughters).

After 10 years in Moab, both of the sons have also died. The mother Naomi wants to return to her homeland and so she urges her daughters-in-law to stay in their native land of Moab and return to their families.

Orpah does remain in Moab, but Ruth determines to leave Moab and go to Judah with her mother-in-law, Naomi.

> *"Then she [Naomi] said, 'Behold, your sister-in-law has gone back to her people and her gods; return after your sister-in-law.' But Ruth said, 'Do not urge me to leave you or turn back from following you; for where you go, I will go, and where you lodge, I will lodge. Your people shall be my people, and your God my God. Where you die, I will die, and there I will be buried. Thus may the Lord do to me, and worse, if anything but death parts you and me.' When she [Naomi] saw that she [Ruth] was determined to go with her, she said no more to her." (1:15-18)*

Upon returning to Naomi's original hometown of Bethlehem, the two women are poverty-stricken. They have no land, no money, no resources and no other close family members.

To keep them both alive, Ruth gleans grain for her mother-in-law and herself to live on. (In those days, as an act of charity, landowners would leave a certain amount of grain in the fields for the poor to come and take for themselves.)

Naomi is a relative of Boaz, the owner of the fields of grain. Boaz is a wealthy man whose mother was Rahab, the prostitute who helped the Israelites capture Jericho.

During the time when Ruth is gleaning grain from Boaz's fields, Boaz falls in love with her and eventually marries her.

Ruth and Boaz have a son and name him Obed. He becomes the father of Jesse, who becomes the father of David, who becomes Israel's second king.

King David is a direct ancestor of Jesus.

INTRODUCTION TO THE BOOKS
OF SAMUEL AND KINGS

The books of Samuel and Kings tell the story of how the prophet Samuel came to begin the process of anointing a leader (a king) for the Israelite people.

The Israelites were, at that time (some 400 years after Moses had brought them out of Egypt) **a loosely connected group of 12 tribes**. There was no common leader and no political structure and the people, observing how other, non-Jewish tribes of people had kings, were longing for the leadership of a king for themselves.

At God's bidding, Samuel wisely tried to tell the people that supporting a monarchy would extract a high price from them. The people, however, persisted and so Samuel, guided by the Lord, anointed Saul, a tall, handsome man from the tribe of Benjamin, as the first king of Israel.

Through time, Saul proved to be less than Samuel had hoped for in a king and so, again, led by the Lord, Samuel searches for a man to be king over Israel. He finds a shepherd boy named David, the youngest son of Jesse, from the house of Judah.

David succeeds Saul as king of Israel and so begins a long line of kings from David - leading ultimately to Jesus.

In the process of kingly succession, however, the kingdom of Israel is divided and two kingdoms result – the Northern Kingdom of Israel (Samaria is its capital) and the Southern Kingdom of Judah (Jerusalem is its capital).

Each kingdom had many kings (*see the chart associated with the notes for 2 Kings, pgs. 58 - 59*). Some are good and follow God's commandments, but many are evil and fall into pagan practices learned from other tribes and groups of people. These pagan practices include worship of many gods, oftentimes involving human sacrifice (not uncommonly, the victims were children), and other rituals which the Lord had forbidden and which were detrimental to the people of Israel.

THE FIRST BOOK OF SAMUEL

It has been suggested that the name Samuel means "The Name of God".

The basic message of the books of Samuel is: God rules in the lives of men and nations. In judgment and in blessing, God works toward His appointed goal – the preparation of a people for the coming of the Messiah, *"a people for His own possession"* who would be an instrument of His redemptive purposes, a *"light of the nations."*

This book deals with the transition from Judges to Kings. The books of Samuel and Kings are a history of the monarchy and the unification of the northern tribes and the southern tribes into one nation under David and Solomon and then as divided nations, until the exile of each.

The books of Samuel and Kings make a complete history of the Great Kingdom and the turmoil of the divided Kingdoms of Judah and Israel.

Samuel was a judge and prophet of Israel (1100 - 1010 B.C.) Samuel's parents were Elkanah and Hannah. Hannah was barren but Eli, the priest, told her she would have a son. When Samuel was born, Hannah dedicated the boy to Eli and when he was weaned she turned him over to Eli for training and education. Hannah would visit Samuel periodically to bring him specially made garments.

One night, after Samuel was grown, he was awakened several times by someone calling him. Each time he would go to Eli and ask him what he wanted (thinking it was Eli who was calling him). Eli finally realized that the Lord had chosen to speak directly to Samuel and told the young man to answer the Lord. The Lord's message was that Samuel would be the one to choose a king for the people. The Lord told Samuel that, although He was their King, the people didn't want Him; they wanted an earthly king, and so if that was what they wanted, that was what they would get. Samuel is then told by the Lord that he would recognize the man who was to be the first king.

Eli had two sons - Hophni and Phineas. The Lord, in speaking to Samuel, also told him that Hophni and Phineas were regularly cheating people at the temple. The Lord told Samuel that Eli's sons would be punished - that they would both die. At some point later, in a battle with the Philistines who capture the Sacred Chest, both Hophni and Phineas are killed. When Eli (98 years old and very heavy) is told about the Sacred Chest being stolen and his sons being killed, he falls over backwards in his chair and dies when his neck is broken by the fall.

Samuel, as a prophet and man of God, had the tremendous job of directing the rebuilding of the social and religious unity of the people.

The man chosen by the Lord to be the first King is Saul, a tall, handsome warrior. Saul is the son of Kish, a wealthy man from the Tribe of Benjamin. At this time, the Israelites were battling the Philistines off and on, and in one battle Saul disobeys the Lord by keeping healthy cattle and sheep after killing an enemy people, when he had been instructed by the Lord to kill all the people and all the animals, and take nothing. The Lord then instructs Samuel that Saul will not remain as king but that Samuel will find the next king in Bethlehem, in the family of Jesse.

Samuel goes to see Jesse and asks to meet his sons. Six of Jesse's seven sons are brought out, one by one, but Samuel does not feel that any one of them is "the one." Samuel asks if there is still another son and Jesse answers yes - his youngest son David, a shepherd. David is a sturdy and attractive young man who takes care of the sheep and plays the lute. Samuel asks if he will serve King Saul and so David becomes Saul's servant.

In a battle with the Philistines, David asks for and receives permission to fight the Philistine's not-so-secret weapon, nine-foot tall Goliath. Goliath thinks it is a joke that they would send a boy. He exclaims that if he kills David, the Philistines will be declared the victors over the Israelites, but that if David kills Goliath, the Israelites will be the victors. Using a stone and his slingshot, David kills Goliath and cuts off his head, winning the war with the Philistines. David's stunning victory makes him very popular with Saul's army and people.

Because Saul had been told by Samuel that he won't be king much longer (having sinned against the Lord), Saul becomes jealous and paranoid when he sees how popular is David. He is determined to kill David, whom he sees as his rival. Saul's son, Jonathan, befriends David and states that he loves David as much as he loves himself. Jonathan saves David's life by warning him of Saul's intent to kill him. Earlier, David had married Saul's daughter, Michal.

A side story is that of Abigail, wife of Nabal. Nabal is rude, insolent and an enemy of David. David sets out to kill Nabal and destroy his army. Abigail intercedes with David by bringing him food. Nabal dies of a heart attack and David takes Abigail as his wife.

Several times Saul attempts to kill David. At one point, David finds Saul in a cave and, unknown to Saul, David gets close enough to cut off a piece of Saul's garment but chooses to let Saul live. When Saul learns of this, he declares to David that he will not harm him.

First Samuel ends with Saul and his forces in battle with the Philistines. Jonathan and two of Saul's other sons are killed. Saul is seriously wounded and entreats his servant to kill him rather than let the enemy rejoice over their having killed him. When the servant refuses, Saul falls on his own sword, thus taking his own life.

THE SECOND BOOK OF SAMUEL

Second Samuel continues the theme – that God is working His divine purpose through all the events of Israel's history - preparing a people through whom the Messiah will come.

A subtheme of 1 Samuel and 2 Samuel is the life of David – the man after God's "own heart." His sins are spelled out in letters as large as his virtues. But the striking difference is David's attitude. When confronted with his sins, he repents.

God's forgiveness of David is a reminder to the nation that they can find forgiveness and mercy at the hands of God.

One of the oldest pieces of historical reporting of any length in the ancient world is found in Chapters 9 through 20 of 2 Samuel and in Chapters 1 and 2 of Kings. Many biblical scholars believe the author was an actual eyewitness to the events of the times – someone who was able to give an intimate picture of David's reign and the problems and intrigues which dealt with the succession to David.

David's life takes many turns. He sins by lusting after - and taking - Bathsheba, the wife of one of his army commanders, Uriah the Hittite, who is away in battle.

Bathsheba becomes pregnant. When she tells David that she is expecting his child, David orders Uriah to return home (in hopes of making Bathsheba's pregnancy look as if it is Uriah's doing). Uriah, however, is so loyal to David that, while on leave, he refuses to visit his wife. David then orders Uriah into battle and directs that all assistance be withdrawn from Uriah, so that he is killed.

David then takes Bathsheba as his wife, after which their baby boy is born. Within a matter of days, their son becomes very ill and although David prays for his son's recovery, it is to no avail. The boy dies.

David goes on to have many wives and many children. The names of some of his children are Amnon, Absalom, Solomon (son of Bathsheba), Adonijah, and also a daughter, Tamar. As a young adult, Tamar is raped by her brother Amnon. Their brother Absalom avenges her by killing Amnon.

As the first and second kings of Israel, both Saul and David had many loyal and fierce military men at their command. Saul's cousin Abner was the commander of Saul's army. After Saul's death, Abner gathered his army and chose Saul's youngest and least capable son, Ishbaal, to take over the throne. All the tribes of Israel gave allegiance to the new king except for the Tribe of Judah, which allied itself with David. David's commander-in-chief was a man named Joab and he had fought beside David in battles against King Saul's army.

Abner and his troops advanced to Gibeon, where they were met by Joab in command of David's forces. Abner and Joab agreed to a fighting tournament between 12 strong men picked from both sides.

After all 12 men were killed and victory still remained uncertain, a real military brawl ensued in which Abner's army was defeated. As David's men pursued Abner's retreating army, Abner killed Joab's brother and so began a personal blood feud between Abner and Joab.

At some later point, Abner resolves to side with David and to bring all of Israel with him. When Joab learns of this new alliance, he tries unsuccessfully to turn David against Abner. Joab then takes matters into his own hands. In a supposed gesture of peace, Joab asks Abner to meet him in Hebron where he murders Abner in cold blood.

Following Tamar's rape by Amnon, and Amnon's murder by Absalom, Absalom breaks away from his father David, and in the ensuing years, he becomes David's rival. Absalom eventually leads a revolt against King David, but Joab's troops crush Absalom's rebellion.

In spite of David's command to his men to treat his rebellious and mutinous son with gentleness, Joab kills Absalom when Absalom's hair becomes so badly entangled in tree branches that he cannot defend himself.

This vengeful murder becomes too much for David and so he removes Joab as commander and replaces him with his nephew, Amasa.

Joab then looks for the right opportunity to kill Amasa and finding it, stabs Amasa to death.

THE FIRST BOOK OF THE KINGS

The First Book of the Kings covers the time period of 970 - 825 B.C. and chronicles the kings of Judah and the kings of Israel (the two kingdoms).

The Israelites were the first people of antiquity to develop a true historiography. Other nations, such as Assyria, Babylonia and Egypt, composed annals (a chronological record of the events of successive years), but among the Gentile nations only the Hittites attempted historical writings.

The histories of the kings of Judah and Israel are never mixed in the bible.

While the books of Kings do not give a complete and detailed history of all the kings of Judah and Israel, they do give great emphasis to prophets Elijah and Elisha, and to less influential kings such as Josiah. It is shown how God's blessing attends those who obey the divine commandments and how tragic events follow those who disobey God's commandments.

In David's day, Egypt's power had waned and Assyria was weak.

Idolatry and image worship were regarded as the worst of all sins.

Near the end of David's life, he learns that his fourth son Adonijah (the son of Haggith) has decided to usurp his throne. Adonijah thought he should be king and he conferred with Joab and Abiathar the priest, but not with Nathan the prophet or other "mighty men" who belonged to David. Nathan advises Bathsheba, the mother of Solomon, of Adonijah's plans to become the next king. Bathsheba then goes to David (who is dying), and reminds him of his promise to her to make their son Solomon the next king.

Nathan also came to David with the news that Adonijah was preparing to be king. Hearing all this, David called Zadok the priest, Nathan the prophet and Benaiah (the son of Jehoiada, the priest) and instructed them to have Solomon ride on David's mule and to bring him down to Gihon and there have Zadok and Nathan anoint Solomon as king over Israel and to blow the trumpet and announce, *"Long live King Solomon" (1:34).*

Nathan and Zadok did as King David commanded and when Adonijah heard that Solomon had been made king, he grew very afraid, *". . . he arose, went and took hold of the horns of the altar. . . and said 'Let King Solomon swear to me today that he will not put his servant to death with the sword.'"* And Solomon answered that if Adonijah, *"will be a worthy man, not one of his hairs will fall to the ground; but if wickedness is found in him, he will die." (1:50-52)*

As David's death drew near, he charged Solomon as follows:

"I am going the way of all the earth. Be strong, therefore, and show yourself a man. And keep the charge of the Lord your God, to walk in His ways, to keep His statutes, His commandments, His ordinances, and His testimonies according to what is written in the law of Moses, that you may succeed in all that you do and wherever you turn so that the Lord may carry out His promise which He spoke concerning me, saying, 'If your sons are careful of their way, to walk before Me in truth with all their heart and with all their soul, you shall not lack a man on the throne of Israel." (2:1-4)

On his deathbed, David gives Solomon a message regarding Joab, *". . . do not let his gray hair go down to Sheol in peace." (2:6)* He also advised Solomon not to let Shimei go unpunished (some time earlier, Shimei had cursed David). Joab fled to the altar for sanctuary, but Solomon commanded his servant Benaiah to strike Joab down, thus bringing an end to Joab's violent life.

Following David 's death, Solomon sat on David's throne and *"his kingdom was firmly established." (2:12)*

After his father's death, Adonijah went to Bathsheba and asked if he could have the beautiful virgin Abishag (who had served as David's nurse before he died) as his wife. When Bathsheba told her son Solomon about Adonijah's request, Solomon decided Adonijah had gone against his promise to stay out of trouble and he sent Benaiah to kill him.

After having slain both Joab and Adonijah, Solomon appointed Benaiah over the army. Solomon then called Shimei to him and told him to build a house in Jerusalem and to stay there and that if he left his house, Solomon would have him killed. Shimei did so, but after three years he left his home to look for runaway servants. When Solomon learned of this, he sent Benaiah to kill Shimei. *"Thus the kingdom was established in the hands of Solomon." (2:46)*

Solomon then formed an alliance with Pharaoh King of Egypt, by marrying his daughter.

The Lord appeared to Solomon in a dream at Gibeon and said,

> *"Ask what you wish Me to give you." (3:5). Solomon said, ". . . O Lord, my God thou has made thy servant king in place of my father David yet I am but a little child; . . . So give thy servant an understanding heart to judge Thy people to discern between good and evil. For who is able to judge this great people of Thine?" (3:7-9)*

God was pleased with Solomon's request and answered, *". . . behold I have done according to your words. Behold I have given you a wise and discerning heart, so that there has been no one like you before you, nor shall one like you arise after you." (3:12)*

Solomon became a wise ruler. He administered his most famous case of justice when two women, each claiming a newborn baby as her own, came to him to decide who shall have the child. Because only the women knew whose baby it really was, Solomon ordered the child to be cut in half and a half given to each woman. The real mother immediately stepped forward and said, *"'Oh my lord, give her the living child and by no means kill him.' The other woman said, 'He shall be neither mine nor yours; divide him!'"* Solomon said, *"'Give the first woman the living child and by no means kill him. She is his mother.'" (3:26-27)*

And so Solomon ruled over all of the kingdom of Israel.

"Now God gave Solomon wisdom and very great discernment and breadth of mind like the sand that is on the seashore. . . And men came from all peoples to hear the wisdom of Solomon, from all the kings of the earth who had heard of his wisdom." (4:29-34)

Solomon then formed an alliance with Hiram king of Tyre and determined to build a house for the Lord. Hiram supplied the cedar and cypress wood in exchange for wheat and oil. Solomon used forced laborers from all Israel (over 100,000 workers) and they began to build the house of the Lord in the 480th year *"after the sons of Israel came out of the land of Egypt. . ." (6:1)*

And as the house of the Lord was being built,

". . . the word of the Lord came to Solomon saying, 'Concerning this house which you are building, if you will walk in My statutes and execute my ordinances and keep all My commandments by walking in them, then I will carry out My word with you which I spoke to David your father. And I will dwell among the sons of Israel and will not forsake My people Israel.'"(6:11-13)

Solomon also built a house for his wife, the Pharaoh's daughter.

After the Lord's temple was completed, the tablets of stone which Moses had brought down from the mountain were placed in the ark.

"And it came about when the priests came from the holy place, that the cloud filled the house of the Lord, so that the priests could not stand to minister because of the cloud, for the glory of the Lord filled the house of the Lord." (8: 10-11)

Solomon dedicated the temple in prayer *(8:22-53)* and the king and all of Israel offered sacrifices before the Lord (22,000 oxen and 120,000 sheep, as well as other offerings).

The Lord then appeared to Solomon again in a dream, at Gibeon, and told him He had heard his prayer. The Lord said:

> *"I will establish the throne of your kingdom over Israel forever, just as I promised to your father David. . .But if you or your sons shall indeed turn away from following Me, and shall not keep My commandments and My statutes. . .and shall go and serve other gods and worship them, then I will cut off Israel from the land which I have given them and the house which I have consecrated for My name. . ." (9:5-7)*

Solomon became so famous that even the Queen of Sheba (a woman of wealth, beauty and power) came to see him. She tested him with difficult questions, *"And Solomon answered all her questions; nothing was hidden from the king which he did not explain to her." (10:3)* The Queen of Sheba and King Solomon exchanged many valuable gifts.

> The city of Sheba is believed to have been located in either Ethiopia or Yemen.

> *"So Solomon became greater than all the kings of the earth in riches and in wisdom. And all the earth was seeking the presence of Solomon to hear his wisdom which God had put in his heart." (10: 23-24)*

> *"Now King Solomon loved many foreign women along with the daughter of Pharaoh: Moabite, Ammonite, Edomite, Sidonian and Hittite women. . ." (11:1)*

These women were from nations that the Lord had told the sons of Israel not to associate with, *". . . for they will surely turn your heart away after their gods." (11:2)*

Solomon had 700 wives and princesses and 300 concubines, *"When Solomon was old, his wives turned his heart away after other gods; and his heart was not wholly devoted to the Lord his God. . ." (11:3-4).*

> *"And Solomon did what was evil in the sight of the Lord. . ." (11:6) "Then Solomon built a high place for Chemosh the detestable idol of Moab. . . and for Molech the detestable idol of the sons of Ammon." (11:7).*

55.

Molech was a god of the Ammonites that involved a cult demanding the sacrifice of children. Chemosh was a god of the Moabites which also involved human sacrifice. The shrine that Solomon built to the god Chemosh was destroyed by Josiah and Jeremiah 300 years later. Both the Moabites and the Ammonites are believed to be descendants of Lot.

The Lord then became angry with Solomon and told him that, because of his turning away and worshipping other gods, the Lord would tear the kingdom from him.

THE SECOND BOOK OF THE KINGS

> **The Northern Kingdom (Israel) falls** - its prophets are Elijah and Elisha.
>
> **The Southern Kingdom (Judah) falls** – its prophets are Hezekiah, Manasseh and Amon.

The great prophet Elijah (the Tishbite) appears in Chapter 17 of Second Kings. He restored life to a young man by praying to the Lord. Elijah opposed Ahab, King of Israel (an evil king who worshiped false gods). Ahab set his wife, Jezebel, against Elijah. Knowing this, Elijah fled from Jezebel and hid in a cave. The Lord came to him and told him that he was to anoint Jehu king over Israel and Elisha as prophet in Elijah's place.

Ahab died in a battle and Ahaziah, his son, became king of Israel. Elijah performed many miracles at the Lord's direction. Elijah's apprentice, Elisha, saw Elijah taken up into heaven in a whirlwind and, having been told by Elijah that this will be a sign that he will be a prophet like Elijah, believed it to be so.

Elisha brought a young man back to life and cured Naaman, the captain of the army, of leprosy.

Benhadad, king of Aram, then besieged Samaria (the capital city of Israel) and there was so great a famine in Israel that people practiced cannibalism.

The following table details (as best as possible) **the parallel histories of the kings of Judah and Israel**

Kings of Judah	# of years	Kings of Israel	# of years
Saul (first king – anointed by Samuel, a priest and prophet)			
David (good)	40	Saul's son, Ish-bosheth	2
Solomon (David's son) (good)	40	Jeroboam (evil – idolatry)	22
Rehoboam (Solomon's son) The kingdom is divided here (evil)	17		
Abijam (son of Rehoboam)	3	Nadab (son of Jeroboam) (evil)	2
Asa (son of Abijam) (good)	41	Baasha (son of Nadab?) (evil)	24
Jehoshaphat (son of Asa) (good – devoted to the Lord)	25	Elah (very evil)	2
		Zimri	7 days
Jehoram (son of Jehoshaphat) (evil)	12	Omri (very evil)	12
Ahaziah (son of Jehoram) (Jehu kills Ahaziah)	1	Ahab (son of Omri) more evil than any other king – married Jezebel, served Baal and worshipped false gods. He did more to provoke the Lord God of Israel than all the kings before him.	22
Athaliah becomes Queen of Judah (she is very evil and was responsible for trying to kill all of Ahaziah's offspring)	7		
Jehoash (son of Ahaziah – escaped the wrath of Athaliah – becomes king at age 7) (good)	40	Ahaziah (son of Ahab) (evil – served and worshipped Baal)	2
Amaziah (son of Joash)	29	Joram (son of Ahab)	12
Azariah aka Uzziah (son of Amaziah)	52	Jehu (son of Jehoshaphat)	28
Jotham (son of Uzziah)	16	Jehoahaz (son of Jehu) (evil)	17
Ahaz (son of Jotham)	16	Joash (son of Jehoahaz)	16
Hezekiah (son of Ahaz) (good) (this was during the time of Isaiah the prophet, who was an advisor to Hezekiah)	29	Jeroboam (son of Johash)	41
		Zehariah (son of Jeroboam) (evil)	
		Menahem (son of Gad) (evil)	10
Manasseh (Hezekiah's son) (one of the most evil kings – he worshipped Baal, made his sons pass through fire, practiced witchcraft, etc.)	55	Pehahiah (son of Menahem) (evil)	2
		Pekah (evil)	20
		Hoshea	9
Amon (Manasseh's son) (also evil)	2		

Kings of Judah	# of years	Kings of Israel	# of years
Josiah (Amon's son)	31		
Jehoahaz (Josiah's son) (evil)	3 months		
Eliakim aka Jehoiakim (son of Josiah) (evil)	11 years	It was during Hoshea's time, that Assyria carried away the people of Israel into captivity)	
At this point, Nebuchadnezzar, the king of Babylon, asserted his power over the kingdom of Judah and Jehoiakim became his servant for 3 years.			
Jehoiachin (Jehoiakim's son) becomes king (evil)	3 months		
It was at this time that Nebuchadnezzar besieged Jerusalem and took king Jehoiachin captive. *"Then he led away into exile all Jerusalem and all the captains and all the mighty men of valor, 10,000 captives and all the craftsmen and the smiths."* *(24:14)*			
Zedikiah (son of the king of Babylon) (evil)	11		
"And they slaughtered the sons of Zedikiah before his eyes, then put out the eyes of Zedikiah and bound him with bronze fetters and brought him to Babylon." *(25:7)*			

Elisha the prophet dies:

"And the sons of Israel did things secretly which were not right, against the Lord their God. . . they set for themselves sacred pillars and Asherim on every high hill. . .and they did evil things provoking the Lord. And they served idols, concerning which the Lord had said to them, 'You shall not do this thing.' Yet the Lord warned Israel and Judah through all His prophets. . saying, 'Turn from your evil ways and keep My commandments.'. . . However, they did not listen. . . they rejected His statutes and His covenant which He made with their fathers. . .and they followed vanity and became vain. . .and they forsook all the commandments of the Lord their God and made for themselves molten images, even two calves, and made an Asherah and worshipped all the host of heaven and served Baal.* Then they made their sons and their daughters pass through the fire, and practiced divination and enchantments, and sold themselves to do evil in the sight of the Lord, provoking Him.

"So the Lord was very angry with Israel, and removed them from His sight; none was left except the tribe of Judah. Also Judah did not keep the commandments of the Lord their God, but walked in the customs which Israel had introduced. And the Lord rejected all the descendants of Israel and afflicted them and gave them into the hands of plunderers, until He had cast them out of His sight." *(17:9-20)*

> ***Definition of Baal:** "Any of various local fertility and nature gods of the ancient Semitic peoples, considered to be false idols by the Hebrews. Any false god or idol." *(The American Heritage Dictionary of the English Language)*

"Josiah was eight years old when he became king and he reigned 31 years. . . and he did right in the sight of the Lord. . . " *(22:1-2)* In his 18th year as king, he directed that the high priest Hilkiah count the money brought in to the house of the Lord. It was then that Hilkiah *". . . found the book of the law in the house of the Lord. . ." (22:8)* and the book was brought to Josiah the king and read to him. And when Josiah heard the words of the book of the law, he tore his clothes. He instructed Hilkiah and others to *"inquire of the Lord for me.. ." (22:13)* because he realized that the Israelites had not been adhering to the Lord's commands. So Hilkiah and the other messengers from King Josiah went to Huldah the prophetess who lived in Jerusalem and she told them that the Lord would bring evil on Israel because the people had forsaken the Lord, burned incense to other gods and had provoked the Lord to anger. But because Josiah had inquired of the Lord, the Lord said He had heard him and knew Josiah was repentant of the sins of Israel.

Josiah, *"Then stood by the pillar and made a covenant before the Lord, to walk after the Lord, and to keep His commandments and His testimonies and His statutes with all his heart and all his soul, to carry out the words of this covenant that were written in this book. . ." (23:3)*

Then King Josiah resolved to reform Israel and he set about burning and destroying all the vessels that were made for Baal which were in the temple. He got rid of the idolatrous priests (and Asherah). *"He also defiled Topheth* [a location in Jerusalem where human sacrifices were made to the pagan gods Molech and Baal] *. . .so that no man might make his son or daughter pass through the fire for Molech."(23:10)* He smashed the pagan and evil altar and symbols where the people had been worshipping evil gods, and slaughtered the priests who were provoking the Lord by worshipping false gods. Josiah then reinstituted Passover and commanded all the people to celebrate the Passover, *"as it is written in this book of the covenant." (23:21)*

Josiah also removed the mediums and spiritists and all the idols and all the abominations in the land. *"And before him there was no king like him who turned to the Lord with all his heart and all his soul and with all his might, according to the law of Moses. . ." (23:25)*

> *"However, the Lord did not turn from the fierceness of His great wrath. . . because of all the provocations with which Manasseh had provoked Him. And the Lord said, 'I will remove Judah also from My sight, as I have removed Israel. And I will cast off Jerusalem, this city which I have chosen, and the temple of which I said, 'My name shall be there.'"(23:26-27)* Then Pharaoh Neco king of Egypt killed Josiah and Johoahaz became king in his place. But he *"did evil in the sight of the Lord." (23:32)* and Pharaoh imprisoned him at Riblah in the land of Hamath, and made Josiah's son Eliahim the king and changed his name to Jehoiakim. Pharaoh took Jehoahaz to Egypt and he died there. *"So Jehoiakim slept with his fathers, and Jehoiachin his son became king in his place. . .and he did evil in the sight of the Lord. . So the king of Babylon took him captive in the eighth year of his reign." (24:6 - 12)*

Then the Babylonians burned the house of the Lord and carried away the Israelites into exile, leaving behind some of the poorest people of the land to be vinedressers and plowmen.

Nebuchadnezzar appointed Gedaliah over the people who were left in Judah, but soon thereafter he was struck down and killed.

> *"Now it came about in the 37th year of the exile of Johoiachin king of Judah. . . the king of Babylon released Johoiachin from prison." (25:27)*

THE FIRST BOOK OF THE CHRONICLES

Although the author is not known, it is commonly thought to be the prophet Ezra.

Written 100 years after Kings, the books of Chronicles, with their goal of maintaining racial and religious purity, are weighted with genealogies. There is also an emphasis on the Law of Moses.

First and Second Chronicles also give additional insight into the kingships of both David and Solomon.

First Chronicles begins with a genealogy from Adam to the family of Abraham, then on to Jacob (Israel), and to the families of David and Solomon, then the sons of Judah (descendants of Simeon), the genealogy of Reuben, the genealogy of Levi (the priestly line of the 12 tribes), the descendants of Issachar, Benjamin, Naphtali, Manasseh, Ephraim and Asher, and lastly, the genealogy from Benjamin, King Saul and the ancestry and descendants of Saul.

The Prayer of Jabez is found in Chapter 4:10:

> *"Oh, that Thou wouldst bless me indeed, and enlarge my border, and that Thy hand might be with me, and that Thou wouldst keep me from harm, that it may not pain me!' And God granted him what he requested."*

Then there is a retelling of the defeat and death of Saul and his sons, followed by a recounting of how David became king over all of Israel and a numbering of the sons from most of the tribes of Israel who helped David.

When the Philistines heard that David had been anointed king over all of Israel, they went in search of him. David asked God if he should go up against the Philistines and the Lord said to him, *"Go up, for I will give them into your hand. . .Then the fame of David went out into all the lands; and the Lord brought the fear of him on all nations." (14:10-17)*

David built houses for himself in the City of David (Jerusalem) and selected members of the tribe of Levi to carry the ark of God to the City of David. David then gave thanks to the Lord in a psalm of thanksgiving which begins:

> *"Oh give thanks to the Lord, call upon His name; make known His deeds among the peoples. Sing to Him; sing praises to Him; speak of all His wonders. Glory in His holy name. . .Let the heart of those who seek the Lord be glad."(16:8-10)*

When David dwelt in his house, the word of God came to Nathan the prophet. God instructed Nathan to tell David,

> *". . .I have been with you wherever you have gone, and have cut off all your enemies from before you; and I will make you a name like the name of the great ones who are in the earth. . . and it shall come about when your days are fulfilled that you must go to be with your fathers; that I will set up one of your descendants after you, who shall be of your sons; and I will establish his kingdom. He shall build for Me a house, and I will establish his throne forever. I will be his father, and he shall be My son; and I will not take My lovingkindness away from him, as I took it from him who was before you. But I will settle him in My house and in My kingdom forever, and his throne shall be established forever." (17:8-12)*

Several successful battles are detailed in which Israel was able to defeat its enemies, but then *"Satan stood up against Israel and moved David to number Israel." (21:1)*

David's commander-in-chief advised David not to number the people of Israel again, but David insisted and God was displeased.

God spoke,

> *"I offer you three things; choose for yourself one of them that I may do it to you. . . either three years of famine or three months to be swept away before your foes, while the sword of your enemies overtakes you, or else three days of the sword of the Lord, even pestilence in the land, and the angel of the Lord destroying throughout all the territory of Israel. . .'"*

And David responded,

> *"'I am in great distress; please let me fall into the hand of the Lord, for His mercies are very great. But do not let me fall into the hand of man.' So the Lord sent a pestilence on Israel; 70,000 men of Israel fell. And God sent an angel to Jerusalem to destroy it; but as he [the angel] was about to destroy it, the Lord saw and was sorry over the calamity, and said to the destroying angel, 'It is enough; now relax your hand. . .' then David. . . saw the angel of the Lord standing between earth and heaven with his drawn sword in his hand stretched out over Jerusalem. Then David and the elders, covered with sackcloth, fell on their faces. And David said to God, 'Is it not I who commanded to count the people? Indeed, I am the one who has sinned and done very wickedly, but these sheep, what have they done? O Lord my God, please let Thy hand be against me and my father's household but not against Thy people that they should be plagued." (21:10-17)*

David then made preparations to build a temple for God and he charged his son Solomon with the task of carrying out this great plan and he made Solomon king over Israel.

In chapters 23 through 27, the responsibilities given to the descendants of the tribes of Israel are set forth, including overseeing the work of the house of the Lord, officers and judges, gatekeepers, musicians, keepers of the treasure, commanders of the army, overseers and counselors.

In Chapter 28, David addresses the officials, princes of the tribes, commanders and overseers and explains that, although he had wanted to build a permanent house for the Lord, because he was a man of war and had shed blood, his son Solomon would be king and would build the house for the Lord.

David then says to Solomon (among other things):

> *"As for you, my son, Solomon, know the God of your father, and serve Him with a whole heart and a willing mind; for the Lord searches all hearts and understands every intent of the thoughts. If you seek Him, He will let you find Him; but if you forsake Him, he will reject you forever." (28:9)*

David then died, having reigned over Israel for 40 years (seven years in Hebron and 33 years in Jerusalem).

THE SECOND BOOK OF THE CHRONICLES

> **Second Chronicles begins with Solomon's death** and details the kings who ruled after Solomon, as well as the exile of the people from Jerusalem.
>
> **Solomon built a palace for himself.** He also completed the temple in Jerusalem (20 years of building), thereby fulfilling David's promise to the Lord - to build a temple.
>
> **Chronicles traces the lineage of the kings - from David** on down.

The second book of Chronicles retells the stories of Solomon as told in 1 Kings. Solomon asks the Lord for wisdom and knowledge and the Lord rewards him with great wisdom along with bountiful riches, wealth and honor.

Solomon decides to carry out the work of building a house for the Lord and he forms an alliance with Huram (also known as Hiram), the king of Tyre. Once the temple was complete, the Ark of the Covenant was brought into the inner sanctuary. King Solomon and all the congregation of Israel assembled and sacrificed so great a number of sheep and oxen they could not be counted.

> *"There was nothing in the ark except the two tablets which Moses put there at Horeb, where the Lord made a covenant with the sons of Israel, when they came out of Egypt. . . then the house of the Lord, was filled with a cloud, so that the priests could not stand to minister because of the cloud, for the glory of the Lord filled the house of God." (5:10-14)*

Following Solomon's death, his son Rehoboam became king, but he lacked his father's wisdom and sound judgment. He was determined to make the peoples' lives harder and he demanded much more of them. *"And he did evil because he did not set his heart to seek the Lord." (12:14)*

It is here that the United Kingdom of Israel becomes the Divided Kingdoms of North and South. The Israelites (from the north) - led by Jeroboam - ask Rehoboam to be easier on them than his father Solomon had been. Instead, following the advice of his young, brash and inexperienced advisors, Rehoboam tells the people of the Northern Kingdom that he will be much harder on them, giving the example that, if his father whipped them with leather straps he will whip them with leather straps which have nails embedded in them.

Jeroboam became Israel's king. He erected images of golden bulls at two major religious centers in the northern kingdom. Since worshipping images was anathema to people who worshipped Yahweh, and since the symbol for Baal (pagan) worship was the bull, this created many problems and this action was constantly referred to as the major sin of Israel (worshipping false gods).

The people of the north rebelled against Jeroboam's leadership and seceded from the union, creating the Divided Kingdom in 922/921 B.C. Israel then became the northern kingdom (with Samaria as its capital) and Judah became the southern kingdom (with Jerusalem as its capital). The animosity toward Samaritans began with these events.

Chronicles goes on to detail the reign of kings of both the Kingdoms of Judah and Israel.

When Asa was king of Judah, Zerah the Ethiopian came out against Asa's army with an army of a million men and 300 chariots.

> *"Then Asa called to the Lord his God, and said, 'Lord, there is no one besides Thee to help in the battle between the powerful and those who have no strength; so help us, O lord our God, for we trust in Thee, and in Thy name have come against this multitude. O Lord, Thou art our God; let not man prevail against Thee.' So the Lord routed the Ethiopians before Asa and before Judah, and the Ethiopians fled." (14:11–12)*

> *"Now the Spirit of God came on* Azariah [the prophet] *the son of Oded, and he went out to meet Asa and said to him, 'Listen to me, Asa, and all Judah and Benjamin: the Lord is with you when you are with Him. And if you seek Him, He will let you find Him; but if you forsake Him, He will forsake you.'" (15: 1-2)*

In Asa's 36th year as king, Baasha, king of Israel came up against Judah in an attempt to prevent anyone from going out or coming in to Asa. Asa then made a treaty with Benhadad king of Aram (in Damascus) and Benhadad sent his armies against the cities of Israel. The seer (prophet) Hanani came to Asa and accused him of relying on the army of the king of Aram, rather than on the Lord. He said,

> *"Were not the Ethiopians and the Lubim an immense army with very many chariots and horsemen? Yet because you relied on the Lord, He delivered them into your hand. For the eyes of the Lord move to and fro throughout the earth that He may strongly support those whose heart is completely His. You have acted foolishly in this. Indeed, from now on you will surely have wars." (16: 8-9)*

Asa became angry and imprisoned Hanani and in the 39th year of Asa's reign as king of Judah, he became diseased in his feet and he died in the 41st year of his reign.

Sometime later, when Ahaziah became king (he reigned for only one year before he was assassinated), he walked in the ways of the house of Ahab, because his mother, Athaliah (granddaughter of Omri) was his counselor and she was very wicked. When Athaliah learned that her son was dead, she ordered that all the royal offspring be murdered. However, one young child, Joash, was hidden away and escaped the evil Athaliah who reigned as queen over Judah for six years.

In the seventh year of Athaliah's reign, Jehoiada the chief priest aligned enough important people against Athaliah and they made young Joash king. When Athaliah learned of this, she declared that treason had been worked against her. They then conspired to kill her *"at the entrance of the Horse Gate of the king's house. . ." (23:15)* The people then tore down the house of Baal. Joash was seven at the time he became king. He reigned for 40 years and he did, *"what was right in the sight of the Lord all the days of Jehoiada the priest." (24:1-2)*

Joash had the temple restored. However, following the death of the priest Jehoiada, Joash had Jehoiada's son murdered, who, as he died, declared, *"May the Lord see and avenge!" (24:22)* The army of the Arameans then came up against Joash and murdered him. His son Amaziah became king.

Amaziah reigned over Judah for 25 years, *"And he did right in the sight of the Lord, yet not with a whole heart. Now it came about as soon as the kingdom was firmly in his grasp, that he killed his servants who had slain his father [Joash], the king." (25:2-3).* And after a successful battle with the Edomites, *". . .he brought the gods of the sons of Seir, set them up as his gods, bowed down before them, and burned incense to them. Then the anger of the Lord burned against Amaziah. . ." (25:14-15)*

Amaziah (king of Judah) then challenged Joash the king of Israel, who advised him not to go into battle against Israel, but Amaziah wouldn't listen, and so Israel and Judah, *"faced each other at Beth-shemesh, which belonged to Judah and Judah was defeated by Israel. . . Then Joash king of Israel captured Amaziah. . . and brought him to Jerusalem [the capital city of Judah] and tore down the wall of Jerusalem from the Gate of Ephraim to the Corner Gate, 400 cubits." (25:21-23)*

> *"And Amaziah, the son of Joash, king of Judah, lived 15 years after the death of Joash, son of Jehoahaz, king of Israel." (25:25) "And from the time that Amaziah turned away from following the Lord, they conspired against him in Jerusalem and he fled to Lachish; but they sent after him to Lachish and killed him there." (25:27)*

Uzziah then became king of Judah when he was 16 years old. He reigned 52 years and *"did right in the sight of the Lord."* With God's help, he warred against the Philistines, and he *"built towers in the wilderness and hewed many cisterns for he had much livestock, both in the lowlands and in the plain. He also had plowmen and vinedressers in the hill country and the fertile fields, for he loved the soil." (26:4-10)*

> *"But when he became strong, his heart was so proud that he acted corruptly, and he was unfaithful to the Lord his God for he entered the temple of the Lord to burn incense on the altar of incense." (26:16)*

And since this was something that only the priests, the sons of Aaron (Levites) were allowed to do, the priests tried to stop Uzziah, but he became enraged with the priests and leprosy broke out on his forehead and he became a leper the rest of his life and he was cut off from the house of the Lord.

At Uzziah's death, Jotham, his son, age 25, became king and he, *"did right in the sight of the Lord" (27:2)* during his reign of 16 years.

Jotham's son Ahaz, became king and he also reigned 16 years, but he committed many sins against the Lord, burning incense and burning his sons in fire. Because of Ahaz's sins, Judah was invaded by the king of Aram and many people were taken captive to Damascus (Syria).

As the kingdom of Judah was in a weakened condition, Israel also preyed upon it and took many of the people of Judah captive. A prophet named Oded told the Israelites that taking the people of Judah and Jerusalem captive would cause the anger of the Lord to burn against them, and so certain men were designated to feed and clothe the captives and lead them on donkeys to Jericho and the Israelites returned to Samaria.

But king Ahaz continued to be unfaithful to the Lord and he *"sacrificed to the gods of Damascus. . . and in every city of Judah he made high places to burn incense to other gods, and provoked the Lord, the God of his fathers, to anger." (28:25)*

 Ahaz died and Hezekiah, his son became king of Judah when he was 25 years old and reigned for 29 years. *"And he did right in the sight of the Lord. . ." (29:2)*

Hezekiah repaired the house of the Lord and had the uncleanness carried out. He declared, *"For our fathers have been unfaithful and have done evil in the sight of the Lord our God and have forsaken Him and turned their faces away from the dwelling place of the Lord. . ." (29:6)*

Hezekiah then restored temple worship. He ordered the Levites to sing praises to the Lord, which they did, and so the services of the house of the Lord were reestablished.

Hezekiah then invited all of Israel and Judah to come to Jerusalem to celebrate Passover, but some of the people laughed and mocked the couriers who carried the invitation. Many people however did come to Jerusalem to celebrate the Feast of Unleavened Bread. Many of them had not consecrated themselves, but went ahead and ate the Passover other than was prescribed.

Hezekiah prayed for the people and the Lord heard Hezekiah and healed them.

> *"And all the assembly of Judah rejoiced with the priests and the Levites, and all the assembly that came from Israel, both the sojourners who came from the land of Israel and those living in Judah, so there was great joy in Jerusalem, because there was nothing like this in Jerusalem since the days of Solomon, the son of David, king of Israel. . . and thus Hezekiah did throughout Judah; and he did what was good, right and true before the Lord his God."* *(30:25-26 and 31:20)*

Then Sennacherib, king of Assyria, invaded Judah, so King Hezekiah cut off the water supply outside the city of Jerusalem and Hezekiah and Isaiah the prophet prayed and cried to heaven, *"And the Lord sent an angel who destroyed every mighty warrior, commander and officer in the camp of the king of Assyria. . ."* *(32: 20-21)*.

When Hezekiah died, his son Manasseh, age 12, became king and reigned for 55 years. *"And he did evil in the sight of the Lord."* *(33:2)* He rebuilt the high places his father Hezekiah had torn down. He erected altars for the Baals, made asherim and made his sons pass through the fire. He practiced witchcraft, divination, sorcery and dealt with mediums and spiritists. *"He did much evil in the sight of the Lord, provoking Him to anger."* *(33:6)*

> *"Thus Manasseh misled Judah and the inhabitants of Jerusalem to do more evil than the nations whom the Lord destroyed before the sons of Israel."* *(33:9)*

The Lord spoke to Manasseh, who, to some extent, repented of his evil ways. When he died, his son Amon, age 22, became king and reigned for two years but he was so evil, in ways like his father, that his servants killed him.

Amon's son, *Josiah*, age 8, then became king and reigned for 31 years. Josiah was a good king and he purged Judah and Jerusalem of the evil pagan images and he sent several trusted officials to repair the house of the Lord.

During the repair process, Hilkiah, the high priest, found the book of the law of the Lord given by Moses. When the book was brought to Josiah, he realized that the wrath of the Lord had come down on Judah because they had not observed the word of the Lord.

Josiah then made a covenant before the Lord to keep His commandments and His testimonies and His statutes. As part of his covenant, Josiah removed all the abominations from the lands belonging to the sons of Israel.

Then Josiah celebrated the Passover to the Lord in Jerusalem, *"And there had not been celebrated a Passover like it in Israel since the days of Samuel the prophet; nor had any of the kings of Israel celebrated a Passover as Josiah did. . ." (35:18)*

After that, Neco the king of Egypt made war at Carchemish and Josiah went out to engage him. Neco asked Josiah why he was not turning away, since Neco wasn't making war with him, but Josiah wouldn't retreat and made war with Egypt. Neco's archers killed Josiah and Jeremiah the prophet chanted a lament for him.

The people then made Josiah's son Joahaz, age 23, the king and he reigned for only three months. The king of Egypt deposed Joahaz and took him to Egypt.

The king of Egypt then made Eliakim (Joahaz's brother) king and changed his name to Johoiahim.

Johoiahim (formerly Eliakim) was 25 when he became king and he ruled for 11 years and he did evil in the sight of the Lord his God.

Nebuchadnezzar, king of Babylon (today's Iraq), took Johoiahim captive to Babylon.

Johoiahim's eight year old son, Johoiachin, then became king and ruled for three months and 10 days and did evil in the sight of the Lord.

Then King Nebuchadnezzar made his kinsman, 21 year old Zedekiah, king. Zedekiah ruled for 11 years in Jerusalem and he did evil in the sight of the Lord his God.

As king, Zedekiah did not humble himself before Jeremiah the prophet and he also rebelled against king Nebuchadnezzar. All the officials of the priests and the people were very unfaithful, followed abominations of the nations, defiled the house of the Lord, and mocked the messengers of God until the wrath of the Lord rose up against the people.

The Chaldeans (people of Babylon) killed many of Israel's young men, burned the house of God, broke down the wall of Jerusalem, burned buildings and destroyed valuable articles.

Those who escaped the Chaldeans were carried away to Babylon to fulfill the word of the Lord by the mouth of Jeremiah.

70 years passed, and then Cyrus king of Persia, in order to fulfill the word of the Lord by Jeremiah, sent a proclamation throughout his kingdom, *"The Lord, the God of heaven, has given me all the kingdoms of the earth, and He has appointed me to build Him a house in Jerusalem, which is in Judah. Whoever there is among you of all His people, may the Lord his God be with him and let him go up!" (36:23)*

The end of 2 Chronicles briefly tells how King Nebuchadnezzar of Babylonia destroyed the City of Jerusalem and carried the people away into captivity ("the exile").

> **While the destruction of Jerusalem isn't given much coverage in the Old Testament**, it is very important. The city of Jerusalem which had been built by King Solomon at the direction of his father, King David, was virtually destroyed - to the point that the Old Testament refers to it as a desert.

THE BOOK OF EZRA

Ezra was a scribe and a most learned interpreter of the law.
There is a tradition that all of the ancient books were lost and Ezra
rewrote them under divine inspiration.

Ezra records God's fulfillment of his promise to Israel through
Jeremiah, to bring His people back to their land after 70 years of
captivity in Babylon (postexilic) and covers the events following
the 70 years of captivity.

Although Ezra comes before Nehemiah in the bible, biblical
scholars think that Ezra may actually have come after Nehemiah,
and that these two prophets may not have been contemporaries,
since Nehemiah lived under Artaxerxes I and Ezra lived under
Artaxerxes II.

**Ezra was a teacher, a priest and a scribe. He was an expert in the
Law** that the Lord had given to Moses. Ezra had spent his life studying
and obeying the Law and teaching it to others.

He played a part in the return of the exiled peoples to Jerusalem.
Ezra was living in exile in Babylonia and was given a letter from King
Artaxerxes of Persia which instructed him to take the people of Israel,
priests and Levites, back to Jerusalem and rebuild the temple.

**Ezra demanded that those Jews who wished to return to life in
Jerusalem** give up the worship of foreign gods and put aside the pagan
wives and families they had taken while in exile. He fasted and then
reminded the people that the Lord God had given Moses instructions
that His people were not to marry outside of their faith. The people
were very sorry for their sins. They cried, moaned and covered
themselves with ashes.

The people of the Northern Kingdom of Israel were never able to return from their exile to Assyria. **Unlike Judah,** the Northern Kingdom had no temple, either in stone, mortar or in their hearts. Israel had no survivors of the royal family after the fall of the Northern Capital of Samaria.

Assyria moved most of the Israelites out of the Northern Kingdom and transplanted foreigners into their lands. This brought about a mixing of the foreigners with the surviving Israelites and gave rise to the Samaritan people – a mixed race hated by the Jews.

Most important, there was no continuing religious leadership or center of worship among the Israelite exiles in Assyria to preserve their religious and cultural identity. Without this identity, they were assimilated into the shifting populations of the ancient Middle East and became known as the 10 lost tribes of the House of Israel. But the history of the exiled kingdom of Judah was different.

It was Babylon (modern day Iraq) which finally captured and burned the City of Jerusalem in 586 B.C.

In Babylonia, the exiled Jews were allowed to settle in their own communities, so they were able to preserve their identities. Judah also had the Davidic line on the throne and a descendant of David went into exile with them. Babylon did not replace the population of Judea, as Assyria had done in Samaria. There were always some Jews left in Jerusalem and those people who had been exiled to Babylon never forgot their Holy City and temple, which lay in ruins on the sacred mountain of Zion.

The exiles from Judah had priests and scribes who preserved and taught the books of the law. The survivors and descendants of the exiled Jews in Babylon became a people whose religious life was centered in the teaching of the Sacred Book.

When the people began to rebuild Jerusalem, after their 70 year exile, they met with much opposition and the work was stopped for a time until Darius, King of Babylon, found the decree to rebuild the house of God, which Cyrus had issued years earlier. *(2 Chronicles 36:23)*

When the rebuilding of the temple was completed, many of the Israelites who had been in exile in Babylon, returned to Jerusalem with Ezra, the Scribe, *"For Ezra had set his heart to study the law of the Lord, and to practice it, and to teach His statutes and ordinances in Israel." (7:10)*

The return to their homeland took place during the reign of king Artaxerxes of Persia (Babylon) who gave a decree to Ezra that *"any of the people of Israel and their priests and the Levites in my kingdom who are willing to go to Jerusalem, may go with you." (7:13)*

The king sent silver and gold with Ezra as an offering, *". . .to the God of Israel, whose dwelling is in Jerusalem." (7:15)*

As the Israelites completed the rebuilding of the temple, certain Israelites came to Ezra, telling him that many of the people had intermarried with people from other lands. This appalled Ezra so much, that he tore his robes, weeping before the house of God. Then the people gathered around Ezra and it was decided to make a covenant with the Lord to put away their foreign wives and their children. A proclamation went throughout Judah that all should assemble in Jerusalem and whoever would not come within three days would be excluded from the assembly of the exiles. There was agreement that foreign wives and children would be separated from the people and they pledged to do so.

While some of Ezra is written in the third person tense (as is most of the bible), part of this book is written in the first person tense, making this story of the return to Jerusalem, and the rebuilding of the temple and the sense of community and culture very personal and real.

THE BOOK OF NEHEMIAH

Nehemiah covers a period of about 25 years (445 – 420 B.C.) when Nehemiah returned from Babylon to cleanse Jerusalem and rebuild the walls of the city.

Nehemiah had two concerns: fidelity to the law and the determination to rebuild the walls of the city of Jerusalem.

This book, like Ezra, is written in the first person tense and it becomes a most personal story of a slave (praying for God's help) who asks his master for a great favor and is granted the favor.

Nehemiah was a cupbearer to the Persian (today's Iran) king Artaxerxes in the City of Susa. He had learned from his brother that although 12 years had passed since the Jews who were exiled from Judah and Jerusalem had returned to Jerusalem (after 70 years in exile), the city of Jerusalem had still not been rebuilt.

Nehemiah asked King Artaxerxes for permission to return to rebuild Jerusalem. Not only did Artaxerxes give him permission, but he also gave Nehemiah letters authorizing both his safe passage and building materials from neighboring regions.

When he returned to Jerusalem and began the work of rebuilding the walls of the City, Nehemiah was subjected to much jealousy from Sanballet, the governor of Samaria (the capital of the Northern Kingdom), as well as several other important people in the region. To counter the sabotage and damage being done, Nehemiah organized the workers so that they took turns building - or guarding others who were building - from those who didn't want to see Jerusalem rebuilt.

When the temple was rebuilt, Nehemiah had a census taken of those Israelites who had returned to Jerusalem from Babylon following the 70 year exile. The census revealed that there were 42,360 Israelites, not counting their servants or animals.

Then all the people gathered together and Ezra the scribe read from the book of the Law of Moses. From the book of the law, the people learned how the Lord had commanded, through Moses, that the sons of Israel should live in booths during the feast of the seventh month. *"And the entire assembly of those who had returned from the captivity made booths and lived in them. . . And there was great rejoicing." (8:17)*

> **The Feast of Booths is now celebrated as "Sukkoth"** – a late summer festival or holiday, in which Jews celebrate the return to Jerusalem from exile, as directed by Ezra.

The people of Israel then separated themselves from all foreigners and they confessed their sins. Nehemiah reminded the people that when Moses was bringing the people out of Egypt, they were met - not with kindness but with hostility - by the Ammonites and Moabites who hired Balaam to curse God's chosen people.

Nehemiah restored recognition of the Sabbath and forbid the buying and selling of goods on the Sabbath. He commanded merchants and traders to spend the night outside Jerusalem if they happened to be there on the Sabbath.

Nehemiah also forbid mixed marriages.

"In those days I also saw that the Jews had married women from Ashdod, Ammon and Moab. As for their children, half spoke in the language of Ashdod and none of them was able to speak the language of Judah. . . So I contended with them and cursed and struck some of them and pulled out their hair and made them swear by God, 'You shall not give your daughters to their sons, nor take of their daughters for your sons or for yourselves. . .'" (13:23-25)

Nehemiah became governor of Jerusalem. He was successful in getting the people together and keeping them focused. Many families took responsibility for rebuilding sections of Jerusalem's walls. The names of some of the areas rebuilt are: Valley Gate, Dragon Spring, Garbage Gate, Fountain Gate, King's Pool, Kidron Valley, Sheep Gate, Hundred Tower, Hananel Tower, Fish Gate, Ancient Gate, West Euphrates Province, Broad Wall and Oven Tower.

While work was going on, there were plots against Nehemiah's life because of the intense jealousy of others. He carefully avoided falling into their traps.

At completion of the rebuilding of Jerusalem, the people came together and Ezra the prophet read from the Book of the Law of Moses.

> As earlier stated, **it is thought that Ezra came so much later than Nehemiah that they were not contemporaries,** but these books of the Old Testament read as though they were.

The people prayed to the Lord God, reviewing their history from Abraham to Egypt and how the Lord had promised to make the Israelite people more numerous than the stars in the sky and how, even though, time after time, the people turned away from the Lord, God always remained faithful to His promises to them.

At the reestablishment of the City, many of the people who returned could remember from 70 years earlier, the splendor of the original city of Jerusalem. The people entered into an agreement with the Lord regarding not marrying foreigners, not buying goods on the Sabbath, tithing grain, taking care of the temple and much, much more. Both Nehemiah and Ezra exhorted the people to put aside their foreign wives and children. Amid much sorrow and grief, many of the people did this in re-pledging their fidelity to their God.

THE BOOK OF ESTHER

Esther is a Persian name, which in Hebrew is Hadassah.

Esther covers a period of about 10 years from the great feast of the Persian king, Xerxes, to the Feast of Purim (now a traditional Jewish holy day).

God is not mentioned a single time, and yet God uses Esther to help His people.

The events recounted in the Book of Esther are set in the time period following the destruction of the temple in Jerusalem (484 B.C. – 474 B.C.) and the carrying off of Jewish people to Babylon (Iraq). Sixteen years after the first Feast of Purim Ezra leads his expedition back to Jerusalem.

The Book of Esther shows the inexorable working of Divine Providence – God's caring for His people who are oppressed.

In Babylon, King Xerxes' wife Vashti refused to obey him when he ordered her to put on her crown and come meet the foreign dignitaries that he was entertaining. The king and his advisors decided that Vashti's punishment should be that she could never see the king again (same as divorce).

King Xerxes took a new wife (Esther) chosen from hundreds of young women who had been "beautified" for one year before meeting the king.

Esther was a Jewish orphan being cared for by her cousin Mordecai. The Jews were living in "ghettoes" in a foreign land (Babylon).

At one point in this story, Mordecai had saved the king from assassination, and the king was very grateful to Mordecai.

A man named Haman was the king's closest advisor. Haman (an egomaniac if ever there was one), ordered everyone to bow down before him when they were in his presence. Mordecai refused to do this and Haman swore vengeance. He swore that he would have Mordecai and all the Jews in the city killed and issued an order to this effect which was to take place in about one year.

Through an emissary, Mordecai begged Esther to make her heritage known to the King and to plead with the King to set aside Haman's order.

However, even though Esther was the queen, no one – not even she – could appear before the King without first being summoned. Esther risked her life by daring to go to the King. Her bravery paid off – the King was happy to see her.

During her visit to the king, Esther invited the King and Haman to have supper with her. The King was charmed with Esther and on two successive nights, he and Haman were her guests at supper.

In the meantime, Haman, who had learned that Mordecai was still around, had a gallows built on which he planned to hang Mordecai.

The King, who momentarily had forgotten what Mordecai had earlier done for him, suddenly remembered - and asked Haman what he thought should be done for someone who had saved his life. Haman, believing that the King's question is in regard to him, declared that the person should have the finest in all things and be given a chariot in which to ride around. The King then ordered Haman to do all these things for Mordecai.

During the second dinner which Esther prepared for the King and Haman, the King asked Esther what he could do for her, telling her that he would give her as much as half of his kingdom, should she ask for it.

Esther told the King that if he really cared for her, he would help her save her people. She told him that a reward has been offered to anyone who killed the Jews. The king asked Esther, "Who would do such a thing?" Esther then told the king that it was the evil Haman. The king then left the room and when he returned, Haman was on his knees, begging Esther to help save him (since he knew he was now in big trouble with the king). The king, seeing Haman on his knees before Esther, accused Haman of attempting to molest the queen, and ordered him hanged from Haman's own gallows which had just built for Mordecai.

Haman begs Esther for his life

Esther became a heroine (along with help from Mordecai) because she risked her life for her people. Esther and Mordecai's acts of bravery established the Feast of Purim.

THE BOOK OF JOB

The Book of Job was possibly written in Solomon's time - or may have been written as early as the time of Abraham, Isaac and Jacob. Job may not have been an Israelite.

The Book of Job deals with mankind's constant need to wrestle with problems of suffering and evil.

Job is a godly man, rich and powerful, from who the devil takes everything to see how Job will react. The devil believes that Job will curse God, after all manner of terrible things befall him.

First the devil destroys all Job's servants, animals, crops and then all 10 of his children.

"Then Job arose and tore his robe and shaved his head, and he fell to the ground and worshiped. And he said, 'Naked I came from my mother's womb and naked I shall return there. The Lord gave and the Lord has taken away. Blessed be the name of the Lord.' Through all this Job did not sin nor did he blame God." (1:20-22)

The devil then afflicts Job with boils all over his body.

"Then his wife said to him, 'Do you still hold fast your integrity? Curse God and die.' But he said to her, 'You speak as one of the foolish women speaks. Shall we indeed accept good from God and not accept adversity?' In all this Job did not sin with his lips." (2:9-10)

Three friends – Eliphaz the Temanite, Bildad the Shuhite and Zophar the Naamathite - enter into a lengthy discourse with Job in regard to what has happened to him and how he should feel about it. Then, a young bystander (Elihu, the son of Barachel the Buzite) speaks to Job.

Then God speaks at length to Job about His might and power. *(38 – 40)* Although, like many of us today, Job can find no answer which explains his misfortune and suffering, he refuses to lose his faith in God.

"Job answered the Lord, and said, 'I know that Thou canst do all things, and that no purpose of Thine can be thwarted. . .(42: 1-2) And the Lord restored the fortunes of Job when he prayed for his friends, and the Lord increased all that Job had twofold. . .And the Lord blessed the latter days of Job more than his beginning, and he had 14,000 sheep, and 6,000 camels, and 1,000 yoke of oxen, and 1,000 female donkeys. And he had seven sons and three daughters. . .And after this Job lived 140 years, and saw his sons, and his grandsons, four generations. And Job died, an old man and full of days." (42:10-17

Perhaps the best lesson to be learned from The Book of Job can be summed up in these words of his regarding God:

"And as for me, I know that my Redeemer lives, and at the last He will take His stand on the earth. Even after my skin is destroyed, yet from my flesh I shall see God; whom I myself shall behold, and whom my eyes shall see and not another. My heart faints within me." (19: 25-27)

What joyful hope this message brings to today's Christians from across the centuries! It foretells of Christ's ultimate sacrifice to redeem fallen mankind and the promise of life eternal in heaven with our God!

THE PSALMS

> **There are 150 Psalms (or psalters)** in the bible. These are hymns, songs, anthems or lamentations, the most famous of which is the 23rd Psalm.
>
> **The time frame** of the writing of the Psalms is not fixed and possibly varies in dates by as much as 1,000 years.
>
> **Although the authorship of many psalms is attributed to David,** it is doubtful that he wrote them.
>
> **Psalms is the largest known collection of ancient lyric poetry.** While they differ in style, length, author and purpose, they are all either about God or are addressed to God.
>
> **The Hebrew language is pictorial**, as can be seen from all of the Old Testament and because of this, psalms are vivid and graphic. Many contemporary church hymns are taken from verses found in the Psalms.

The following are but a sampling of the beautiful prayers found in the Book of Psalms.

A psalm asking for the Lord's mercy:

"O Lord, do not rebuke me in Thine anger, nor chasten me in Thy wrath. Be gracious to me, O Lord, for I am pining away; heal me, O Lord, for my bones are dismayed. And my soul is greatly dismayed; But Thou, O Lord – how long?. . . . .Depart from me, all you who do iniquity, for the Lord has heard the voice of my weeping. The Lord has heard my supplication, the Lord receives my prayer. . ." (6: 1-3, 8-9)

Our Lord, Jesus Christ was a scholar and committed much of the Hebrew testament to memory. As He hung in agony on the cross at Calvary waiting for death, he spoke these words:

"My God, my God, why hast Thou forsaken me?" (22:1)

The rest of that part of Psalms is as follows:

*"Far from my deliverance are the words of my groaning.
O my God, I cry by day, but Thou dost not answer; and by night, but
I have no rest. Yet Thou art holy, O Thou who art enthroned upon
the praises of Israel. In Thee our fathers trusted; they trusted, and
Thou didst deliver them. To Thee they cried out, and were
delivered; in Thee they trusted, and were not disappointed." (22:1-
5).*

*"Commit yourself to the Lord; let Him deliver him; let Him rescue
him, because He delights in him." (22:8)*

**It is prophetic that the following lines found in Psalms were written
centuries before Jesus' birth**, and yet they describe, in part, his day of
crucifixion.

*"For dogs have surrounded me; a band of evildoers has
encompassed me; they pierced my hands and my feet. I can count
all my bones. They look, they stare at me; they divide my garments
among them, and for my clothing they cast lots." (22:16-18)*

**The 23rd Psalm is perhaps the best known and best loved psalm of
all:**

*"The Lord is my shepherd, I shall not want. He makes me lie down
in green pastures; He leads me beside quiet waters. He restores my
soul; He guides me in the paths of righteousness for His name's
sake. Even though I walk through the valley of the shadow of death,
I fear no evil; for Thou art with me; Thy rod and Thy staff, they
comfort me. Thou dost prepare a table before me in the presence of
my enemies; Thou hast anointed my head with oil; my cup
overflows. Surely goodness and lovingkindness will follow me all
the days of my life, and I will dwell in the house of the Lord
forever." (23:1-6)*

A psalm asking for the Lord's protection in times of danger:

*"To Thee, O Lord, I lift up my soul. O my god, in Thee I trust.
Do not let me be ashamed; do not let my enemies exult over me.
Indeed, none of those who wait for Thee will be ashamed;
those who deal treacherously without cause will be ashamed."
(25:1-3)*

A psalm asking God to keep us close to Him and far from sin:

*"Make me know Thy ways, O Lord; Teach me Thy paths.
Lead me in Thy truth and teach me, for Thou art the God of my
salvation; for Thee I wait all the day. Remember, O Lord, Thy
compassion and Thy lovingkindnesses, for they have been from of
old. Do not remember the sins of my youth or my transgressions;
according to Thy lovingkindness remember Thou me, for Thy
goodness' sake, O Lord." (25:4-7)*

A psalm for those who trust in the Lord:

*"Do not fret because of evildoers, be not envious toward
wrongdoers. For they will wither quickly like the grass,
And fade like the green herb. Trust in the Lord, and do good;
Dwell in the land and cultivate faithfulness. Delight yourself in the
Lord; and He will give you the desires of your heart. Commit your
way to the Lord, trust also in Him, and He will do it."(37: 1-5)*

"Rest in the Lord and wait patiently for Him. . ." (37:7)

*"Cease from anger, and forsake wrath; do not fret, it leads only to
evildoing." (37:8)*

"Depart from evil, and do good, so you will abide forever." (37:27)

Asking God's protection in times of trouble:

*"God is our refuge and strength, a very present help in trouble.
Therefore we will not fear, though the earth should change,
And though the mountains slip into the heart of the sea;
Though its waters roar and foam, though the mountains quake at its
swelling pride." (46:1-3)*

A psalm for deliverance from enemies of all kinds:

"O God, Thou art my God; I shall seek Thee earnestly; my soul thirsts for Thee, my flesh yearns for Thee, in a dry and weary land where there is no water. Thus I have beheld Thee in the sanctuary to see Thy power and Thy glory. Because Thy lovingkindness is better than life, my lips will praise Thee. So I will bless Thee as long as I live; I will lift up my hands in Thy name. My soul is satisfied as with marrow and fatness, and my mouth offers praises with joyful lips. When I remember Thee on my bed, I meditate on Thee in the night watches, for Thou hast been my help, and in the shadow of Thy wings I sing for joy. My soul clings to Thee; Thy right hand upholds me. For those who seek my life, to destroy it, will go into the depths of the earth. They will be delivered over to the power of the sword; they will be a prey for foxes. But the king will rejoice in God; everyone who swears by Him will glory, for the mouths of those who speak lies will be stopped." (63:1-11)

A prayer of the Afflicted:

"Hear my prayer, O Lord! And let my cry for help come to Thee. Do not hide Thy face from me in the day of my distress; incline Thine ear to me; in the day when I call answer me quickly. For my days have been consumed in smoke, and my bones have been scorched like a hearth. My heart has been smitten like grass And has withered away, Indeed, I forget to eat my bread. Because of the loudness of my groaning my bones cling to my flesh. I resemble a pelican of the wilderness; I have become like an owl of the waste places. I lie awake, I have become like a lonely bird on a housetop. . ." (102: 1-7)

"But Thou, O Lord, dost abide forever; and Thy name to all generations. Thou wilt arise and have compassion on Zion; for it is time to be gracious to her, for the appointed time has come. . ." (102:12-13)

"I say, 'O my God, do not take me away in the midst of my days.'"(102:24)

Praise for the Lord's Mercies:

"Bless the Lord, O my soul; and all that is within me, bless His holy name. Bless the Lord, O my soul, and forget none of His benefits; Who pardons all your iniquities; Who heals all your diseases; Who redeems your life from the pit; who crowns you with lovingkindness and compassion; Who satisfies your years with good things, so that your youth is renewed like the eagle." (103:1-4)

In Psalm 105 is found the story of the Patriarchs of the Old Testament from Abraham, to Isaac, Jacob and Joseph to Moses and Aaron.

Psalm 150, the last of the Psalms, is a Psalm of Praise to our God:

"Praise the Lord! Praise God in His sanctuary; praise Him in His mighty expanse. Praise Him for His mighty deeds; praise Him according to His excellent greatness. Praise Him with trumpet sound; Praise Him with harp and lyre. Praise Him with timbrel and dancing; praise Him with stringed instruments and pipe. Praise Him with loud cymbals; Praise Him with resounding cymbals. Let everything that has breath praise the Lord. Praise the Lord!"(150:1-6)

THE PROVERBS

Proverbs is meant as a way to teach moral and ethical
principles and does so by drawing many contrasts between good
and evil.

Good in the proverbs is represented by words such as
instruction, understanding, justice, equity, knowledge, discretion,
learning, counsel, and, most especially, wisdom.

The wisdom of the proverbs is attributed to King Solomon.
Although his name occurs in three parts of this book, it is not
known whether he wrote any or all of them.

It is known that King Hezekiah of Judah was responsible for
transcribing some of the proverbs.

A sampling of Proverbs. . .

The rewards of wisdom:

> *"Trust in the Lord with all your heart, and do not lean on your own
> understanding. In all your ways acknowledge Him, and He will
> make your paths straight. Do not be wise in your own eyes; fear the
> Lord and turn away from evil. It will be a healing to your body,
> and refreshment to your bones. Honor the Lord from your wealth,
> and from the first of all your produce; so your barns will be filled
> with plenty, and your vats will overflow with new wine. My son, do
> not reject the discipline of the Lord, or loathe His reproof, for
> whom the Lord loves He reproves, even as a father, the son in
> whom he delights."(3:5-12)*

Parental Counsel:

*"Go to the ant, O sluggard, observe her ways and be wise,
which, having no chief, officer or ruler, prepares her food in the
summer, and gathers her provision in the harvest. How long will you
lie down, O sluggard? When will you arise from your sleep?
'A little sleep, a little slumber, a little folding of the hands to rest' –
And your poverty will come in like a vagabond, and your need like
an armed man." (6:6-11)*

*"There are six things which the Lord hates, yes, seven which are an
abomination to Him; haughty eyes, a lying tongue, and hands that
shed innocent blood, a heart that devises wicked plans, feet that run
rapidly to evil, a false witness who utters lies, and one who spreads
strife among brothers." (6: 16-19)*

Wisdom's Invitation:

*"The fear of the Lord is the beginning of wisdom, and the
knowledge of the Holy One is understanding." (9:10)*

Comparing the upright and the wicked :

*"A false balance is an abomination to the Lord, but a just weight is
His delight. When pride comes, then comes dishonor, but with the
humble is wisdom. The integrity of the upright will guide them, but
the falseness of the treacherous will destroy them." (11:1-3)*

*"He who is steadfast in righteousness will attain to life, and he who
pursues evil will bring about his own death." (11:19)*

*"As a ring of gold in a swine's snout, so is a beautiful woman who
lacks discretion." (11:22)*

*"He who diligently seeks good seeks favor, but he who searches
after evil, it will come to him." (11:27)*

*"Truthful lips will be established forever, but a lying tongue is only
for a moment." (12:19)*

*"A wise son accepts his father's discipline, but a scoffer does not
listen to rebuke." (13:1)*

"The one who guards his mouth preserves his life; the one who opens wide his lips come to ruin." (13:3)

"The wise woman builds her house, but the foolish tears it down with her own hands." (14:1)

"In all labor there is profit, but mere talk leads only to poverty." (14:23)

A gentle answer turns away wrath, but a harsh word stirs up anger." (15:1)

"A joyful heart makes a cheerful face, but when the heart is sad, the spirit is broken." (15:13)

"Better is a little with the fear of the Lord, than great treasure and turmoil with it." (15:16)

"Better is a dish of vegetables where love is, than a fattened ox and hatred with it." (15:17)

"Bright eyes gladden the heart; good news puts fat on the bones." (15:30)

"Commit your works to the Lord, and your plans will be established." (16:3)

"Better is a dry morsel and quietness with it than a house full of feasting with strife." (17:1)

"A brother offended is harder to be won than a strong city." (18:19)

"A man of many friends comes to ruin, but there is a friend who sticks closer than a brother." (18:24)

"Listen to counsel and accept discipline, that you may be wise the rest of your days." (19:20)

On life and conduct:

"A good name is to be more desired than great riches, favor is better than silver and gold. The rich and the poor have a common bond, the Lord is the maker of them all."(22:1-2)

"Train up a child in the way he should go, even when he is old he will not depart from it." (22:6)

"Do not associate with a man given to anger; or go with a hot-tempered man, lest you learn his ways, and find a snare for yourself." (22:24-25)

"Do not let your heart envy sinners, but live in the fear of the Lord always." (23:17)

Warnings and Instructions:

"Do not be envious of evil men, nor desire to be with them; For their minds devise violence, and their lips talk of trouble." (24:1-2)

"My son, eat honey, for it is good, yes, the honey from the comb is sweet to your taste; know that wisdom is thus for your soul; if you find it, then there will be a future, and your hope will not be cut off." (24:13-14)

"Let your foot rarely be in your neighbor's house, lest he become weary of you and hate you." (25:17)

"Do not boast about tomorrow, for you do not know what a day may bring forth. Let another praise you, and not your own mouth;" (27:1-2)

"Know well the condition of your flocks, and pay attention to your herds; for riches are not forever, nor does a crown endure to all generations."(27:23-24)

"A fool always loses his temper, but a wise man holds it back." (29:11)

"Do not slander a slave to his master, les he curse you and you be found guilty." (30:10)

"The leech has two daughters, 'Give' 'Give.'" (30:15)

"Four things are small on the earth, but they are exceedingly wise: the ants are not a strong folk, but they prepare their food in the summer; the badgers are not mighty folk, yet they make their houses in the rocks; the locusts have no king, yet all of them go out in ranks; the lizard you may grasp with the hands, yet it is in kings' palaces." (30:24-28)

Description of a worthy woman:

"An excellent wife, who can find? For her worth is far above jewels. The heart of her husband trusts in her, and he will have no lack of gain. She does him good and not evil all the days of her life. . .She rises also while it is still night and gives food to her household. . .She girds herself with strength, and makes her arms strong. She extends her hand to the poor; and she stretches out her hands to the needy.. . .Strength and dignity are her clothing, and she smiles at the future. . .She looks well to the ways of her household, and does not eat the bread of idleness." (31:10-27)

Proverbs ends on this note:

"Charm is deceitful and beauty is vain, but a woman who fears the Lord, she shall be praised. Give her the product of her hands, And let her works praise her in the gates." (31:30-31)

THE BOOK OF ECCLESIASTES

"Ecclesiastes" is the Hebrew word for "assembly" translated into Greek and is a collection of sayings, proverbs, parables and allegories.

Although Ecclesiastes appears to claim Solomon as the author, this is doubtful. It is believed that the unknown author used Solomon as a literary device to convey the message.

This book explores Life's futilities and asks the reader to consider what life is all about.

Ecclesiastes can perhaps be summed up by the fact that humans - in every generation - look for happiness oftentimes in the wrong places.

Ecclesiastes condemns what seems to be the popular, materialistic understanding of life.

The futility of all endeavor:

"The words of the Preacher, the son of David, king in Jerusalem. 'Vanity of vanities,' says the Preacher. . .' All is vanity.'" (1:1-2)

"I, the Preacher, have been king over Israel in Jerusalem. . . And I set my mind to know wisdom and to know madness and folly; I realized that this also is striving after wind. Because in much wisdom there is much grief, and increasing knowledge results in increasing pain." (1:12-18)

"So I turned to consider wisdom, madness and folly. . . And I saw that wisdom excels folly as light excels darkness." (2:12-13)

"Then I said to myself, 'As is the fate of the fool, it will also befall me. Why then have I been extremely wise?'. . .So I hated life, for the work which had been done under the sun was grievous to me; because everything is futility and striving after wind." (2:15-17)

The words most often quoted from Ecclesiastes:

"There is an appointed time for everything.
And there is a time for every event under heaven –
A time to give birth, and a time to die;
A time to plant, and a time to uproot what is planted.
A time to kill, and a time to heal;
A time to tear down, and a time to build up.
A time to weep, and a time to laugh;
A time to mourn, and a time to dance.
A time to throw stones, and a time to gather stones;
A time to embrace, and a time to shun embracing.
A time to search, and a time to give up as lost;
A time to keep, and a time to throw away.
A time to tear apart, and a time to sew together;
A time to be silent, and a time to speak.
A time to love, and a time to hate;
A time for war, and a time for peace. . ." (3:1-8)

God sets Eternity in the heart of man:

"What profit is there to the worker from that in which he toils? I
have seen the task which God has given the sons of men with which
to occupy themselves. He has made everything appropriate in its
time. He has also set eternity in their heart, yet so that man will not
find out the work which God has done from the beginning even to
the end. I know that there is nothing better for them than to rejoice
and to do good in one's lifetime. . it is the gift of God." (3:9-13)

Ecclesiastes ends with these admonitions:

"Remember also your Creator in the days of your youth, before the
evil days come and the years draw near when you will say, 'I have
no delight in them'; before the sun, the light, the moon, and the
stars are darkened. . .Remember Him before the silver cord is
broken and the golden bowl is crushed. . .then the dust will return to
the earth as it was, and the spirit will return to God who gave it.
'Vanity of vanities,' says the Preacher, 'all is vanity!'" (12:1-8)

"The conclusion, when all has been heard, is: fear God and keep
His commandments, because this applies to every person. For God
will bring every act to judgment, everything which is hidden,
whether it is good or evil." (12:13-14)

THE SONG OF SOLOMON

> **A beautiful, thought-provoking love poem with several interpretations.**
>
> **Like the Book of Esther**, God is not mentioned in The Song of Solomon.
>
> **It is thought that The Song of Solomon** could be about one of the following: love between God and His chosen people, love between Solomon and a Shulamite girl, love between Christ and His church, or human love between a man and a woman.

A sampling of The Song of Solomon:

"The Song of Songs, which is Solomon's. May he kiss me with the kisses of his mouth! For your love is better than wine." (1:1-2)

"I am the rose of Sharon, the lily of the valley. Like a lily among the thorns, so is my darling among the maidens. Like an apple tree among the trees of the forest, so is my beloved among the young men. In his shade I took great delight and sat down, and his fruit was sweet to my taste." (2:1-3)

"On my bed night after night I sought him whom my soul loves. I sought him but did not find him." (3:1)

"Awake, O north wind, and come, wind of the south, make my garden breathe out fragrance, let its spices be wafted abroad. May my beloved come into his garden and eat its choice fruits." (4:16)

"I am my beloved's and his desire is for me. Come, my beloved, let us go out into the country, let us spend the night in the villages. Let us rise early and go to the vineyards; let us see whether the vine has budded and its blossoms have opened, and whether the pomegranates have bloomed. There I will give you my love." (7:10-12)

THE BOOK OF ISAIAH

> The Book of Isaiah is perhaps the most widely quoted of the Old Testament prophets.
>
> Isaiah foretold the birth and life of Christ.
>
> During the latter half of the 8th Century B.C., Israel (the 10 tribes of the Northern Kingdom) suffered a catastrophic decline after the death of Jeroboam II. Samaria (the capital city of the Northern Kingdom) was destroyed in 722 B.C. The long succession of ungodly kings and the dwindling of biblical faith caused the downfall of Israel.
>
> Judah (the Southern Kingdom) was about ready to follow the decline of Israel (the Northern Kingdom).
>
> Isaiah was an esteemed citizen of Jerusalem and an advisor to King Hezekiah (circa 739 B.C.)
>
> In 622 B.C., Hezekiah made progress against the idolatrous "high places" and promoted a return to belief in God among the people.
>
> During his service to King Hezekiah (see 2 Kings 19-20), Isaiah was a stern and determined protester against the unfaithfulness of Judah (the Southern Kingdom).
>
> It is believed that Isaiah was probably martyred by King Manasseh (possibly the worst and most ungodly of the kings) by being cut in half.

Chapter 9 of Isaiah begins:

"But there will be no more gloom for her who was in anguish; in earlier times He treated the land of Zebulun and the land of Naphtali with contempt, but later on He shall make it glorious, by the way of the sea, on the other side of Jordan, Galilee of the Gentiles. The people who walk in darkness will see a great light; those who live in a dark land, the light will shine on them. . ." (9:1-2)

Isaiah, 9: 6-7, prophesizes the birth of our savior, Jesus Christ:

"For a child will be born to us, a son will be given to us; And the government will rest on His shoulders; and His name will be called Wonderful Counselor, Mighty God, Eternal Father, Prince of Peace. There will be no end of the increase of His government or of peace, on the throne of David and over his kingdom, to establish it and to uphold it with justice and righteousness from then on and forevermore. The zeal of the Lord of hosts will accomplish this."

A further promise of the Redeemer, Isaiah 42:1-4:

"Behold, My Servant, whom I uphold; My chosen one in whom My soul delights. I have put My Spirit upon Him; He will bring forth justice to the nations. He will not cry out or raise His voice, nor make His voice heard in the street. A bruised reed He will not break, and a dimly burning wick He will not extinguish; He will faithfully bring forth justice. He will not be disheartened or crushed, until He has established justice in the earth; and the coastlands will wait expectantly for His law."

Later, in Isaiah, 52: 13-15, Jesus' impact on the world is revealed:

"Behold, My servant will prosper, He will be high and lifted up, and greatly exalted. Just as many were astonished at you, My people, so His appearance was marred more than any man, And His form more than the sons of men. Thus He will sprinkle many nations, kings will shut their mouths on account of Him; For what had not been told them they will see, and what they had not heard they will understand."

And in Isaiah 53: 4-6, Jesus' suffering is foretold:

*"Surely our griefs He Himself bore, and our sorrows He carried;
Yet we ourselves esteemed Him stricken. Smitten of God, and
afflicted. But He was pierced through for our transgressions,
He was crushed for our iniquities; the chastening for our well-being
fell upon Him, and by His scourging we are healed. All of us like
sheep have gone astray, each of us has turned to his own way; but
the Lord has caused the iniquity of us all to fall on Him."*

**Isaiah 53: 7-11 prophesizes Jesus' death and the reason for his
death:**

*"He was oppressed and He was afflicted, yet He did not open His
mouth; like a lamb that is led to slaughter, and like a sheep that is
silent before its shearers, so He did not open His mouth. By
oppression and judgment He was taken away; and as for His
generation, who considered that He was cut off out of the land of
the living. For the transgression of my people to whom the stroke
was due? His grave was assigned with wicked men, yet He was with
a rich man in His death, because He had done no violence, nor was
there any deceit in His mouth. But the Lord was pleased to crush
Him, putting Him to grief; if He would render Himself as a guilt
offering, He will see His offspring, He will prolong His days, and
the good pleasure of the Lord will prosper in His hand. As a result
of the anguish of His soul, He will see it and be satisfied; by His
knowledge the Righteous One, My servant, will justify the many, as
He will bear their iniquities. Therefore, I will allot Him a portion
with the great, and He will divide the booty with the strong;
Because He poured out Himself to death, and was numbered with
the transgressors; yet He Himself bore the sin of many, and
interceded for the transgressors."*

700 years later, Jesus read these words of Isaiah in the synagogue at Nazareth:

> *"The Spirit of the Lord God is upon me, because the Lord has anointed me to bring good news to the afflicted; He has sent me to bind up the broken-hearted, to proclaim liberty to captives, and freedom to prisoners; to proclaim the favorable year of the Lord, and the day of vengeance of our God; to comfort all who mourn. . ." (61:1-2)*

When Jesus had finished His prophetic reading from Isaiah, he said, *"Today this scripture has been fulfilled in your hearing." (Luke 4:21)*

Although Isaiah had long been a respected Jewish prophet, his words of prophesy, read by Jesus about Himself, were considered revolutionary and incited those present in the temple that day to rise up against Jesus.

THE BOOK OF JEREMIAH

> **Jeremiah was a prophet to King Josiah** *(see 2 Chronicles 35:25)*, the last good king of the many kings of Judah.
>
> **Jeremiah continued into the early years of the Exile**. He died in Egypt after the destruction of Jerusalem (587 B.C.).
>
> **The death of Jeremiah brings the history of the Hebrew kingdom to an end.** The proclamation of Cyrus, which permitted the exiles to return from Babylon to Jerusalem opened what is called the Second Commonwealth epoch.
>
> **In Jeremiah there is a poignant dialogue between this prophet and the Lord**. God expresses His displeasure with His people for having turned away from Him, their worship of foreign gods and their evil ways of pagan worship. Throughout Jeremiah, the Lord tells His people what will become of them.

Some of the dialogue between The Lord and Jeremiah:

"'Before I formed you in the womb I knew you, and before you were born I consecrated you. I have appointed you a prophet to the nations.' Then I said, 'Alas, Lord God! Behold, I do not know how to speak, because I am a youth.' But the Lord said to me, 'Do not say, 'I am a youth,' because everywhere I send you, you shall go, and all that I command you, you shall speak. Do not be afraid of them, for I am with you to deliver you,' declares the Lord." (1:5-8)

The Lord then instructed Jeremiah to be a prophet to the people of Judah:

"For My people have committed two evils: they have forsaken Me, the fountain of living waters, to hew for themselves cisterns, broken cisterns that can hold no water." (2:13)

Jeremiah states that the Lord sees how Israel became unfaithful to Him and how Judah also sinned against the Lord:

"Thus says the Lord, 'Stand by the ways and see and ask for the ancient paths, where the good way is, and walk in it; And you shall find rest for your souls.' But they said, 'We will not walk in it.' And I set watchmen over you, saying, 'Listen to the sound of the trumpet!' But they said, 'We will not listen.'" (6:16-17)

"Hear, O earth: behold, I am bringing disaster on this people, the fruit of their plans, because they have not listened to My words, And as for My law, they have rejected it also." (6:19)

"Therefore, thus says the Lord, 'Behold, I am laying stumbling blocks before this people. And they will stumble against them, fathers and sons together; neighbor and friend will perish.'" (6:21)

In Chapter 13, Jeremiah relates a parable that the Lord told him regarding the people of Judah:

"Thus the Lord said to me, 'Go and buy yourself a linen waistband, and put it around your waist, but do not put it in water.' So I bought the waistband in accordance with the word of the Lord and put it around my waist. Then the word of the Lord came to me a second time, saying, 'Take the waistband that you have bought, which is around your waist, and arise, go to the Euphrates and hide it there in a crevice of the rock.'

"So I went and hid it by the Euphrates, as the Lord had commanded me. And it came about after many days that the Lord said to me, 'Arise, go to the Euphrates and take from there the waistband which I commanded you to hide there.'

"Then I went to the Euphrates and dug, and I took the waistband from the place where I had hidden it; and lo, the waistband was ruined, it was totally worthless.

"Then the word of the Lord came to me, saying, 'Thus says the Lord, 'Just so will I destroy the pride of Judah and the great pride of Jerusalem. This wicked people, who refuse to listen to My words, who walk in the stubbornness of their hearts and have gone after other gods to serve them and to bow down to them, let them be just like this waistband, which is totally worthless. For as the waistband clings to the waist of a man, so I made the whole household of Israel and the whole household of Judah cling to Me,' declares the Lord, 'that they might be for Me a people, for renown, for praise, and for glory; but they did not listen.'" (13:1-11)

Jeremiah goes on to relate that God has given up on His people and He will allow them to be carried into exile (into Babylon).

Jeremiah states to God that other prophets have told the Hebrews that they will have lasting peace. God responds that these prophets are giving His people a false vision.

God then tells Jeremiah that He will make the people, *"an object of horror among all the kingdoms of the earth because of Manasseh, the son of Hezekiah, the king of Judah, for what he did in Jerusalem."* (15:4)

Manasseh was regarded as possibly the most evil of the kings of Judah and Israel. *(The Second Book of the Chronicles, 33:6)*

God also told Jeremiah that when the people ask why God is deserting them, he is to say to them,

". . . 'It is because your forefathers have forsaken Me', declares the Lord, 'and have followed other gods and served them and bowed down to them: but Me they have forsaken and have not kept My law. You too have done evil, even more than your forefathers; for behold, you are each one walking according to the stubbornness of his own evil heart, without listening to Me. So I will hurl you out of this land into the land which you have not known, neither you nor your fathers; and there you will serve other gods day and night, for I shall grant you no favor." (16:11-13)

The Lord, through Jeremiah, then reveals that after His people have been taken into exile (Babylon):

> *"Then I Myself shall gather the remnant of My flock out of all the countries where I have driven them and shall bring them back to their pasture; and they will be fruitful and multiply. I shall also raise up shepherds over them and they will tend them; and they will not be afraid any longer, nor be terrified, nor will any be missing. . . Behold, the days are coming. . . when I shall raise up for David a righteous Branch; and He will reign as king and act wisely and do justice and righteousness in the land. In His days Judah will be saved, and Israel will dwell securely; and this is His name by which He will be called, 'The Lord of Righteousness.'" (23:3-6)*

The Lord, using an allegory of two baskets of figs, (a basket of good figs representing Judah and a basket of rotten figs representing King Zedekiah and his officials) then told Jeremiah that, although He would abandon Zedekiah king of Judah and his officials who had gone to Egypt, He would salvage the people of Judah who had been taken into captivity and would return them to the land He promised them. The Lord then, through Jeremiah, revealed that His people would be in captivity for 70 years. *(24)*

After all the people were taken into captivity in Babylon by Nebuchadnezzar, Jeremiah wrote a letter to them. In his letter he urged them, on behalf of the Lord, to live their lives productively, to build houses to live in, to marry and have families, *"And seek the welfare of the city where I have sent you into exile and pray to the Lord on its behalf; for in its welfare you will have welfare." (29:7)*

> *"For thus says the Lord, 'When seventy years have been completed for Babylon, I will visit you and fulfill My good word to you, to bring you back to this place. For I know the plans that I have for you,' declares the Lord, 'plans for welfare and not for calamity to give you a future and a hope. Then you will call upon Me and come and pray to Me, and I will listen to you. And you will seek Me and find Me, when you search for Me with all your heart. And I will be found by you,' declares the Lord, 'and I will restore your fortunes and will gather you from all the nations and from all the places where I have driven you,' declares the Lord, 'and I will bring you back to the place from where I sent you into exile.'"(29:10-14)*

The Lord then told the people, through Jeremiah, that He would restore them in their own land, and punish their oppressors, *"And you shall be My people, and I will be your God." (30:22)*

Jeremiah further prophesied how good it would be for the people of Judah and Israel when they were returned to their land after the 70 years of exile.

Although Jeremiah tried in many ways to warn the king of Judah and the people that calamity would befall them if they did not turn from their evil ways, the king would not heed the warnings. Attempts were made to kill Jeremiah. At the Lord's command, Jeremiah dictated all his words of warning to Baruch the son of Neriah and this scroll was read to the people and ultimately to the king who, as he heard the words, cut the scroll and burned it.

At the Lord's direction, Jeremiah dictated another, replacement, scroll. Jeremiah was imprisoned, briefly put into a cistern and various attempts were made on his life.

When Jerusalem was besieged and captured by the Babylonians, King Zedekiah's sons and all the nobles were killed. King Zedekiah was blinded and taken in fetters to Babylon.

Nebuchadnezzar king of Babylon gave orders that Jeremiah not be harmed and that he was free to go where he wished.

THE LAMENTATIONS OF JEREMIAH

In the form of poems, Jeremiah's lamentations express the anguish, grief and mourning of the Jewish people at the destruction of Jerusalem, the Temple, and the "carrying off" or exile of the people under the Babylonians.

It is thought that the Jewish people who were carried off into exile and who later returned became the Samaritans.

There later was enmity between the Samaritans and the Jews, because, during their exile, the Samaritans had inbred with the Babylonians.

A sampling of The Lamentations of Jeremiah:

"How lonely sits the city that was full of people! She has become like a widow who was once great among the nations! She who was a princess among the provinces has become a forced laborer! She weeps bitterly in the night, and her tears are on her cheeks; she has none to comfort her among all her lovers. All her friends have dealt treacherously with her; they have become her enemies. Judah has gone into exile under affliction, and under harsh servitude; she dwells among the nations, but she has found no rest; all her pursuers have overtaken her in the midst of distress." (1:1-3)

A Prayer for Mercy:

"Remember, O Lord, what has befallen us; look, see our reproach! Our inheritance has been turned over to strangers, our houses to aliens. We have become orphans without a father, our mothers are like widows. . .We are worn out, there is no rest for us. . .Elders are gone from the gate, young men from their music. The joy of our hearts has ceased; our dancing has been turned into mourning. The crown has fallen from our head; woe to us, for we have sinned!" (5:1-16)."

"Restore us to Thee, O Lord, that we may be restored; renew our days as of old. . ." (5:21)

THE BOOK OF EZEKIEL

The Prophet Ezekiel followed Jeremiah,

By Divine revelation, Ezekiel was God's spokesperson and watchman to the exiled Israelites (the Babylonian exile).

Before the fall of Jerusalem, Ezekiel was primarily a preacher of repentance and judgment.

He brought constant warnings to the rebellious Israelites who were inclined to idolatry and susceptible to a pagan environment.

After the fall of Jerusalem, he became a consoler and an expositor of the necessity of inner religion.

Ezekiel experienced visions of creatures from heaven and, *". . .the appearance of the likeness of the glory of the Lord, and when I saw it, I fell on my face and heard a voice speaking. . . 'Son of man, I am sending you to the sons of Israel, to a rebellious people who have rebelled against Me; they and their fathers have transgressed against Me to this very day. . .for they are a rebellious house – they will know that a prophet has been among them. . .but you shall speak My words to them. . ." (2:1-7)*

Throughout this book, Ezekiel is told of the devastation which will befall the Israelites and the city of Jerusalem. *"This is Jerusalem; I have set her at the center of the nations, with lands around her. But she has rebelled against My ordinances more wickedly than the nations and against My statutes more than the lands which surround her; for they have rejected My ordinances and have not walked in My statues. . . 'Therefore,' thus says the Lord God, 'Behold, I, even I, am against you, and I will execute judgments among you in the sight of the nations."* *(5:5-8)*

After many visions and warnings, Ezekiel receives a promise of restoration: *". . .Though I* [God] *have removed* [the people]*. . .and though I had scattered them among the countries, yet I was a sanctuary for them. . . .I shall gather you from the peoples and assemble you out of the countries among which you have been scattered, and I shall give you the land of Israel. . .And I shall give them one heart, and shall put a new spirit within them. . .that they may walk in My statues and keep My ordinances. . . Then they will be My people, and I shall be their God." (11:16-20)*

Ezekiel prophesied about the restoration of Israel:

"For thus says the Lord God, 'Behold I Myself will search for My sheep and seek them out. As a shepherd cares for his herd in the day when he is among his scattered sheep, so I will care for My sheep and will deliver them from all the places to which they were scattered on a cloudy and gloomy day. And I will bring them out from the peoples and gather them from the countries and bring them to their own land; and I will feed them on the mountains of Israel, by the streams, and in all the inhabited places of the land. I will feed them in a good pasture, and their grazing ground will be on the mountain heights of Israel. . .I will seek the lost, bring back the scattered, bind up the broken, and strengthen the sick; but the fat and the strong I will destroy. I will feed them with judgment.'" (34:11-16)

"Thus says the Lord God, 'When I gather the house of Israel from the peoples among whom they are scattered. . .they will live in their land which I gave to My servant Jacob. . .and they will build houses, plant vineyards, and live securely, when I execute judgments upon all who scorn them. . . Then they will know that I am the Lord their God." (28:25)

It is the prophet Ezekiel to whom the Lord showed the vision of all the dead being restored to life:

" 'Behold, I will open your graves and cause you to come up out of your graves, My people; and I will bring you into the land of Israel. Then you will know that I am the Lord. . .And I will put My Spirit within you, and you will come to life, and I will place you on your own land. Then you will know that I, the Lord, have spoken and done it,' declares the Lord." (37:12-14)

THE BOOK OF DANIEL

> **Both the books of Ezekiel and Daniel were written during the time of exile** when the Jews were displaced from their country after the destruction of their temple, capital city and commonwealth by Nebuchadnezzar in 586 B.C.
>
> **Daniel looked into the future to prophesy the events of the end times** (similar to Revelation), when the Lord will, for one last time, reveal Himself and bring the earthly ages to a close and establish His eternal reign, bringing full salvation to His people.

Daniel wrote about three upstanding young Hebrew men - Haneniah, Misheael, and Azoniah - who were tested by King Nebuchadnezzar. The king first ordered a large golden image of himself to be made and then ordered that, at the sound of the music, everyone was to fall down and worship the golden image.

When the three young men refused to worship the king's image, the king ordered them thrown into a burning furnace. Instead of the men being burned alive, they walked around in the midst of the fire, unharmed, saved by their faithfulness to God.

Nebuchadnezzar then had dreams that greatly alarmed him. When he called for Daniel to interpret the dreams, Daniel advised the king to, *". . .break away now from your sins by doing righteousness, and from your iniquities by showing mercy to the poor. . ." (4:27)*

A year later, a voice from heaven, noting that the king had not amended his life, declared that his sovereignty was being taken from him. He was driven away from mankind and lived like the beasts of the field. At the end of *"seven periods of time,"* Nebuchadnezzar raised his eyes towards heaven and *". . .blessed the Most High and praised and honored Him who lives forever." (4:33-34)*

Later, Belshazzar, the acting king of Babylon, held a great feast and had Daniel brought in to interpret a writing that had mysteriously appeared on the palace wall. Daniel, in essence, told the king that he had raised himself up against the Lord of heaven. *". . .you and your nobles. . .have praised the gods of silver and gold. . . but do not see, hear or understand. But the God in whose hand are your lifebreath and your ways, you have not glorified." (5:23)*

That night king Belshazzar was slain and Darius the Mede became king.

Darius appointed Daniel as one of three commissioners over the kingdom, but because *"he possessed an extraordinary spirit,"* the other officials *". . .tried to find grounds to accuse Daniel."* Although they found *"no evidence of corruption, inasmuch as he was faithful,"* they convinced the king to cast him into the lions' den." (6:3:12)

> *"Then the king gave orders, and Daniel was brought in and cast into the lions' den. The king spoke and said to Daniel, 'Your God whom you constantly serve will Himself deliver you.'"* (6:16)

And while the king himself spent a restless night, Daniel was spared. The lions refused to touch him, while others who were thrown into the den were immediately torn apart.

Regarding one of his visions, Daniel said:

> *"I kept looking in the night visions, and behold, with the clouds of heaven one like a Son of Man was coming, and He came up to the Ancient of Days and was presented before Him. And to Him was given dominion, glory and a kingdom, that all the peoples, nations, and men of every language might serve Him. His dominion is an everlasting dominion which will not pass way; and His kingdom is one which will not be destroyed."* (7:13-14)

THE BOOK OF HOSEA

Hosea prophesied to the Northern Kingdom during the time that Isaiah was prophesying in Judah (the Southern Kingdom).

Israel's unfaithfulness to God at that time in history is depicted in Hosea in terms of a wife who has turned her back on a faithful husband.

Hosea married a woman named Gomer who was known to be a harlot (perhaps a temple prostitute). He divorced her, but his love for her persisted and he later remarried her.

Hosea's personal life is, perhaps, a metaphor for God's dealings with Israel. After vowing faithfulness for the Lord, Israel went lusting after Baal and other gods of Canaan until God brought about a temporary rejection (the exile of His people from the land He had promised them).

> *"Return O Israel, to the Lord your God, for you have stumbled because of your iniquity. . ." (14:1)*

THE BOOK OF JOEL

Joel was a citizen of southern Palestine and probably a resident of Jerusalem.

Joel uses the word "Israel" for Judah, which no pre-exilic prophet would have done. The term was used only for the ten northern tribes prior to 722 BC.

The immediate occasion for this writing was the devastation of the land by locusts and drought.

"The Day of the Lord is coming" is the central theme of the book of Joel - the day when the Lord will manifest himself in the destruction of his enemies and the exaltation of his friends.

This day will be accompanied by a display of extraordinary phenomena in nature.

The attitude of a man's heart and life before the Lord will determine his reaction to that day.

> *"The sun and moon grow dark, and the stars lose their brightness, and the Lord roars from Zion and utters His voice from Jerusalem, and the heavens and the earth tremble. But the Lord is a refuge for His people. . ." (3:15-16)*

THE BOOK OF AMOS

Amos, a prophet about 760 B.C., was a shepherd from Tekoa, which is in the desert of Judah about 12 miles south of Jerusalem.

The call of God came to Amos while he was tending his flock. His claim that the Lord called him directly puts him in line with all the prophets who experienced a direct revelation from God.

Although a native of Judah, Amos prophesied in the Northern Kingdom and aroused such antagonism that he returned to Judah where he committed his message to writing.

Amos is the great prophet of the righteousness of God. As such, he demanded an ethical content to religion.

Amos believed religion involved justice toward one's fellowman and conferred great responsibility as well as blessing.

During Amos's time, Uzziah ruled Judah and Jeroboam II ruled Israel. Uzziah was influenced by Jeroboam who didn't exclude worship of the Lord, but did encourage cults, idols, adultery, robbery, murder - a time of injustice and oppression.

"'Behold days are coming,' declares the Lord God, 'when I will send a famine on the land, not a famine for bread or a thirst for water, but rather for hearing the words of the Lord.'" (8:11)

Regarding the restoration of Israel, the Lord said to Amos,

". . .I will restore the captivity of My people Israel, and they will rebuild the ruined cities and live in them, they will also plant vineyards and drink their wine, and make gardens and eat their fruit. I will also plant them on their land, and they will not again be rooted out from their land which I have given them. . ." (9:14-15)

THE BOOK OF OBADIAH

Obadiah means "servant of the Lord" or worshipper of the Lord.

Obadiah alludes to a historical situation in which the Edomites (descendants of Esau – Jacob's twin brother) were allied with the enemies of Israel (descendants of Jacob) and participated in the sack of Jerusalem.

This poem is under-girded by a sense of justice. Kinsmen had violated tribal bonds and committed terrible crimes. Their sins had to be punished. The Israelites did not punish the Edomites. Instead, they recognized God as the Judge of all the nations and believed He would execute justice on the crimes committed.

"For the day of the Lord draws near on all the nations. As you have done, it will be done to you. Your dealings will return on your own head. . ." (1-15)

THE BOOK OF JONAH

> **Jonah is referred to as a prophet** in 2 Kings 14:25. The book of Jonah is considered a parable, a legend, myth and prophetic allegory.
>
> **As an allegory,** the city of Nineveh represents the vast non-Jewish world that awaits the awakening only the true message of God can bring. The parable portrays the justice and mercy of God towards anyone who will repent of sin.
>
> **The books of Jonah, Nahum and Habakkuk** all deal with the evil city of Nineveh.

God instructs Jonah to go and preach to the people of Nineveh, a hated, wicked and ruthless city – much in need of intercession with God.

Jonah resists God and instead takes passage on a ship due to sail to Spain, which, at that time, was considered to be the far edge of the known world.

During a fierce storm, the pagan sailors cast lots to determine who is to blame for the terrible plight the ship is in. Jonah loses and is cast overboard. He is swallowed by a huge fish where he prays for salvation. God rescues him.

This time, Jonah obeys God and goes to Nineveh to preach repentance. The people of Nineveh respond with earnestness and God hears their pleas for mercy. Jonah, however, is angry that God took mercy on the people of Nineveh and says, *"Therefore now, O Lord please take my life from me, for death is better to me than life."* (4:3)

Jonah then went out from Nineveh and sat where he could observe the city to see what would happen.

The Lord appointed a plant to grow up quickly to give Jonah shelter and Jonah was very happy about the plant. God then sent a worm to destroy the plant which caused Jonah to again become very angry. But God said to Jonah, *"You had compassion on the plant for which you did not work and which you did not cause to grow. . . should I not have compassion on Nineveh. . .?"* *(4:10-11)*

Jonah is identified with the true mission of Israel to declare God's truth to the world - which Israel had failed to do.

The "great fish" (which swallowed Jonah) is considered to be Babylon, which swallowed the Israelites. When the fish spits Jonah up and onto the land, it is the allegory of the Jews returning from exile.

Jonah's misfortune in being swallowed by a fish is directly related to his reluctance – refusal – to do God's will. God finds a way (the fish) to get Jonah's attention.

THE BOOK OF MICAH

Micah began his work at the time of Jotham, Ahaz and Hezekiah (750 BC). These were days of unrest, insecurity and hardship, especially for villages and peasants.

Micah's summary of true religion is,

> ". . .What does the Lord require of you but to do justice, to love kindness, and to walk humbly with your God?" (6:8)

> "But as for me, I will watch expectantly for the Lord; I will wait for the God of my salvation. My God will hear me. Do not rejoice over me, O my enemy. Though I fall I will rise; though I dwell in darkness, the Lord is a light for me." (7:7-8)

> "I will bear the indignation of the Lord because I have sinned against Him, until He pleads my case and executes justice for me. He will bring me out to the light, and I will see His righteousness. Then my enemy will see, and shame will cover her who said to me, 'Where is the Lord your God?'. . ." (7:9-10)

THE BOOK OF NAHUM

Nahum was a consoler or oracle about 612 BC.

The book of Nahum, like the book of Jonah, centers around the city of Nineveh

Nahum was a witness to the Southern Kingdom (the Northern Kingdom having been carried off into captivity by Assyria a century earlier - 722 BC).

"A jealous and avenging God the Lord; the Lord is avenging and wrathful. . .The Lord is slow to anger and great in power, and the Lord will by no means leave the guilty unpunished." (1:2-3)

THE BOOK OF HABAKKUK

> **Possibly written toward the end of the reign of Josiah** (640 - 609 BC).
>
> **Probably written before** the destruction of Nineveh.

Habakkuk's spiritual message is that sin is a broken relationship and rebellion from God. Faith is the restoration of that broken relationship by repentance and humble trust in God.

"How long, O Lord, will I call for help, and Thou wilt not hear? I cry out to Thee, 'Violence!' Yet thou doest not save. Why dost Thou make me see iniquity, and cause me to look on wickedness? Yes, destruction and violence are before me; strife exists and contention arises. Therefore, the law is ignored and justice is never upheld. For the wicked surround the righteous; therefore justice comes out perverted." (1:2-4)

"Woe to him who says to a piece of wood, 'Awake'; to a dumb stone, 'Arise! ' And that is your teacher? Behold, it is overlaid with gold and silver, and there is no breath at all inside it. But the Lord is in His holy temple. Let all the earth be silent before Him!" (2:19-20)

"Though the fig tree should not blossom, and there be no fruit on the vines, though the yield of the olive should fail, and the fields produce no food, thought the flock should be cut off from the fold, and there be no cattle in the stalls, yet I will exult in the Lord, I will rejoice in the God of my salvation. The Lord God is my strength, and He has made my feet like hinds' feet, and makes me walk on my high places." (3:17-19)

THE BOOK OF ZEPHANIAH

Zephaniah means "the power of God to hide his worshipers in time of danger."

Zephaniah prophesized during the reign of Josiah (640 - 609 BC).

The people were indulging in idolatrous practices in secret. Their hypocrisy stirred the young prophet Zephaniah (probably of royal descent) into action.

Early in King Josiah's reign, Zephaniah began to warn his people of the impending judgment of God. The earlier fate of Samaria (in 722 B.C.) had been a solemn reminder of God's power and justice.

"Seek the Lord, all you humble of the earth who have carried out His ordinances; seek righteousness, seek humility. Perhaps you will be hidden in the day of the Lord's anger." (2:3)

THE BOOK OF HAGGAI

The prophet Haggai was a contemporary of Zechariah (520 BC).

Haggai ministered to those Jews who returned from Babylonian exile/captivity.

He urged the rebuilding of the Temple - and predicted the future establishment of God's earthly kingdom (Jesus Christ).

"In the second year of Darius the king. . .the word of the Lord came by the prophet Haggai. . . 'You have sown much, but harvest little; you eat, but there is not enough to be satisfied; you drink, but there is not enough to become drunk; you put on clothing, but no one is warm enough; and he who earns, earns wages to put into a purse with holes.' Thus says the Lord of hosts, 'Consider your ways! Go up to the mountains, bring wood and rebuild the temple, that I may be pleased with it and glorified," says the Lord.'" (1:8)

"For thus says the Lord of hosts, 'Once more in a little while, I am going to shake the heavens and the earth, the sea also and the dry land. And I will shake all the nations; and they will come with the wealth of all nations; and I will fill this house with glory,' says the Lord of hosts." (2:6-7)

THE BOOK OF ZECHARIAH

> **Zechariah means "The Lord remembers."**
>
> **Zechariah was a contemporary of Haggai (520 B.C.).**

This prophet also urged the rebuilding of the Temple in Jerusalem.

"Thus says the Lord of hosts, 'I am exceedingly jealous for Zion, yes, with great wrath I am jealous for her!' Thus says the Lord, 'I will return to Zion and will dwell in the midst of Jerusalem, then Jerusalem will be called the City of Truth, and the mountain of the Lord of hosts will be called the Holy Mountain.' Thus says the Lord of hosts, 'Old men and old women will again sit in the streets of Jerusalem, each man with his staff in his hand because of age, and the streets of the city will be filled with boys and girls playing in its streets.'" (8:2-5)

Zechariah prophesied concerning Jesus as the Messiah:

"Rejoice greatly, O daughter of Zion! Shout in triumph, O daughter of Jerusalem! Behold, your king is coming to you; He is just and endowed with salvation, humble and mounted on a donkey, even on a colt, the foal of a donkey." (9:9)

THE BOOK OF MALACHI

Malachi means "messenger of the Lord." (432 - 520 BC).

Following the Babylonian captivity and the rebuilding of the Temple, Malachi urges the Jews who have been rebellious, to return to God.

"'But for you who fear My name the sun of righteousness will rise with healing in its wings; and you will go forth and skip about like calves from the stall. And you will tread down the wicked, For they shall be ashes under the soles of your feet on the day which I am preparing,' says the Lord of hosts." (4:2-3)

This marks the end of the Hebrew Scriptures - also known as the Old Testament

THE TIME BETWEEN THE HEBREW SCRIPTURES (THE OLD TESTAMENT) AND THE CHRISTIAN SCRIPTURES (THE NEW TESTAMENT)

Having somewhat of an understanding of the Old Testament (the Hebrew Scriptures) is important as a basis for reading the New Testament (the Christian Scriptures).

There are many references made by Jesus, Paul and Peter which relate back to Hebrew prophets and key persons in the Israelites' history, along with important events which formed the basis for many Christian beliefs.

A period of about 400 years elapsed between the last known writings belonging to the Hebrew Scriptures (B.C.) and the beginning of the Christian Era (A.D.)

This intertestamental period was an extremely active time. The events that took place during this period shaped the political atmosphere into which Jesus Christ was born.

The Persian Period:
For about a hundred and fifty years after the Israelites were allowed to return to Jerusalem and rebuild the temple (Ezra and Nehemiah's times), they did well under the control of the Persian Empire (today's Iran, Iraq, Syria, Jordan and Lebanon).

At that point in time, the lineage of the Jewish priests could still be traced directly back to Aaron, (Moses' brother). However, the Jewish priesthood then began to become politicized, sowing the seeds of future trouble. Contests for the office of High Priest were marked by jealousy, intrigue and sometimes even murder.

The country of Judea was under the domination of Persia, the world power of the time. However, Persia's failure to conquer Greece encouraged Egypt to attempt to throw off Persian rule. And Judea - located between these two powers - couldn't escape involvement.

A substantial number of Jews had earlier migrated to Egypt, "and by the fifth century before Christ, a Jewish colony of mercenary soldiers was located at Elephantine Island near modern Aswan, at the first cataract of the Nile River. Contrary to Mosaic Law, they built a temple for themselves and combined their devotion to the God of their fathers with pagan elements."

Alexander the Great:
During the time that Persia was still the world power, a man named Philip of Macedon (Greece) became that country's leader. His son was Alexander the Great. In a battle between the Greeks and the Persians, Alexander and his Greek army were victorious and Greece became the most powerful country in the world, bringing an end to the Persian Empire.

Alexander the Great, a student of the Greek philosopher Aristotle, was convinced that Greek culture could unify the world.

In 333 B.C., Alexander and his army passed from Macedonia (northern Greece) into Asia Minor (the area of today's Turkey), then southward through Syria and Judea to Egypt.

In 331 B.C., Alexander built the city of Alexandria in Egypt and encouraged Jews to settle there, giving them privileges comparable to his Greek subjects.

Alexander then moved eastward through Babylon (today's Iraq) and Persia (today's Iran).

Alexander was determined to establish a new city in every country of his growing empire - to serve as a model for the reordering of the life of each country along Greek lines. People were encouraged – but not forced - to take Greek names and to adopt both Greek dress and language – in short, to become Hellenized.

During this time, trade and commerce flourished, libraries and schools were built along with other fine public buildings and gymnasiums. Many Jews welcomed the Greek culture, which led to the breakdown of their adherence to some of the traditional Jewish ordinances.

In studying the prophesies of Daniel, Alexander the Great saw predictions that he believed pointed towards him being the notable goat with the horn in his forehead who would come from the west, destroy the power of Persia and conquer the known world. Alexander believed so firmly in this prophesy that he promised to save the city of Jerusalem from siege.

In 323 B.C., at the age of 32, Alexander the Great died in Babylon, but in his short life, he had changed the world so significantly that nothing was ever the same as it had been before his reign. Because he left no heir, the empire he had built soon became rife with dissension.

The Ptolemies and the Seleucids:
Following the death of Alexander the Great, two of his four generals – Ptolemy and Seleucus - divided his empire. Ptolemy took Egypt and northern Africa and his power base was centered in Alexandria, Egypt. Seleucus took Syria (to the north of Judea).

Judea then found itself torn between these two opposing generals and was caught in ongoing conflicts between Syria and Egypt.

Between the third and second centuries B.C., at King Ptolemy's request, 72 persons – six from each of the Twelve Tribes of Israel - were sent from Judea to Egypt to translate the Hebrew Scriptures into Greek. This translation came to be known as the Septuagint (relating to the number of persons involved in the translation).

During this period, the greatest figure among the Jews was a High Priest named Simon The Just, who was credited with rebuilding the walls of Jerusalem (which had been demolished by Ptolemy I), repairing the temple and directing the excavation of a great reservoir to provide fresh water for Jerusalem in time of drought. There were, however, several other historical figures called "Simon the Just," so exactly which one deserves credit for these deeds is not clear.

After the division of Alexander the Great's empire, when Seleucus I gained Syria, the Syrian rulers came to be called "Seleucids."

During this period of time, Judea was annexed by Egypt as part of Ptolemy's kingdom and for the next century, Judea was caught in what has been described as a "meat grinder" in the conflicts between Syria to the north and Egypt to the south.

The Seleucids eventually wrested Judea from the Ptolemies after the Battle of Panion, which took place about the year 200 B.C., near the border of what is today modern Israel.

This Seleucid victory marked the beginning of a new era of Jewish history. While the Ptolemies had been tolerant of Jewish institutions, the Seleucids were determined to force Hellenism (Greek culture) on the Jews.

The Hellenists and the Pharisees:
A crisis arose when two Jewish brothers - Jason (who favored Greek culture) and the High Priest Onias III (a strictly orthodox Jew) - opposed each other.

As an outcome, the Jewish people were split between two political groups – the Hellenists and the Pharisees. The Hellenists were those interested in liberalizing some of the Jewish laws and bringing Greek culture and thought to the nation. They formed a party which came to be known in the New Testament as the Sadducees (or liberals). They avoided strict interpretation of the Mosaic law and stopped believing in the supernatural.

The Pharisees (meaning "to separate") were composed of Hebrew nationalists determined to adhere to tradition and to the Mosaic order. In their opposition to Hellenism, the Pharisees became more legalistic and rigid, to the point of becoming religious hypocrites.

The Sadducees' and Pharisees' opposition with each other created a breach which gave the Syrians an opportunity to wrest Jerusalem from the Egyptians. In the year 203 B.C., on a Sabbath day (when it was known that Orthodox Jews wouldn't fight), Antiochus the Great (from Syria) captured Jerusalem. Many Jews were slaughtered and the city's walls were destroyed.

When Antiochus the Great died, his brother took power, becoming a vicious persecutor of the Jewish people. He unseated the high priest in Jerusalem, thereby ending the long line of priestly descendants of Aaron.

In 171 B.C., under the second Antiochus, Syria invaded Egypt, causing Judea to once again be caught in the rivalry between the two countries.

When it was reported that Antiochus had been murdered in Egypt, the Jewish people rose up, organized a revolt and overthrew the person who had been placed in power over them by the Syrians.

Unfortunately, word of Antiochus' death was false and when he learned what was happening in Jerusalem, he fought to regain his hold over that city. In so doing, more than 40,000 persons were killed in three days of fighting. An attempt was made to eradicate all traces of the Jewish faith, to the point where swine were offered in sacrifice on the Temple altar. Jews were forbidden to practice circumcision, observe the Sabbath or celebrate the feasts of the Jewish calendar.

The Maccabean Revolt:
The oppressed Jews found a champion in an older priest named Mattathias and his five sons, who began waging guerrilla warfare on both the Syrians and the Hellenistic Jews.

Mattathias' third son, Judas (known as the "Maccabee" or "hammer") along with other Jews led the fight – thus the name, "the Maccabees".

The Maccabees were able to stand up against the Syrians and Hellenistic Jews. They worked their way to Jerusalem, and took over everything but the Akra (a Syrian garrison or fortress). They removed the pagan god statues from the temple and erected a new altar to Israel's God.

The prophet Daniel had predicted that the temple Holy of Holies would be polluted for 2,300 days *(Daniel 8:14)*. And, in accordance with that prophesy, it was six and a half years (2,300 days) before the temple was cleansed under the leadership of Judas Maccabaeus.

That December marked the end of the three year period following the desecration of the Temple. In celebration of the cleansing of the temple, an eight day Feast of Dedication was held, which, through the years, came to be known as Hanukkah or the Festival of Lights.

Their peace didn't last long, however. In the ensuing struggle for control, civil war again broke out when the Syrians defeated the Maccabees in a battle near Jerusalem in which Judas "the Maccabee" was killed.

Another of Mattathias's sons, Jonathan, stepped into the breach caused by Judas' death, and successfully made treaties with both Sparta (a prominent city-state in Greece) and Rome.

Later, after Jonathan's death, still another brother, Simon, became High Priest. Simon made major diplomatic strides in working with the Syrians, secured immunity from taxation for the Jews and was able to starve out the Syrian garrison.

Simon was the last of the sons of Mattathias.

The Hasmonaens:
Simon's son, John Hyrcanus, became the hereditary head of the Jewish state and his dynasty became known as the Hasmonaens.

The name Hasmonean is derived from the name of an ancestor of the Maccabees who was called Hashmon.

The Syrians recognized the government of John Hyrcanus on the condition that he consider himself subject to Syria. For the next hundred years, the Hasmonean family ruled over Judea.

During this time, Judea had succeeded in overthrowing foreign domination – and "before John Hyrcanus died in 104 B.C., the borders of the Jewish state had been extended on every side." However, it was also during this time that a pact had been entered into with Rome which called for Rome's help in the event of another attack from Syria.

Although the Maccabean struggle was long past, new rivalries developed. The older Hellenist Jews were discredited, but their ideas continued to be perpetuated in the party of the Sadducees. And the Orthodox Jews of Maccabean times became the Pharisees of pre-Christian Judaism.

Sadly, the heirs of the Maccabees had become thoroughly Hellenized and John Hyrcanus' children struggled with each other for control of the dynasty.

John Hyrcanus's eldest son, Aristobulus (Greek word for the Hebrew name of Judah) became victor and took the title of king to himself. His reign lasted only one year.

Aristobulus' brother, Alexander Jannaeus, succeeded him and managed to expand the Jewish state's territory, which included the whole of Judea and adjacent areas from the borders of Egypt to Lake Hulch, north of the Sea of Galilee. It was at that time that Galilee became an important center of the Jewish world.

Meanwhile, the Pharisees were aligning themselves with Syria. This angered Alexander Jannaeus so much that he ordered the crucifixion of 800 Pharisees. After Jannaeus' death, his widow, Salome Alexandra (who had earlier been married to Jannaeus's eldest brother, Aristobulus) reigned for seven years. Alexandra's own brother was a leader among the Pharisees, which served to promote peace between opposing factions of Judaism.

Under Alexandra's rule, the Pharisees began making significant contributions to Jewish life. Among other things, they promoted education which focused on the Hebrew scriptures.

While the Pharisees were becoming recognized, the Sadducees were losing power. The Pharisees, seeking to avenge the murder of their leaders by Jannaeus, spilled Sadducean blood, which created an atmosphere for yet another civil war.

It was then that Pompey (a Roman general who had an army in Damascus) and his Roman legions restored peace in Judea as a way of promoting Rome's agenda.

The Romans:
The Roman Empire was growing in size and strength. As Roman armies were conquering lands and people, they moved to the east: North Africa, Egypt, Asia Minor, modern day Turkey and Syria.

In approximately 63 B.C., Pompey laid siege to Jerusalem. After three months of fighting, he breached the fortifications, entered the city and captured it for Rome. He reportedly was responsible for the murder of 12,000 Jews. It was then that Judea came under the power and authority of Rome. Pompey did, however, allow the continuation of temple worship.

Jerusalem then became subject to the Romans and its last shred of independence was removed. Judea was incorporated into the Roman province of Syria and it lost its coastal cities, the district of Samaria and the non-Jewish cities east of the Jordan. A yearly tax from all of Judea was due Rome and these monies were zealously collected. Jews who worked for Rome as tax collectors were generally hated.

Roman rulers were successful in controlling all aspects of life in Judea due to their cruel and ruthless treatment of anyone who dared, in any way, to oppose them. Their methods of controlling Jewish citizens included taxation so severe it forced citizens into abject poverty and death by crucifixion (considered to be the harshest and most humiliating method of torture and death).

The Romans also brought paganism to Judea, in that they built temples and worshipped many gods.

During this time, Julius Caesar was murdered and Cassius became the Roman ruler. Herod the Great (also known as Herod I), the son of the Idumaean* governor Antipater, was given the title of Procurator of Judea with the promise that he would someday be king.

Although Judea was governed by Herod the Great, Rome was the force behind him and was known to be both the source of well-being and the problems that plagued the Jewish state.

> ***Idumaeans are Edomites – descendants of Esau**. Looking back to earlier biblical times, Abraham's son Isaac and his wife Rebekah had twin sons Esau (the actual firstborn) and Jacob (later to have his name changed to Israel). Israel became the father of 12 sons – the 12 Tribes of Israel). Esau became the father of the Arab peoples.
>
> **Genesis 25:23:**
> *"And the Lord said to her [Rebekah], 'two nations are in your womb; and two peoples shall be separated from your body; and one people shall be stronger than the other; and the older shall serve the younger.'"*

In 41 B.C., the Parthians (who lived in what is today the northeastern part of Iran) attacked Jerusalem.

Herod the Great was forced to flee to Rome at a time when Marc Anthony had succeeded Cassius as the Roman ruler. And because Herod had earlier bribed his way into Marc Anthony's favor, he was officially named as the King of Judea. After the Parthians were driven out of Jerusalem by Herod, with the help of the Roman armies, he returned to Jerusalem as king.

Herod ruled from 37 B.C. to 4 B.C. He is infamous as the king who feared the birth of a rival and decreed the murder of infants in Bethlehem at the time of the birth of Jesus. Although this barbarism isn't documented in secular records, his other atrocities are well known. For example, "Herod's 10 wives and many children were violently removed when they interfered with his plans or were suspected of disloyalty."

Although Herod was hated by the Jews, he worked to win them over by building cities and fortresses, baths, parks, market places, roads and other Greek luxuries.

In 20/19 B.C., Herod began rebuilding the Jewish Temple in Jerusalem, but the work wasn't completed until 62-64 A.D. Less than 10 years later, it was completely destroyed by the armies of the Roman Emperor Titus, in the siege of Jerusalem.

With the death of Herod (which no one mourned) the intertestamental period comes to an end and we move into the New Testament period.

Although much of today's literature regarding this important time in history refers to Judea as "Palestine", the name Palestine did not come into usage until the second century A.D.

The then-Roman Emperor Hadrian wanted to rid the world of the name of Israel and erase all memory of the country. Therefore, he chose to rename Judea "Palestine," because it is a derivation of the name "Philistines," who were enemies of the Israelites.

THE TEN COMMANDMENTS - TYING TOGETHER THE HEBREW SCRIPTURES AND THE CHRISTIAN SCRIPTURES

The following sermon by Pastor Tania Haber, Westwood Lutheran Church, St. Louis Park, MN, on March 26, 2006, entitled "**A Closer Walk**" illustrates, in part, the significance of the Old Testament - the Hebrew Scriptures – as being "the Law" and the New Testament – the Christmas Scriptures – as being the Spirit of Love.

"The 10 Commandments have hit the news a lot in recent years. Can they hang on courthouse walls or be printed on a plaque in a public square? Big lawsuits have ensued. Kind of interesting that these rules given by God to Moses on the top of a mountain, thousands of years ago, have caused so much controversy in our high-tech, unchurched society today. What's with these 10 rules anyway?

"Here's my read on it: I believe it's an indication that in the world we're living in today, we're looking for boundaries to the chaos that reigns, for rules perhaps. We're looking for some order to contain the disorder we live in.

"Perhaps that's why some churches that attempt to answer all of people's questions and give them strict rules to live by are so popular. On one level, we crave the law.

"What if there were no laws? No one would stop at an intersection. Or, perhaps here in Minnesota, no one would go! When my kids were little, they used to think it was so nice when at a 4-way stop, everyone would sit there and motion the other person to go...before they understood that there actually were rules about that. So we create laws for the good of all of us.

"We even have laws, rules, about war...that both sides are supposed to follow, like the Geneva Convention, giving a code of conduct for how prisoners of war should be treated. It does seem a bit ludicrous that it's not against the rules to drop a bomb, thousands of bombs, but it IS against the rules to, for example, air pictures of a prisoner of war on TV?

"What this says to me is that even amidst the utter chaos of war, we crave some boundaries to the evil....some rules or guidelines that allies and enemies alike can live by. . . It seems to me that we have a fundamental need for order. Without rules and laws, we would be doomed to chaos.

"Enter the 10 Commandments. Despite the story that they came down from on high, really they came up from the cries below....from the need for help on how it is that sinful, impatient, lustful, selfish people live together in any kind of community.

"The Hebrew people were ready to kill Moses, and probably each other as well. They were tired, hungry, thirsty, had no homes, no possessions, no schools, no churches, no society. They were wandering in the wilderness...literally and figuratively.

"And God knew that the only way they were going to make it to the Promised Land, was to create out of this motley mess of humanity, some sense of community. They needed rules to live by. And God gave them exactly what they needed. God crafted these laws so perfectly that even today, if we lived by them, we would have for ourselves a society of peace and equality and faithfulness, beyond what this planet has ever seen.

"Martin Luther once said that when God speaks to us, God talks 'baby talk'. . . But it's true. God speaks to us as if we were kids on a playground, playing with no rules. God is direct, succinct, very clear. 'You don't kill. You don't steal. Love me above all the other things that you are tempted to love more.' Can we understand that? Yes, it's quite clear.

"The 10 Commandments come out of the part of the Hebrew Bible called the 'Torah'. We call this part of the scriptures 'the Law'. But the Hebrew word 'torah' means 'the way'....or more literally 'the finger pointing the way'. Isn't that kind of a nice way to view the 10 Commandments? ...as God's finger pointing the way?!

"So these 10 laws, that we sometimes see as restrictive, limiting our fun, are in fact the finger that points us to the good life. You want the good life? Honor each other. Don't steal or even long for that which isn't yours...be content with what you have. Take one day a week to rest and to worship. Don't kill or hurt each other...physically or emotionally. Aren't those good rules?

"These commandments are a gift from God....to show us how much God loves us! But, here's the dilemma: If following all the laws were what created a relationship between us and God, I'd be in trouble. They're good laws, they make perfect sense, and I'd love to keep all 10 of them. But I don't. Do you?

"Do you ever put something in first place in your life besides God? Do you ever speak words that kill a person's self-esteem, or kill someone's enthusiasm? Are you ever less than satisfied with what you have?

"Who of us can answer 'yes' to all of the above, and more? In the course of a few days we could probably check off all 10 Commandments as being broken. Do you remember me telling you about a Far Side cartoon of a church called 'Church Lite'. On their sign it said, 'We only observe 6 Commandments...you choose which ones.' That might be a little easier to keep.

"But seriously, the Commandments can help us be disciplined in our walk with God, but the bottom line is, they can't bring us life. This God-thing is not about following rules. I mean, I feel pretty good about myself when I'm behaving properly...but that's not what saves me....that's not what brings us comfort, peace, love, an abundant life. The rules are not the bottom line for God.

"Did you hear that? People get this confused a lot. Jesus never said it's all about keeping the law, did he? Obeying the rules is not what brings us into a relationship with God. We are able to walk closely with God not because we keep all of these wonderful laws, but simply because of God's love for us in Jesus Christ.

"One theologian today said that God was doing through the 10 Commandments in the Old Testament, what God later did through Jesus in the New Testament. The 10 Commandments were one way that God showed his love for his people. And we are to still honor and obey those laws. But we all know it takes more than laws to create a relationship, right?

"When I sign a Marriage License, a marriage is not created, right? I'm sealing the deal legally, but....it takes very concrete actions of love to create the relationship of marriage, right? Spouses could follow all the legal rules about getting married, but if there isn't some visible love, some affection, some exchange of conversation, some time spent together, some acts of service towards the other, it's really not much of a marriage.

"Enter Jesus. It took God talking 'baby talk' to us again...God saying, 'Let me try it this way. I want so much to be in a relationship with you that I'll come down to you, so you can see me and know me...so that I can love you...and die for you. Then, perhaps you will understand how desperately I want to be in relationship with you.'

"Would you read with me verses 16 and 17 from our Gospel lesson, where John, in his words, tells us this: *'For God so loved the world that he gave his only Son, that whoever believes in him should not perish but have eternal life. For God sent the Son into the world, not to condemn the world, but that the world might be saved through him.'*

"The law, the Torah, is the finger that points us to God. And the law is good, and necessary. But it is a relationship with the very real person of Jesus Christ that offers us the gift of life and salvation.

"Both ends of the scale are needed to keep our lives in balance. The Commandments call us to a life of discipline. But freedom, deep joy, abundant life in this world and the next, comes when we know Jesus and accept his incredible love for us. For us as Christians, Jesus Christ is the torah, 'the way' that has been given to us to be in a relationship with God.

"My daughters. . . are in a Suzuki violin program with a very strict teacher, who says that we should 'practice only on the days we eat'....like it or not. When the girls were younger, I tried every trick in the book to get the girls to practice. I set up reward systems....I created games....I was firm and consistent....I stooped to bribery....but here's what I have discovered works: When Sophie and Ali hear a student a few years ahead of them perform a beautiful Sonata, their hearts are touched. They fall in love with the music and come home and pick up their instruments and begin to play.

"You see, although it was the discipline of the law, the practicing, that enabled them to play in the first place, it is not the law that has touched their hearts....it is love. It is sitting in a room and hearing music so beautiful that tears come to your eyes. It is that concrete experience of being lifted to a new place that changes us.

"I invite you this morning, to open your heart again to the music of God's love for you. Let that love wash over you and nourish you and sustain you, as you continue your walk with God. Amen."

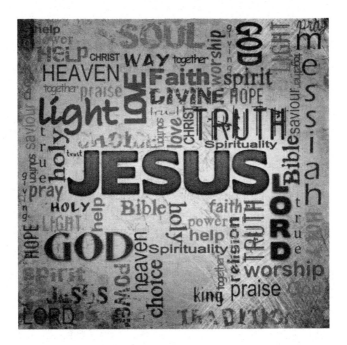

INTRODUCTION TO THE 27 BOOKS OF THE NEW TESTAMENT (THE CHRISTIAN SCRIPTURES)

"Many ages after the world was created,
when God, in the beginning,
formed the heavens and the earth –
long after the great flood –
some 2000 years after the birth of Abraham –
15 centuries after Moses and the passing over of Israel –
a thousand years after the anointing of David as King –
in the 65th week as Daniel's prophecy takes note –
in the 194th Olympiad –
the 752nd year from the founding of the City of Rome –
the 42nd year of Octavian Augustus' rule –
in the 6th age of the world, all the earth being at peace –
Jesus Christ, Eternal God, Son of the Father,
willing to hallow the world by His coming in mercy,
was born of the Virgin Mary in Bethlehem of Judea.

"GOD BECAME FLESH!"
- Anonymous

THE POLITICAL CLIMATE OF JUDEA
AT THE TIME OF JESUS' BIRTH

The Roman Empire ruled Judea and the Jews resented and resisted being under Roman rule.

Because Judea was the frontier of the Roman Empire in that part of the world, it was important for Rome to quell even the slightest sign of uprising in order to protect its border from the recently revived Persian Empire.

Within the Jewish community at the time were several quasi-religious "parties." These parties or sects represented different reactions to the continuing clash between Hellenism and traditional Jewish religious life.

The most important of the religious parties was the sect known as the Pharisees. They were lay persons who didn't get involved in politics and were more interested in religious matters. They believed in a life after death and a resurrection to reward or punishment. They also believed in angels and demons. They strictly upheld the authority of the Torah (the first five books of the Old Testament) and accepted oral traditions. The Pharisees were influential and were connected with the temple or synagogue. Scribes were probably drawn from the Pharisees. Modern Judaism traces its roots to the Pharisees.

A second group composed primarily of priests were the Sadducees and they were most closely associated with the Torah. They didn't believe in resurrection and rejected oral tradition or any doctrine related to a Messiah, as well as belief in angels and demons. They believed that each person had the freedom to choose to do good or evil and each was responsible for the choices he or she made. Because they were priests, they were closely involved with the temple and its cultures. We hear nothing more of the Sadducees after 70 A.D., when the temple was destroyed.

Both the Pharisees and the Sadducees sat on the Sanhedrin (an "assembly" or "council") which had jurisdiction over the province of Judea. The Sanhedrin was composed of 70 men (chief priests, scribes and elders), plus the high priest who served as its president. The Sanhedrin had its own police force which could arrest people, as it did with Jesus.

While the Sanhedrin heard both civil and criminal cases, and could impose the death penalty, it did not have the authority to execute convicted criminals. That power was reserved to the Romans, which explains why Jesus was crucified – a Roman punishment – rather than being stoned, according to Mosaic law. The Sanhedrin was abolished with the fall of Jerusalem and the destruction of the temple in 70 A.D.

A third group was the Essenes. They believed in separating themselves from what they considered as evil society. They were often celibate, usually monk-like and lived simple and hard working lives. Each member was required to take on certain tasks of labor so as to make the community, as a whole, self-supporting. The Dead Sea Scroll community at Qumran (discovered and uncovered from 1947 to 1956) was a community of Essenes. They emphasized religious and ceremonial purity and looked for the establishment of the kingdom of the righteous at any time.

A fourth group, commonly known as Zealots, was cut from the cloth of the Maccabean period and was inspired by zeal for Jewish purity, independence and political power. Zealots were "super-patriots who were determined to resist Rome at all costs" and so were openly rebellious against Rome's rule and hold over Judea. Several of Jesus' followers were Zealots.

A fifth group was known as Herodians (a political party) – who appear to have been influential Jews inclined towards the Herodian rule and, consequently, to the Romans who supported the Herods. The Herodians, on at least two occasions in the New Testament, displayed a negative disposition towards Jesus.

An even more fanatical group in Israel at the time was called the Sicarii ("dagger-men" or "contract killers"). They were a splinter group of the Zealots. Their mission was to expel the Romans from Judea by assassinating the Romans and their sympathizers.

Following the world-changing advent of Jesus Christ, the Roman Empire continued to maintain control over Judea for a large part of the first century A.D. Several members of the Herod family (who ruled Judea under the Roman regime) are referred to in the New Testament. As an example, some historians believe that Herod the Great (Herod I) was still alive when both John the Baptist and Jesus were born, although the date of his death is generally in dispute.

Herod the Great has been described as a madman who murdered members of his own family as well as a great many rabbis. He is also known, however, for his great many building projects in Jerusalem and elsewhere, including the rebuilding of the Second Temple in Jerusalem.

One of Herod's sons – Archelaus – replaced his father as ruler over the southern part of Judea but ruled only briefly. Antipas, another of Herod's sons was given the main part of his father's realm. He enjoyed a long time in office and is mentioned in the first three Gospels.

Agrippa I, a grandson of Herod the Great, ruled over the territory of Northeast Judea. Agrippa II, a great-grandson of Herod the Great, participated in the trial of Paul and recognized Paul's innocence.

Roman governors functioned in Judea for much of the first century A.D. Pontius Pilate handed down the final sentence for Jesus. Antonius Felix and Porcius Festus were involved in Paul's fate after his arrest in Jerusalem and during his two year Caesarean imprisonment.

The entire New Testament was written in Greek, the language of everyday life throughout the Roman Empire, as well as in Judea where Aramaic and Hebrew also were used. Some of Jesus' utterances were probably in Aramaic but when they are quoted in the New Testament, they have been translated into Greek.

The original manuscripts of the New Testament no longer exist, having perished long ago from much use. This is not a cause for concern, however, since thousands of translations were made into Greek so that the quotations of the earliest Christians have been preserved.

THE NEW TESTAMENT BEGINS WITH THE FOUR GOSPELS ("GOOD NEWS"): MATTHEW, MARK, LUKE AND JOHN

All four gospels give an accounting of the life of Jesus, but, as with any four writers writing about the same person and events, their accounts differ in approach and emphasis.

The four gospels cover a period from approximately 5 B.C. to 30 A.D. when Jesus was crucified and raised from the dead.

Unlike other chapters in the New Testament, the four gospels contain Jesus' words. A summary of the gospels cannot do justice to Jesus' actual words, activities, directions, healings, life, suffering, death and resurrection.

Reading the four gospels in their entirety – is essential in order to fully understand and appreciate Jesus' life on earth and his love and sacrifice for mankind.

THE GOSPEL ACCORDING TO MATTHEW

Matthew's gospel is the gospel of the Son of David.

This gospel ties the Old Testament to Christ through the law and the prophets. There are many references to, or direct quotations from, the Old Testament.

This is the first of the three synoptic gospels (Matthew, Mark and Luke). The word "synoptic" used here means synopsis of the life of Jesus. There are similarities between these three Gospels but like all writers, each approaches the life of Jesus from a slightly different viewpoint, making each of them all the more interesting.

Matthew's Gospel demonstrates that Jesus fulfilled the Messianic prophecy and was Israel's Messiah.

The Gospel of Matthew seems aimed at Jewish converts to Christianity. It was probably written prior to 70 A.D., for there is no mention of the destruction of Jerusalem.

Matthew was a Jewish tax collector for Rome (a "publican"). Because he could read and write (he knew business shorthand), and worked with numbers, his depiction of Jesus' life has an air of credibility and accuracy.

Because he was a despised employee of the Roman Empire and therefore thought to be a sinner, Matthew was someone with whom the Jewish people would have nothing to do.

Several of Jesus' disciples were so openly opposed to Roman rule they were considered radicals ("Zealots").

Although Matthew knew he was despised, he wanted to be closer to Jesus and so Jesus invited him to become a disciple.

Because of his trade, Matthew was precise in his writings. He tells us about the genealogy of Jesus, going back to the family of King David and then also going back all the way to the family of Abraham.

Matthew names the 42 generations from Abraham to David and then David to Jesus. From Abraham to David there are 14 generations; from David to the deportation to Babylon another 14 generations; and from the deportation from Babylon to the time of Christ, another 14.

The number 14 is significant. It is a sacred number, being **twice 7** (the Sabbath) but more importantly, it is the numerical equivalent of the name of David, the Great King. This is **Matthew's way of emphasizing that Jesus is the son of David, the promised Messiah of God!**

Matthew begins telling us about the birth of Jesus Christ:

> *"And she will bear a Son; and you shall call His name Jesus, for it is He who will save His people from their sins."* *(1:21)*

The Gospel according to Luke gives us a more complete picture of this monumental event in time.

Matthew affirms that there are three persons in one God. He recognizes the Trinity of God, citing Jesus' baptism by John the Baptist:

> *"And after being baptized, Jesus went up immediately from the water; and behold, the heavens were opened, and he saw the Spirit of God descending as a dove, and coming upon Him, and behold, a voice out of the heavens, saying, 'This is my beloved Son, in whom I am well-pleased!'"* *(3:16-17)*

It is in Matthew's gospel that we learn about Jesus preparing for his life of public ministry by going into the wilderness and fasting for 40 days and 40 nights, after which He is subjected to temptation by the devil.

It is through Matthew that we have the Sermon on the Mount, during which Jesus taught the Beatitudes *(5:1-12 – see also the Gospel of Luke, 6:20-38).* At that same time, Jesus also said:

> *"Let your light shine before men in such a way that they may see your good works, and glorify your Father who is in heaven." (5:16)*

THE SERMON ON THE MOUNT.

171.

It was also during the Sermon on the Mount that Jesus gave us the Lord's Prayer.

> *"Pray then in this way: Our Father who art in heaven, hallowed be Thy name. Thy kingdom come, Thy will be done on earth as it is in heaven. Give us this day our daily bread, and forgive us our debts as we forgive our debtors. And do not lead us into temptation, but deliver us from evil,[for Thine is the kingdom, and the power, and the glory, forever. Amen"]. (6:9-13)*

> *"For if you forgive men for their transgressions, your heavenly Father will also forgive you. But if you do not forgive men, then your Father will not forgive your transgressions." (6:14-15)*

Jesus also encourages us to come to Him with our cares and needs:

> *"Ask, and it shall be given to you; seek, and you shall find; knock, and it shall be opened to you. For everyone who asks receives, and he who seeks finds, and to him who knocks, it shall be opened." (7:7-8)*

Matthew tells us about Jesus curing a leper, the centurion's servant, a paralytic, and many, many others. He also relates how, on two occasions, Jesus fed great numbers of the people who had come to hear Him, from small amounts of food - several fishes and only a few loaves of bread.

> **Here, as in the Old Testament Book of Genesis, God uses the symbol of bread** to feed His people, once again foretelling of the Bread of Life which is our Savior, Jesus Christ, the Son of God.

Matthew names Jesus' 12 apostles: Peter (Simon), Andrew (Peter's brother), James and John (both sons of a man named Zebedee). All four of these men are fishermen. Philip and Bartholomew, Thomas and Matthew (the tax-gatherer), James (son of Alphaeus), Thaddaeus, Simon the Zealot and Judas Iscariot (who eventually betrays Jesus). *(10:1-4)*

Jesus sends His disciples out, telling them to preach that the Kingdom of Heaven is at hand. He adjures them to heal the sick, raise the dead, cleanse lepers, cast out demons, saying to them, *"Freely you received; freely give." (10:5-8)*

Jesus talks about the unforgivable sin:

> *"Therefore I say to you, any sin and blasphemy shall be forgiven men, but blasphemy against the Spirit shall not be forgiven. And whoever shall speak a word against the Son of Man, it shall be forgiven him; but whoever shall speak against the Holy Spirit, it shall not be forgiven him, either in this age, or in the age to come." (12:31-32)*

Jesus used parables to teach important concepts and to help people see the relationship between God and man and between heaven and earth. Parables were important teaching tools and Jesus often took the time to explain the meaning of his parables to His disciples.

> *". . . the kingdom of heaven is like a dragnet cast into the sea, and gathering fish of every kind; and when it was filled, they drew it up on the beach; and they sat down, and gathered the good fish into containers, but the bad they threw away. So it will be at the end of the age; the angels shall come forth and take out the wicked from among the righteous, and will cast them into the furnace of fire; there shall be weeping and gnashing of teeth." (13:47-50)*

In Chapter 13, Jesus' brothers are mentioned: James, Joseph, Simon and Judas. Mention is also made of sisters, but they are not named. *(13:55-56)*

In Chapter 16, Jesus founds His church. When He asks Peter who he thinks He is, Peter responds, *"Thou art the Christ, the Son of the living God."* Hearing this, Jesus responds:

> *"Blessed are you, Simon Barjona, because flesh and blood did not reveal this to you, but My Father who is in Heaven. And I also say to you that you are Peter, and upon this rock I will build My church; and the gates of Hades shall not overpower it. I will give you the keys of the kingdom of heaven; and whatever you shall bind on earth shall be bound in heaven, and whatever you shall loose on earth shall be loosed in heaven." (16:17–19)*

In Chapter 17 Jesus is transfigured before Peter, James and his brother John. In His transfiguration, Moses and Elijah appear with Jesus, talking with Him.

> *". . .He was transfigured before them; and His face shone like the sun, and His garments became as white as light." (17:2)*

Matthew tells us that Jesus cast out demons. *(17:14-18)*

In Chapter 22, Jesus is asked,

> *"Teacher, which is the great commandment in the law? And He said to him, 'You shall love the Lord your God with all your heart, and with all your soul, and with all your mind. This is the great and foremost commandment. The second is like it, you shall love your neighbor as yourself. On these two commandments depend the whole Law and the Prophets.'" (22:36-40)*

In Chapter 23, Jesus talks about the scribes and Pharisees who led the Jewish people in the law of Moses and how they have perverted God's law by making outward appearances more important than justice and mercy.

In Chapter 23, Jesus also talks about the importance of forgiveness. **He used a parable to illustrate** that if we don't forgive others, God will not forgive us.

In Chapter 24, Jesus talks about the signs of the end of the world, and says, among other things,

> *". . .For nation will rise against nation, and kingdom against kingdom. . .Many will fall away and will deliver up one another and hate one another. . .and because lawlessness is increased, most peoples' love will grow cold. But the one who endures to the end, he shall be saved." (24:7, 10, 12-13)*

Matthew details Jesus' last days on earth - and how the chief priests and the elders of the people were plotting against Him with an intent to seize Him and kill Him. One of Jesus' disciples, Judas Iscariot, betrayed Jesus by promising to lead them to Jesus in return for 30 pieces of silver.

Jesus, knowing that those who wanted Him dead were plotting His capture and that His life on earth was soon to end, told His disciples to prepare a place for them to eat the Passover meal together. During that meal,

> *". . .Jesus took some bread, and after a blessing, He broke it and gave it to the disciples, and said, 'Take, eat, this is My body.' And when He had taken a cup and given thanks, He gave it to them, saying, 'Drink from it all of you; for this is My blood of the covenant, which is poured out for many for forgiveness of sins. . .'" (26:26-28)*

After supper the group accompanied Jesus to the Garden of Gethsemane.

> Jesus said, *"Sit here while I go over there and pray." (26:36)* He took Peter and the two sons of Zebedee with Him and said to them, *"My soul is deeply grieved, to the point of death; remain here and keep watch with Me. . .Keep watching and praying, that you may not enter into temptation; the spirit is willing, but the flesh is weak." (26:38-41)*

Jesus, knowing the suffering and death He was about to undergo, prayed to His Father, saying, *"My Father, if this cannot pass away unless I drink it, Thy will be done." (26:42)*

Jesus, who had earlier been betrayed by Judas Iscariot in exchange for 30 pieces of silver, is taken before Caiaphas, the high priest, where the scribes and the elders were gathered together.

Peter, who had followed Jesus being taken away, gains entrance into the courtyard of the high priest. When questioned as to his relationship with Jesus, Peter three times denies knowing Jesus. Meanwhile, Jesus, being questioned by the high priest, acknowledges that He is the Son of God. The high priest tears his robes and declares that Jesus has blasphemed, and so Jesus is spat upon, beaten and slapped by those who are seeking His death.

> When morning came, *the chief priests and the elders of the people counseled, ". . .against Jesus to put Him to death; and they bound Him and led Him away and delivered Him up to Pilate the governor." (27:1-2)*

When Judas Iscariot learned what was happening to Jesus, he tried to return the 30 pieces of silver to the chief priests and elders saying, *"'I have sinned by betraying innocent blood.' But they said, 'What is that to us? See to that yourself!'"* (27:3-4) Judas threw the 30 pieces of silver into the sanctuary and went away and hanged himself.

Pontius Pilate, in questioning Jesus, asked Him, *"'Are you the king of the Jews?' And Jesus said to him, 'It is as you say.'"* (27:11)

Because the time all this was happening was right before the beginning of Passover, *". . .the governor was accustomed to release to the multitude any one prisoner whom they wanted. And they were holding at that time a notorious prisoner, called Barabbas."* (27:15-16).

And even though Pilate's wife said to Pilate, *"Have nothing to do with that righteous man, for last night I suffered greatly in a dream because of Him,"* when Pilate asked the crowd what he should do with Jesus, they all said, *"'Let Him be crucified!'"* (27:19-22)

Pilate, seeing that the crowd was about to riot, took water and washed his hands in front of the crowd saying, *"I am innocent of this Man's blood; see to that yourselves.'"* (27:24)

Pilate then released Barabbas, *". . .but after having Jesus scourged, he delivered Him to be crucified."* (27:26) The Roman soldiers then put a crown of thorns on Jesus' head, spat on Him, beat Him, mocked Him and, *". . .led Him away to crucify Him."* (27:31)

A man named Simon who was from Cyrene was in Jerusalem that day, and he was, *". . .pressed into service to bear His cross."* Jesus' crucifixion took place at Golgotha, *". . .which means Place of a Skull."* (27:32-33)

Matthew does not tell us how Jesus was nailed to the cross, nor does he tell us with what intense pain Jesus suffered as His body was raised with the cross. We know that crucifixion was, in those times, a common way to deal with those condemned to death. The body - nailed to the cross at the wrists with the arms extended on the cross bar – hangs by its weight, putting tremendous pressure on the bones, muscles, tendons, ligaments and flesh of the arms and chest. The feet are also nailed to the cross, making movement even more excruciating as the person attempts to brace the body to relieve the pain of hanging from the wrists.

The weight of the body prohibits the person from drawing a deep breath, and death sometimes comes from asphyxiation.

If the person being crucified doesn't die within a certain period of time, the soldiers may choose to break the person's legs in order to hasten asphyxiation. Jesus' legs were not broken, because death came before that could happen.

A sign which had been placed over His head read, *"THIS IS JESUS THE KING OF THE JEWS." (27:37)*

Matthew tells us that two robbers were crucified with Jesus, *". . .one on the right and one on the left." (27:38)* The chief priests and scribes, as well as passersby, hurled insults at Jesus.

> *"Now from the sixth hour darkness fell upon all the land until the ninth hour. And about the ninth hour Jesus cried out with a loud voice, saying, 'Eli, Eli, Lama Sabachthani?' That is, 'My God, My God, why hast Thou forsaken Me?'" (27:45-46) ". . .And Jesus cried out again with a loud voice, and yielded up His spirit." (27:50)*

At the time of Jesus' death,

> *". . .The veil of the temple was torn in two from top to bottom, and the earth shook; and the rocks were split, and the tombs were opened; and many bodies of the saints who had fallen asleep were raised; and coming out of the tombs after His resurrection they entered the holy city and appeared to many." (27:51-53)*

The centurion and others keeping guard became frightened and said, *"Truly this was the Son of God!" (27:54)*

> *"And many women were there looking on from a distance, who had followed Jesus from Galilee, ministering to Him." (27:55)*

Each of the four gospels gives a different account of the women who were there. Matthew names *"Mary Magdalene, Mary the Mother of James and Joseph, and the mother of the sons of Zebedee." (27:56)*

Joseph of Arimathea, a disciple of Jesus, asked Pilate for Jesus' body. Being granted this great privilege, Joseph wrapped Jesus' body in clean linen and laid Him in his own new tomb, hewn out of rock, and then rolled a large stone against the entrance of the tomb. *(27:57-60)*

The chief priests and Pharisees, fearing the fulfillment of Jesus' words, *"After three days I am to rise again,"* went to Pilate asking for a guard for Jesus' tomb. *"And they went and made the grave secure, and along with the guard they set a seal on the stone." (27:62-66)*

"Now after the Sabbath. . .Mary Magdalene and the other Mary went to the grave where they found the stone had been rolled away and, *". . .an angel of the Lord descended from heaven and came and rolled away the stone and sat upon it. . .The guards shook for fear. . .and became like dead men. And the angel. . .said to the women, 'Do not be afraid; for I know you are looking for Jesus who has been crucified. He is not here, for He has risen, just as He said. . .'" (28:2-6)*

The women ran to tell Jesus' disciples, and met Jesus on the way. *He said to them, "Do not be afraid; go and take word to My brethren to leave for Galilee, and there they shall see Me." (28:10)*

Matthew tells us that the guards, having run away, told the chief priests what had happened. The guards were then given *". . .a large sum of money,"* and told to say that Jesus' disciples had taken His body away while they were asleep. (28:12)

". . .The eleven disciples proceeded to Galilee to the mountain which Jesus had designated. And when they saw Him, they worshipped Him; but some were doubtful. And Jesus came up and spoke to them saying, 'All authority has been given to Me in heaven and on earth. Go therefore and make disciples of all the nations, baptizing them in the name of the Father and the Son and the Holy Spirit, teaching them to observe all that I commanded you; and lo, I am with you always, even to the end of the age.'" (28:16-20)

It is in this way that Matthew comes full circle from his initial recognition of the three persons in one God – the Holy Trinity – Father, Son and Holy Spirit.

✝

THE GOSPEL ACCORDING TO MARK

Mark is the Gospel of the Son of God.

Although the author of this gospel is anonymous, there is sufficient evidence pointing to Mark, since the author is familiar with Palestine and with Jerusalem in particular, and because he makes geographical references which are correct in fine detail.

This gospel is known as "The Marcan Gospel." It is a synoptic gospel, along with the gospels of Matthew and Luke, meaning they are similar in outline.

There is an "on-the-scene" quality to Mark's Gospel. The word "immediately" is used many times and the gospel appears to be an unvarnished reporting of the facts.

It is in Acts 12:12, that we first hear of Mark in connection with a prayer meeting in his mother's house.

It is possible that the Apostle Peter was the main source for this Gospel, since Mark was an attendant to Peter and may have been his son.

Mark was not an apostle, but traveled with Paul and Barnabas as far as Perga on Paul's first missionary journey. When Mark chose to return home early, Paul became angry with him and refused to have Mark come on a second journey. However, when Paul was later imprisoned in Rome, he sent for Mark.

This gospel opens with John the Baptist preaching a baptism of repentance for the forgiveness of sins. Mark then reports the baptism of Jesus *(1:4)* and later, that John the Baptist is taken into custody by King Herod and is beheaded. *(6:17-28)*

Jesus begins recruiting his disciples - Simon (Peter) and Andrew, both fishermen; then James and John (also fishermen), sons of a man named Zebedee.

Jesus enters the synagogue in Capernaum and begins teaching there. He casts out an unclean spirit, which aroused everyone's interest. Word about this Man of God spreads quickly. He heals Peter's mother-in-law and then many others.

Jesus often rises early in the morning in order to be by himself (going off to rest and pray after being with large groups of people). He soon becomes so much of a sensation that He can no longer enter a city without a lot of fanfare, so instead chooses to stay in unpopulated areas. People, however, flock to Him everywhere.

Jesus heals a paralytic in the midst of a crowd. The scribes question this healing and accuse Him of blaspheming. Jesus answers this accusation by saying, *"Which is easier, to say to the paralytic 'Your sins are forgiven' or to say 'Arise and take up your pallet and walk'?"* Jesus explains He healed the man to show His authority on earth to forgive sins. *(2:9)*

Jesus recruits Matthew (also known as Levi) the son of Alphaeus. Matthew is a Jewish tax collector for Rome and, as such, is hated by other Jews. Jesus eats at Matthew's house with tax gatherers and sinners, and the Pharisees criticize Him for this. Jesus explains that he, *"did not come to call the righteous, but sinners." (2:17)*

The Pharisees also criticize Jesus because His disciples aren't fasting, as required by Jewish law. Jesus replies with the metaphor that while the bridegroom is with them, the attendants don't fast. The Pharisees then criticize Jesus' disciples for picking heads of grain to eat on the Sabbath (a common practice when walking through fields, except on the Sabbath). Jesus states, among other things, *"The Sabbath was made for man and not man for the Sabbath." (2:27)* Jesus was telling them that the Son of Man is Lord even of the Sabbath.

Jesus then heals a man with a withered hand (in the Temple, no less) and is again criticized. Jesus then goes up to the mountain and calls those whom he wants and appoints his twelve apostles: Simon (Peter), James and John (the sons of Zebedee), Andrew, Philip, Bartholomew, Matthew, Thomas, James (son of Alphaeus), Thaddaeus, Simon the Zealot and Judas Iscariot. *(3:16-19)*

He gave them authority to cast out demons (pretty strong stuff for a carpenter from Nazareth!) and when *"His own people heard of this"* they wanted to take charge of Him, since they were saying, *"He has lost His senses."* And, not surprisingly, the scribes said that Jesus was, *"possessed by Beelzebul."* *(3:22)*

But Jesus calls them to Himself and begins speaking in parables regarding, *"How can Satan cast out Satan?"* (meaning Satan wouldn't destroy – or cast out – himself). *(3:23)*

About this time, Jesus' mother and brothers arrive and send word to Jesus. It could be that they are concerned about His well-being. When told that His mother and brothers are looking for Him, Jesus replies, *". . . whoever does the will of God, he is my brother and sister and mother."* *(3:33-35)*

In Chapter 4, Jesus begins to teach again by the sea. So many people come to hear Him, that He gets into a boat in order to talk to, and teach, the gathered crowds from there. He uses His parable of the sower and the seed to illustrate how people respond to God's word and whether they allow God's word to take root in them or they let Satan take away the word which God has sown. Jesus then uses another parable to illustrate God's word – the parable of a lamp being placed on a lamp stand to give light, or placed under a "peck measure" (basket) or under a bed where it can't give light.

Jesus goes on to use two more parables to help the people understand God's word – the first being the parable of the seed, in which He likens the Kingdom of God to a man who casts seed upon the soil and how some of the seed falls on rocks and can't grow, some seed gets eaten by the birds, and some seed falls on fertile soil where it grows and produces a crop. He then compares the Kingdom of God to the mustard seed – so small a seed, but growing up to be much larger than all the other garden plants, so that even the birds can nest under its shade. Although Jesus spoke to the people in parables, He later explained everything to His disciples in private.

At the end of that day, Jesus said to His disciples, *"Let's go over to the other side,"* *(4:35)* and so they got into the boat He was in, along with other boats. While Jesus was sleeping, a storm came up. The disciples became alarmed and woke Jesus up. He calmed the sea and the wind by saying, *"Hush, be still!"* *(4:39)*

When they reached the other side of the sea and went into the country of the Gerasenes they encountered a man who was possessed by many unclean spirits, crying out and cutting himself with stones. When Jesus commanded the legion of spirits to come out of the man, they did so and went into a herd of swine which then rushed over a cliff and drowned in the water below.

The herdsmen who saw this happen talked about this to others in the city and the country so that many people came to see what had happened. The man who had been possessed asked Jesus if he could accompany Him. Jesus told him to, *"Go home to your people and report to them what great things the Lord has done for you and how He had mercy on you." (5:19)*

Jesus then accomplished other miracles and healings, bringing back to life the daughter of a synagogue official and curing a woman who had been hemorrhaging for 12 years.

Mark relates many miracles which Jesus accomplished. He tells how, on two occasions, Jesus fed thousands of people who came out to hear His words. The first time, Jesus took five loaves of bread and two fishes and then blessed the food. He broke the loaves and divided up the two fishes, giving them to His disciples to feed the five thousand people gathered to hear Him.

At a later time, Jesus is again confronted with thousands of people who have traveled a long way to hear Him. He again blesses seven loaves of bread and a few small fish and feeds the entire assemblage, having seven large baskets of food left over.

Jesus tells His disciples that He – the Son of Man – *"must suffer many things and be rejected by the elders and the chief priests and the scribes, and be killed, and after three days, rise again."(8:31)* Peter rebukes Jesus for saying this and Jesus replies that Peter is, *"not setting his mind on God's interests, but man's." (8:33)*

Six days later, Jesus takes Peter, James and John to a high mountain and is transfigured before them, His garments becoming exceedingly white *"as no launderer on earth can whiten them."* Elijah and Moses appear with Jesus, a cloud forms overhead and a voice is heard from the cloud, *"'This is my beloved Son, listen to Him!' And all at once they looked around and saw no one with them anymore, except Jesus alone."* *(9:2-8)*

When they came down from the mountain, Jesus is confronted by a man asking Him to cast out a spirit from his son. The man said to Jesus, *". . .If You can do anything, take pity on us and help us!"* And Jesus said to him, *"'If you can'! All things are possible to him who believes.'"* The boy's father responded, *"I do believe; help my unbelief.'"* *(9:14-25)* Jesus then rebuked the unclean spirit which first cried out, then threw the boy into convulsions, then finally coming out of the boy.

Jesus later told His disciples what was soon to happen to Him*:*

> *"The Son of Man is to be delivered into the hands of men, and they will kill Him; and when He has been killed, He will rise three days later." (9:31)*

In teaching His disciples, Jesus oftentimes used hyperbole (teaching with exaggerated examples). In so doing, He cautioned them that,

> *". . .if your hand. . .your foot. . .your eye causes you to stumble [causes you to commit sin], cast it off; it is better for you to enter the kingdom of God [without those sinful parts of the body] than having [a perfect body] to be cast into hell where. . .[your] worm does not die, and the fire [of hell] is not quenched." (9:43-46)*

Jesus had this to say about marriage:

> *". . .from the beginning of creation, God made them male and female. For this cause a man shall leave his father and mother, and the two shall become one flesh; consequently they are no longer two, but one flesh. What therefore God has joined together, let no man separate." (10:6-9)*

Jesus said this about children (and all of us),

> *"Permit the children to come to Me; do not hinder them; for the kingdom of God belongs to such as these. Truly I say to you, whoever does not receive the kingdom of God like a child shall not enter it at all." (10:14-15)*

When asked by a rich man what he should do to inherit eternal life, Jesus mentioned some of the 10 commandments and encouraged the man to, *". . .go and sell all you possess, and give to the poor, and you shall have treasure in heaven; and come, follow me." (10:17-21)* When the man's face fell in disappointment and he went away grieved, Jesus commented, *"How hard it will be for those who are wealthy to enter the kingdom of God!" (10:22-23)*

As Jesus and His disciples were then approaching Jerusalem, He directed two disciples to go into the nearby village, *". . .you will find a colt tied, on which no one has ever sat; untie it and bring it here." (11:1-2)*

The disciples did as they were told and found the colt just as Jesus had said they would. Jesus, sitting on the colt, rode into Jerusalem. Some of the people who were following along, cut leafy branches and spread them on the road while others took garments and did likewise.

> *"And those who went before, and those who followed after, were crying out, 'Hosanna! Blessed is He who comes in the name of the Lord. Blessed is the coming kingdom of our father David; Hosanna in the highest!" (11:9-10)*

Upon arriving in Jerusalem, Jesus entered the temple and drove out those who were buying and selling there. He, *". . .overturned the tables of the money changers"* and wouldn't allow anyone to carry goods through the temple. *(11:15-16)* Jesus' actions further spurred the chief priests and the scribes to more seriously seek ways to destroy Him.

Each evening Jesus and His disciples would go out of the city. On one such occasion He told them, *"Therefore I say to you, all things for which you pray and ask, believe that you have received them and they shall be granted you." (11:24)*

In response to this question asked of Him,

> *"What commandment is the foremost of all? Jesus answered, 'The foremost is, 'Hear, O Israel! The Lord our God is one Lord; and you shall love the Lord your God with all your heart, and with all your soul, and with all your mind, and with all your strength.' The second commandment is this, 'You shall love your neighbor as yourself.' There is no commandment greater than these.'" (12:28-31)*

In Chapter 13, Jesus tells Peter, James, John and Andrew that the temple in Jerusalem will be torn down and that others will come who will attempt to mislead His followers. He also describes for His disciples the end times.

> *"For nation will arise against nation, and kingdom against kingdom; there will be earthquakes in various places; there will also be famines. These things are merely the beginning of birth pangs. . .and unless the Lord has shortened those days, no life would have been saved; but for the sake of the elect whom He chose, He shortened the days. . .for false Christs and false prophets will arise, and will show signs and wonders, in order, if possible, to lead the elect astray. . ." (13:8-22)*

Jesus then goes on to tell those four disciples about His return to earth.

> *". . .Therefore, be on the alert – for you do not know when the master of the house [Jesus Himself] is coming. . .and what I say to you I say to all, 'Be on the alert.'" (13:35-37)*

In Chapter 14, we learn that Jesus' time of trial was coming in two days. While He was at the home of Simon the leper, *". . .reclining at the table,"* a woman came in and poured costly perfume over His head. Some of those who were with Him were upset about this, saying that the perfume had been wasted. But Jesus said, *". . .she has anointed My body beforehand for the burial. . ." (14:1-8)* It was then that Judas Iscariot left the group in order to betray Jesus by meeting with those who sought His death.

At Jesus' request, His disciples then set about preparing for their celebration of the Passover. When His 12 disciples were gathered with Jesus for their last Passover meal, He told the group that one of them would betray Him. During the meal, He took bread,

> *". . .and after a blessing He broke it; and gave it to them and said, 'Take it; this is My body.' And when He had taken a cup, and given thanks, He gave it to them; and they all drank from it. And He said to them, 'This is My blood of the covenant, which is poured out for many. Truly I say to you, I shall never again drink of the fruit of the vine until that day when I drink it new in the kingdom of God.'"* *(14:22-25)*

Jesus and His disciples then went out to the Mount of Olives, to the Garden of Gethsemane. Jesus went apart from them to pray. And while praying, He said, *"Abba! Father! All things are possible for Thee; remove this cup from Me; yet not what I will, but what Thou wilt."* *(14:36)* When Jesus returned to where His disciples were, and saw that they had fallen asleep, He said to Peter, *"Simon, are you asleep? Could you not keep watch for one hour? Keep watching and praying, that you may not come into temptation; the spirit is willing, but the flesh is weak."* *(14:37-38)*

As Jesus was speaking, Judas Iscariot (having earlier arranged for Jesus' betrayal) accompanied by a multitude, delivered Him into the hands of those who sought to silence and destroy Him. Jesus was led away to the high priest where the chief priests and the scribes tried, without success, to obtain testimony against Him in order to put Him to death.

When Jesus was asked, *"Are You the Christ, the Son of the Blessed One?"* He responded, *"I am; and you shall see the Son of Man sitting at the right hand of Power, and coming with the clouds of heaven."* *(14:61-62)* With that, the high priest tore his clothes in frustration and said, *"What further need do we have of witnesses?"* *(14:63)*

Peter, who had managed to enter into the courtyard below, was asked three times, in various ways, if he knew Jesus. Each time Peter denied Jesus. When a cock crowed a second time, Peter suddenly recalled that Jesus had earlier said to him, *"Before a cock crows twice, you will deny Me three times."* *(14:72)*

Early in the morning, Jesus was brought before the council of the chief priests and elders. Upon consultation, they bound Jesus and, *". . .delivered Him up to Pilate." (15:1)* Pilate, having questioned Jesus, found no guilt in Him and proceeded to ask the crowd that had gathered who they wished to be released in honor of the Feast of Passover – Jesus or Barabbas who had been jailed for murder and insurrection. The crowd demanded Barabbas' release and the crucifixion of Jesus. When Pilate said to the crowd, *"'Why, what evil has He done?'"* They shouted all the more, *"'Crucify Him!'" (15:14)*

The Roman soldiers took Jesus, dressed Him in purple, put a crown of thorns on His head, mocked Him, spat upon Him and beat Him about His head. They then proceeded to the place of crucifixion, a place called *"Golgotha" or "Place of a Skull."* They crucified Jesus with two robbers.

> *"And when the sixth hour had come, darkness fell over the whole land until the ninth hour. And at the ninth hour Jesus cried out with a loud voice, 'Eloi, Eloi, Lama Sabachthani?' which is translated, 'My God, My God, why has Thou forsaken Me?'* Shortly, thereafter, *". . . Jesus uttered a loud cry, and breathed His last. And the veil of the temple was torn in two from top to bottom." (15:34-38)*

Looking on from a distance were some women, among whom were Mary Magdalene and Mary the Mother of James the Less and Joses and Salome. When Jesus had been in Galilee, they had followed Him and ministered to Him.

Joseph of Arimathea, a prominent member of the Jewish Council (who had come to know and believe in Jesus) asked Pilate for the body of Jesus so that He could be buried before the start of the Sabbath (sundown that same day). Pilate, upon ascertaining from the centurion who was watching Jesus, that Jesus was, in fact, dead, gave permission for Joseph to take the body of Jesus for burial.

Joseph wrapped Jesus' body in a linen cloth, *". . . and laid Him in a tomb which had been hewn out in a rock; and he rolled a stone against the entrance of the tomb." (15:46)*

> *"And when the Sabbath was over, Mary Magdalene and Mary the mother of James, and Salome, brought spices, that they might come and anoint"* the body of Jesus. *(16:1)*

But when the women arrived at the tomb, they found that the heavy stone that had sealed the entrance, had been rolled away. When they entered the tomb, they found a young man there, wearing a white robe.

"And he said to them, 'Do not be amazed; you are looking for Jesus the Nazarene, who has been crucified. He has risen. . .go tell His disciples and Peter: He is going before you into Galilee; there you will see Him, just as He said to you.'" (16:5-7)

After His resurrection from death, Jesus first appeared to Mary Magdalene,

"And after that, He appeared in a different form to two of His disciples as they were walking in the country" (on their way to Emmaus, as reported by Luke in his gospel). He then appeared to His eleven disciples, *"as they were reclining at the table. He reproached them for their unbelief. . .because they had not believed those who had seen Him after He had risen. And He said to them, 'Go into all the world and preach the gospel to all creation. He who has believed and has been baptized shall be saved; but he who has disbelieved shall be condemned. . .So then, when the Lord Jesus had spoken to them, He was received up into heaven, and sat down at the right hand of God." (16:14-19)*

THE GOSPEL ACCORDING TO LUKE

Luke is the Gospel of the Universal Savior – the Savior of the poor and the rich, male and female, Jew and Gentile, slave and free.

Luke is the last of the three synoptic gospels.

This gospel is considered to be the most comprehensive in terms of giving us an active glimpse into the life of Jesus and it gives a more complete accounting of Jesus' life than the other gospels.

As the Gospel of the Universal Savior, Luke relates more of Jesus' story through parables and describes individual characters. Luke includes the walk to Emmaus, which none of the other gospels contain in full. Only Luke tells the story of the Good Samaritan, as well as the story of the rich man who ignored a suffering beggar. Luke focuses on Jesus lifting men out of their sins and bringing them back to life and hope.

Luke was a gentile physician and companion to Paul. Paul refers to Luke three times in his epistles as "the beloved physician." As a physician, Luke is a learned man who knows how to read and write.

Although Luke was not one of Jesus' disciples, and did not personally know Jesus, he presents a very readable picture of our Savior. It is believed he was a convert, possibly from Antioch, where Paul served with Barnabas at the beginning of Paul's ministry.

It is believed that Luke may have gotten his information about Jesus' life directly from Mary, the Mother of Jesus, Mary Magdalene and other women.

If Luke traveled in Judea during Paul's imprisonment at Caesarea, he could have interviewed many persons who had seen and heard Jesus firsthand.

Luke is also identified as the author of The Acts of the Apostles, which could, therefore, be considered the second book of Luke.

Luke shows clearly that Jesus' mission is two-fold: first, to make His Godhead - His supremacy - known to man in order to redeem man's sinfulness, and to help man return to God's fold. Secondly, to establish a new way for individuals to deal with each other - a socially interested way. *"For the Son of Man did not come to destroy men's lives, but to save them." (9:56)*

Luke's Gospel unfolds the career of Jesus like a living picture, since it begins with His birth.

The first two chapters of Luke may be based on first-hand accounts from Jesus' mother, Mary. These chapters contain information only someone who'd been there (Mary) could know. He gives us information about a priest named Zacharias and his wife Elizabeth who are related to Mary and who, although they are elderly, became the parents of John the Baptist.

Luke's gospel opens with him stating,

> *". . .it seemed fitting for me. . .having investigated everything carefully from the beginning, to write it out for you in consecutive order, most excellent Theophilus; so that you might know the exact truth about the things you have been taught." (1:3-4)*

When it was Zacharias' turn to again perform priestly duties in the temple, the angel Gabriel appeared to him and told him that he and Elizabeth would conceive and have a son and that, *". . .you will give him the name John." (1:13)* The angel told Zacharias that his son, *". . .will be great in the sight of the Lord. . .he will be filled with the Holy Spirit, while yet in his mother's womb." (1:15)* Zacharias could not understand how such a thing could possibly take place because of his and Elizabeth's advanced ages, and so the angel caused Zacharias to not be able to speak, *". . .until the day when these things take place, because you did not believe my words. . ." (1:18-20)*

When Zacharias came out of the temple that day, *". . .he was unable to speak. . ." (1:22)* When his priestly service had ended, Zacharias returned home. Shortly after, Elizabeth became pregnant and then kept herself in seclusion for five months.

"Now in the sixth month, the angel Gabriel was sent from God to a city in Galilee called Nazareth to a virgin engaged to a man whose name was Joseph, of the descendants of David; and the virgin's name was Mary." (1:26-27)

The Angel Gabriel addressed Mary by saying,

"Hail, favored one! The Lord is with you." (1:28) Although Mary was afraid, the angel reassured her by saying, *"Do not be afraid, Mary; for you have found favor with God. And behold you will conceive in your womb and bear a son and you shall name Him Jesus. He will be great, and will be called the Son of the Most High and the Lord God will give Him the throne of His father David; and He will reign over the house of Jacob forever; and His kingdom will have no end." (1:30-33)*

The angel Gabriel then told Mary that her cousin Elizabeth had also conceived a son and was now in her sixth month, *"For nothing will be impossible with God." (1:37)*

Mary's response to God's angel was, *"Behold, the bondslave of the Lord; be it done to me according to your word." (1:38)*

So Mary left her home and traveled to the home of Elizabeth and Zacharias some distance away. Upon seeing Mary come, Elizabeth immediately recognized that Mary was pregnant with a holy child, and said to her, *"Blessed among women are you, and blessed is the fruit of your womb!" (1:42)*

Mary's response, called the Magnificat, is an acknowledgement of God's having bestowed upon her the highest honor of being chosen to bear the savior. *". . .For behold, from this time on all generations will count me blessed. For the Mighty One has done great things for me; and holy is His name.. ." (1:46-55)*

Luke tells us that Mary stayed with Elizabeth and Zacharias for three months and then returned to her home.

After Elizabeth gave birth – and when, on the eighth day Zacharias brought their baby to the temple for his circumcision, Zacharias wrote on a tablet that the child's name is John. It was at that point Zacharias' speech was returned to him.

"And. . .Zacharias was filled with the Holy Spirit and prophesied, saying, 'Blessed be the Lord God of Israel, for He has visited us and accomplished redemption for His people, and has raised up a horn of salvation for us. . .And you, child, will be called the prophet of the Most High; for you will go on before the Lord to prepare His ways; to give to His people the knowledge of salvation by the forgiveness of their sins, because of the tender mercy of our God. . ." (1:67-78)

The child, John, grew up, *". . .strong in spirit, and he lived in the deserts until the day of his public appearance to Israel." (1:80)*

It is from Luke's second chapter that we are given details of the birth of our Lord Jesus Christ. In those days, the Roman Emperor Caesar Augustus, decreed that a census be taken of, *". . .all the inhabited earth. . ." (2:1)* which meant all of the countries ruled by Rome. People were told to register – or be counted – in their own city. For Joseph, this meant traveling from Nazareth to Bethlehem, because he was descended from the house and family of King David who had come from Bethlehem.

It is in Matthew's Gospel where we learned that Mary, *"had been betrothed to Joseph [but] before they came together [to consummate their relationship] she [Mary] was found to be with child by the Holy Spirit." (Matthew 1:18)*

When Joseph and Mary arrived in Bethlehem, Mary's time came *". . .for her to give birth. . .to her first-born son, and she wrapped him in cloths, and laid Him in a manger, because there was no room for them in the inn." (2:6-7)*

Nearby there were shepherds watching over their flocks when an *". . .angel of the Lord suddenly stood before them, and the glory of the Lord shone around them; and they were terribly frightened." (2:9)*

> *"And the angel said to them, 'Do not be afraid; for behold, I bring you good news of a great joy which shall be for all the people; for today in the City of David there has been born for you a Savior, who is Christ the Lord. And this will be a sign for you; you will find a baby wrapped in cloths, and lying in a manger.'" (2:10-12)*

> A multitude of the Heavenly host then appeared, *". . .praising God, and saying, 'Glory to God in the highest, and on earth peace among men with whom He is pleased." (2:13-14)*

The shepherds went, *"in haste"* to Bethlehem and there found Mary, Joseph and the baby, as He lay in the manger. They then, *". . .made known the statement"* which had been told to them about this Child." *(2:17)*

At eight days after His birth and before His circumcision, Mary and Joseph named the child Jesus, *". . .the name given by the angel before He was conceived in the womb." (2:21)*

When Mary and Joseph brought the baby Jesus to the temple, *". . .according to the law of Moses,"* two devout, elderly people – first Simeon, and then Anna a prophetess, recognized the baby Jesus as the Messiah and both praised God for the privilege of being able to see the Christ Child.

Soon thereafter Joseph, Mary and Jesus returned to their home in Nazareth, where, *". . .the child continued to grow and become strong, increasing in wisdom; and the grace of God was upon Him." (2:39-40)*

The only glimpse that we are given of Jesus' childhood is when He was twelve, at a time when His family was making their annual trip to Jerusalem during the Feast of the Passover. When it came time to return home to Nazareth, Mary and Joseph, believing Jesus to be with relatives in the caravan, did not miss Jesus for a day. When they discovered that Jesus, indeed, was not in their travel group, Mary and Joseph returned to Jerusalem to find him. After three days' searching, they found Jesus in the temple, *". . .sitting in the midst of the teachers, both listening to them and asking them questions." (2:46)* When confronted by His mother, Jesus said, *" 'Why is it that you were looking for Me? Did you not know that I had to be in My Father's house?'. . .And all who heard Him were amazed at His understanding and His answers." (2:47-52)*

Jesus returned to Nazareth with his parents, *". . .and continued in subjection to them; and His mother treasured all these things in her heart. And Jesus kept increasing in wisdom and stature, and in favor with God and men." (2:51-52)*

In Chapter 3, Luke traces Jesus' lineage all the way back to Adam and to the *"Son of God."* (as Matthew also does, except Matthew started with Abraham).

In Chapter 3, Luke returns to John the Baptist (now a grown man) and tells us how he came into the area around the Jordan River, preaching a baptism of repentance for the forgiveness of sins. John is quoted by Luke as saying, *"As for me, I baptize you with water, but One is coming who is mightier than I and I am not fit to untie the thong of His sandals. He will baptize you with the Holy Spirit and fire." (3:16)*

During this time Jesus was baptized by John, *". . .and while he* [John] *was praying, heaven was opened, and the Holy Spirit descended upon Him [Jesus] in bodily form, like a dove, and a voice came out of heaven, 'Thou art My beloved Son, in Thee I am well-pleased.'" (3:21-22)*

The Holy Spirit is illustrated in the bible with several signs, i.e., fire, wind, water, being sealed, oil, and a dove. It is clear that the Holy Spirit is God and is equal to God the Father. Our understanding of the Holy Trinity (three persons in one God) is built on these biblical truths and revelations.

In Chapter 4, Jesus, full of the Holy Spirit, spends 40 days in the wilderness being tempted by the devil who says to Him (among other things), if You worship me, I will give You all the world. Jesus replies (among other things), *"You shall worship the Lord your God and serve Him only." (4:8)*

According to Luke, Jesus' public ministry begins when He returns to Galilee, His home territory, and goes, as is His custom, to the synagogue on the Sabbath. On this particular Sabbath, He stands up and reads from the Prophet Isaiah, *"The Spirit of the Lord is upon Me, because He appointed Me to preach the gospel to the poor. He has sent Me to proclaim release to the captives, and recovery of sight to the blind, to set free those who are down-trodden, to proclaim the favorable year of the Lord." (4:18-20)* When He had finished reading this passage, He sat down and said to the congregation, *"Today this scripture has been fulfilled in your hearing." (4:21)*

Although the people in the synagogue spoke well of Jesus, they also remarked that this was the son of Joseph, a carpenter. Jesus replied that, *"Truly, I say to you, no prophet is welcome in his home town." (4:24)*

The people in the synagogue then rose up in anger and proposed to kill Jesus by throwing Him over a cliff, but He passed through their midst. Shortly after, He went to Capernaum, also a city in Galilee, and there, while preaching in the synagogue on the Sabbath, He cast out a demon which had possessed a man. Word about Jesus spreads.

After leaving the synagogue, Jesus goes to the home of Simon Peter and cures Simon's mother-in-law of a high fever. He then continues healing many others who come to Him. Demons were coming out of people and were proclaiming of Jesus, *"You are the Son of God!" (4:41)*

Luke fleshes out some of Jesus' encounters – for example, Jesus' recruitment of Simon Peter is told more fully in Chapter 5. Jesus comes to the Lake of Gennesaret and finds Simon fishing. He sits down in Simon's boat and begins teaching the crowd of people who are on the shore. He then tells Simon, *"to put out into the deep water and let down your nets for a catch." (5:4)*

Although Simon declares they have worked all night with no results, he does Jesus' bidding and catches a great number of fish. In fact, so many fish are caught that their nets begin to break and their boats to sink. When Simon Peter saw this, he fell down at Jesus' feet, saying,

> *"'Depart from me, for I am a sinful man, O Lord!'" (5:8) "Jesus said to Simon, 'Do not fear, from now on you will be catching men.' And when they had brought their boats to land, they [Simon Peter and his partners, James and John, the sons of Zebedee] left everything and followed Him." (5:10-11)*

Going into a city, Jesus cured a leper, but directed him to not tell anyone. However, news about Jesus was spreading and, *"great multitudes were gathering to hear Him and to be healed of their sicknesses. But He Himself would often slip away to the wilderness and pray." (5:12-16)*

At one time, Pharisees (teachers of Jewish law) came to see and hear Jesus from, ". . .*every village of Galilee and Judea and from Jerusalem; and the power of the Lord was present for Him to perform healing."* *(5:17)* Because there was so large a crowd, a paralyzed man, being carried by others, was having difficulty reaching Jesus, and so a hole was cut in the roof of the house where Jesus was, and in that way the man was brought to Jesus. And Jesus, seeing his faith, said to the paralyzed man, *"'Friend, your sins are forgiven you.'"* *(5:20)* The Pharisees and scribes at once began criticizing Jesus for this. *"But Jesus, aware of their reasonings, answered and said, '. . .Which is easier to say, 'Your sins have been forgiven you,' or to say, 'Rise and walk'? But in order that you may know that the Son of Man has authority on earth to forgive sins' - He said to the paralytic - 'I say to you, rise, and take up your stretcher and go home.'"* The crowd was amazed and, *"began glorifying God."* *(5:21-24)*

After Jesus had left that house, He came across a tax-gatherer named Levi (later known as Matthew), ". . .*and He said, 'Follow me.' And he [Levi] left everything behind and rose and began to follow Him."* *(5:27-28)*. Levi gave a big reception for Jesus, but the Pharisees criticized Jesus for eating and drinking, ". . .*with tax-gatherers and sinners."* *(5:30)* Jesus' response to this criticism was that He was needed, not by those who are well but rather those who are sick. *"'I have not come to call the righteous but sinners to repentance.'"* *(5:32)*

After going off by Himself to the mountain, Jesus, having spent the whole night in prayer to God, ". . .*when day came, He called His disciples to Him and chose His 12 apostles from the group. "Simon, whom He also named Peter, and Andrew his brother; and James and John; and Philip and Bartholomew; and Matthew [Levi] and Thomas; James the son of Alphaeus, and Simon who was called the Zealot; Judas the son of James, and Judas Iscariot, who became a traitor."* *(6:12-16)*

Jesus and His disciples then descended the mountain. A multitude of people, ". . .*had come to hear Him and to be healed of their diseases; and those who were troubled with unclean spirits were being cured."* *(6:17-18)*

"And turning His gaze on His disciples, He began to say, 'Blessed are you who are poor, for yours is the kingdom of God. Blessed are you who hunger now, for you shall be satisfied. Blessed are you who weep now, for you shall laugh. Blessed are you when men hate you, and ostracize you, and cast insults at you, and spurn your name as evil, for the sake of the Son of Man. Be glad in that day, and leap for joy, for behold your reward is great in heaven; for in the same way their fathers used to treat the prophets. But woe to you who are rich, for you are receiving your comfort in full. Woe to you who are well-fed now, for you shall be hungry. Woe to you who laugh now for you shall mourn and weep. Woe to you when all men speak well of you, for in the same way their fathers used to treat the false prophets. But I say to you who hear, love your enemies, do good to those who hate you, bless those who curse you, pray for those who mistreat you. Whoever hits you on the cheek, offer him the other also; and whoever takes away your coat, do not withhold your shirt from him either. Give to everyone who asks of you, and whoever takes away what is yours, do not demand it back. And just as you want people to treat you, treat them in the same way, and if you love those who love you, what credit is that to you? For even sinners love those who love them. And if you do good to those who do good to you, what credit is that to you? For even sinners do the same. And if you lend to those from whom you expect to receive, what credit is that to you? Even sinners lend to sinners, in order to receive back the same amount. "But love your enemies, and do good and lend, expecting nothing in return; and your reward will be great, and you will be sons of the Most High; for He Himself is kind to ungrateful and evil men. Be merciful, just as your Father is merciful. And do not judge and you will not be judged; and do not condemn, and you will not be condemned; pardon and you will be pardoned. Give and it will be given to you; good measure, pressed down, shaken together, running over, they will pour into your lap. For by your standard of measure it will be measured to you in return.'" *(6:20-38)*

In Chapter 7, Luke tells us about specific miracles of healing which Jesus performed, i.e., healing the son of a centurion's slave, after the centurion entreats Jesus, *"Lord, do not trouble Yourself further, for I am unworthy for You to come under my roof."* *(7:2-6)* And bringing back to life the only son of a mother who was grieving. *(7:12-14)*

"And it came about soon afterwards, that He began going about from one city and village to another, proclaiming and preaching the kingdom of God, and the twelve were with Him." (8:1)

Luke tells us that there were women who also were with Jesus as He moved about. *"Mary who was called Magdalene from whom seven demons had gone out; Joanna the wife of Chuza, Herod's steward, and Suzanna and many others who were contributing to. . .*[the support of Jesus and His disciples] *out of their private means." (8:2-3)*

Jesus continued teaching the crowds who gathered, often using parables such as the sower of seeds – relating to how His word, regarding how one should live, might take root and produce good results, or be rejected as seed that falls on rocky soil, producing nothing.

Luke, like Mark, tells us how Jesus, in the country of the Gerasenes, was met by a man possessed of demons and how He drove the demons from the man and into a nearby herd of swine, which then rushed into a lake and was drowned.

More and more people, hearing of Jesus and His works, were coming to see and to hear Him. Luke tells us how Jesus saved the dying daughter of an official of the synagogue and cured a woman who had suffered from a loss of blood for many years.

Jesus called His twelve apostles together and giving them power over demons and the power to cure diseases, *". . .He sent them out to proclaim the kingdom of God and to perform healing." (9:1-2)*

Word about Jesus had spread so far that Herod the tetrarch, who had had John the Baptist beheaded at the request of his brother's wife's daughter, had heard about Him and was disturbed, thinking, *". . .that John had risen from the dead. . .and he kept trying to see Him [Jesus]." (9:7-9)*

Luke tells us how Jesus fed five thousand persons who had come to see and hear Him with five loaves of bread and two fish. *"And they all ate and were satisfied; and the broken pieces which they had left over were picked up, twelve baskets full." (9:12-17)*

Afterwards, Jesus asked His disciples, *"'Who do the multitudes say I am?'"* And they answered that some thought He was John the Baptist and others thought He was Elijah. *"And He said to them, 'But who do you say I am?' And Peter answered and said, 'The Christ of God.' But He warned them, and instructed them not to tell this to anyone, saying, 'The Son of Man must suffer many things, and be rejected by the elders and chief priests and scribes, and be killed, and be raised up on the third day.' And He was saying to them all, 'If anyone wishes to come after Me, let him deny himself, take up his cross daily, and follow Me. For whoever wishes to save his life shall lose it, but whoever loses his life for My sake, he is the one who will save it. For what is a man profited if he gains the whole world, and loses or forfeits himself?'"* (9:18-25)

Some eight days later, Jesus took Peter and John and James up to the mountain to pray. And while He was praying, *"The appearance of His face became different; and His clothing became white and gleaming." (9:28-29)* And the three apostles saw Moses and Elijah speaking with Jesus and talking, *". . .of His departure which He was about to accomplish at Jerusalem." (9:30-31)* A cloud then formed overhead, *"And a voice came out of the cloud saying, 'This is My Son, My chosen One; listen to Him!'" (9:35)* After the voice had spoken, Jesus was found alone. The three apostles kept silent about what they had seen and heard.

In Chapter 10, Luke tells us that, at one time, Jesus appointed 70 of His disciples to go out to the cities and places where He was planning to go. He said to them, *"'. . .heal those. . .who are sick and say to them. . .'The kingdom of God has come near to you.'"* He cautioned them that if they were not well-treated, they should shake off the dust of that place and leave it. *"'The one who listens to you listens to Me. And the one who rejects you rejects Me; and he who rejects Me rejects the One who sent Me.' And the seventy returned with joy, saying, 'Lord, even the demons are subject to us in Your name.'" (10:9-17)*

When, at one time, a lawyer asked Jesus who is his neighbor, that he should love him as himself, Jesus told the parable of the Good Samaritan – a man who, finding another by the roadside who had been beaten and was half dead, bandaged his wounds and took care of him. *"And Jesus said to the lawyer, 'Go and do the same.'" (10:30-37)*

In Chapter 11: 2-4, Luke, like Matthew, sets forth the prayer Jesus taught His disciples:

> *"When you pray, say: Father, hallowed be Thy name. Thy kingdom come. Give us each day our daily bread, and forgive us our sins, for we ourselves also forgive everyone who is indebted to us, and lead us not into temptation."*

In Chapter 11: 9-10, Jesus said:

> *"And I say to you, ask, and it shall be given to you; seek and you shall find; knock, and it shall be opened to you. For everyone who asks, receives; and he who seeks, finds, and to him who knocks, it shall be opened."*

In Chapter 12, Luke tells us that, at one time, so many thousands of people had gathered to hear Jesus they were stepping on each other. Jesus said, among other things,

> *"Beware of the leaven of the Pharisees, which is hypocrisy. But there is nothing covered up that will not be revealed, and hidden that will not be known. Accordingly, whatever you have said in the dark shall be heard in the light, and whatever you have whispered in the upper rooms shall be proclaimed upon the housetops. And I say to you, My friends, do not be afraid of those who kill the body, and after that have no more that they can do. But I will warn you whom to fear: fear the One who after He has killed has authority to cast into hell; yes, I tell you, fear Him!" (12:1-5)*

> *"And I say to you, everyone who confesses Me before men, the Son of God shall confess him also before the angels of God; but he who denies Me before men shall be denied before the angels of God. And everyone who will speak a word against the Son of Man, it shall be forgiven him; but he who blasphemes against the Holy Spirit, it shall not be forgiven him.'" (12:8-10)*

Someone in the crowd asked Jesus to *". . .tell my brother to divide the family inheritance with me,"* but Jesus replied, *"Man, who appointed Me a judge or arbiter over you?. . .Beware and be on your guard against every form of greed; for not even when one has an abundance does his life consist of his possessions." (12:13-15)*

> *". . .Do not be afraid, little flock, for your Father has chosen gladly to give you the kingdom. Sell your possessions and give to charity; make yourselves purses which do not wear out, an unfailing treasure in heaven, where no thief comes near, nor moth destroys. For where your treasure is, there will your heart be also.'" (12:32-34)*

> *"Now tax-gatherers and the sinners were coming near Him to listen to Him. And both the Pharisees and the scribes began to grumble, saying, 'This man receives sinners and eats with them.'" (15:1-2)*

And Jesus told parables meant to show that He came to save sinners and redeem those who most need Him – parables about a shepherd who has a hundred sheep and when he loses one, searches for the lost sheep until he finds it; about a woman who has 10 silver coins and losing one coin, searches diligently until the coin is found; about a father with two sons, one of whom is good and obedient – the other disobedient – who leaves family and home and who, at length, returns destitute, hungry and despairing of all he has wasted, but whom the father greets with great joy and forgiveness; and about a rich man whose steward forgave, in part, those who owed his master money.

Jesus also told a parable about a rich man who scorned and refused to help a poor beggar named Lazarus. When both the rich man and Lazarus died, the rich man was cast into hell, and Lazarus went to heaven, into the arms of Abraham. When the rich man cried out for Lazarus to but give him a drop of water to ease his agony in hell, Abraham told the rich man,

> *"Child, remember that during your life you received your good things, and likewise Lazarus bad things; but now he is being comforted here, and you are in agony. . .between us [in heaven] and you there [in hell] is a great chasm fixed, in order that those who wish to come over from here to you may not be able, and that none may cross over from there to us."*

> **The rich man then begged for the opportunity to warn his brothers** who were still among the living, *". . .lest they come to this place of torment."* But he was told, *"If they [the living] do not listen to Moses and the prophets, neither will they be persuaded if someone rises from the dead." (16:25-31)*

In Chapter 18, Jesus tells His followers a similar parable about two men worshipping in the temple. One was a Pharisee and the other a tax-gatherer. The Pharisee thanked God that he was better than other men, while the tax-gatherer asked God to have mercy on him, because of his sinfulness. Jesus finishes this parable by saying, *"I tell you, this man went down to his house justified rather than the other; for everyone who exalts himself shall be humbled, but he who humbles himself shall be exalted." (18:11-14)*

Later, Jesus took His twelve apostles aside and told them that they would be going to Jerusalem soon,

> *". . .and all things which are written through the prophets about the Son of Man will be accomplished. For He will be delivered to the Gentiles, and will be mocked and mistreated and spit upon, and after they have scourged Him they will kill Him; and on the third day He will rise again." (18:31-33)*

When Jesus and His disciples went through Jericho, a rich tax-gatherer named Zaccheus tried hard to see Jesus. Because of the crowds surrounding Jesus, Zaccheus ran ahead and climbed a tree in order to see Jesus as He passed underneath. When Jesus was nearby, He called to Zaccheus and told him He would stay at his house. And those around Jesus were grumbling, saying that Jesus was going to be the guest of a sinner.

> *"And Zaccheus. . .said to the Lord, 'Behold Lord, half my possessions I will give to the poor, and if I have defrauded anyone of anything, I will give back four times as much.' And Jesus said to him, "Today salvation has come to this house. . .For the Son of Man has come to seek and to save that which was lost.'" (19:1-10)*

Luke tells us how Jesus began preparing for His ultimate sacrifice. With Passover approaching, Jesus sent two of His disciples into the village near Mount Olivet, to find and bring to Him a colt on which no one had yet ridden. Jesus then sat upon the colt and as the group approached the descent of the Mount of Olives,

> *". . .the whole multitude of the disciples began to praise God joyfully with a loud voice for all the miracles which they had seen, saying, 'Blessed is the King who comes in the Name of the Lord. . .'" (19:37-38)*

Pharisees who witnessed this outcry told Jesus to rebuke His disciples. But Jesus answered them, *"I tell you, if these become silent, the stones will cry out!" (19:39-40).*

When Jesus entered the temple, He cast out those who were selling there, saying, *"'It is written, 'And My house shall be a house of prayer', but you have made it a robbers' den.'" (19:45-46)*

Jesus began *". . .teaching daily in the temple, but the chief priests and the scribes and the leading men among the people were trying to destroy Him." (19:47)*

Among His teachings and parables, Jesus predicted that,

"Nation will rise against nation and kingdom against kingdom, and there will be great earthquakes, and in various places plagues and famines; and there will be. . .great signs from heaven. . .signs in sun and moon and stars, and upon the earth dismay among nations, in perplexity at the roaring of the sea and the waves. . .for the powers of the heavens will be shaken. And then they will see the Son of Man coming in a cloud with power and great glory. But when these things begin to take place, straighten up and lift up your heads, because your redemption is drawing near." (21:10-28)

As the Feast of Passover drew near, *". . .Satan entered into Judas who was called Iscariot. . .and he went away and discussed with the chief priests and officers how he might betray Him* [Jesus] *to them." (22:1-4)*

Jesus sent Peter and John to prepare a place for Him and His apostles to eat the Passover meal. And when Jesus and the 12 reclined at the Passover table, Jesus said to them, *"I have earnestly desired to eat this Passover with you before I suffer: for I say to you, I shall never again eat it until it is fulfilled in the kingdom of God." (22:14-16)*

Jesus then took bread, gave thanks, broke the bread and gave it to His apostles saying, *" 'This is My body which is given for you, do this in remembrance of Me.' And in the same way He took the cup after they had eaten, saying, 'This cup which is poured out for you is the new covenant in My blood. But behold, the hand of the one betraying Me is with Me on the table. For indeed, the Son of Man is going as it has been determined; but woe to that man by whom He is betrayed." (22:19-22)*

The apostles then began disputing among themselves as to which one of them is the greatest. And Jesus interjected, among other things, *". . .just as My father has granted Me a kingdom, I grant you that you may eat and drink at My table in My kingdom, and you will sit on thrones judging the twelve tribes of Israel." (22:29-30)*

Then speaking directly to Simon Peter, Jesus warned him,

> *". . .behold, Satan has demanded permission to sift you like wheat; but I have prayed for you, that your faith may not fail; and you, when once you have turned again, strengthen your brothers." (22:31-32)*

Soon thereafter, Jesus (followed by his apostles) went to the Mount of Olives, as was His custom, to pray. He then withdrew from them, *". . .About a stone's throw. . .and being in agony He was praying very fervently; and His sweat became like drops of blood. . ." (22:40-44)*

When Jesus returned to where His apostles were, He found them asleep. He awakened them, saying, *"Rise and pray that you may not enter into temptation."* Thereupon, Judas approached Him with those who wanted Jesus dead, and kissing Jesus, he betrayed Him. One of His apostles (identified as Simon Peter in John's Gospel) struck the slave of the high priest with a sword, cutting off his right ear. *"But Jesus said, 'Stop! No more of this.' And He touched his [the slave's] ear and healed him." (22:46-51)*

Jesus was then taken to the house of the high priest and Peter followed at a distance. While in the courtyard, Peter was trying to avoid recognition as a follower of Jesus. When he was challenged by a servant girl, three times he denied knowing, or having anything to do with, Jesus. Then, just as Jesus had earlier told Peter, a cock crowed a second time and Peter, remembering that Jesus had foretold his denials, *". . .went out and wept bitterly." (22:56-62)*

In custody, Jesus was beaten and mocked and blasphemed. Early the next day Jesus was led into the council chamber of the elders of the people – both chief priests and scribes - who demanded to know if He was the Christ. Jesus answered,

> *"'If I tell you, you will not believe. . .But from now on the Son of Man will be seated at the right hand of the power of God.' And they all said, 'Are You the Son of God, then?' And He said to them, 'Yes, I am.' And they said, 'What further need do we have of testimony? For we have heard it ourselves from His own mouth.'" (22:66-71)*

Jesus was brought before Pilate, who asked Him, *"'Are you the king of the Jews?' And He answered him and said, 'It is as you say.'" (23:1-3)*

Pilate failed to find Jesus guilty of the crimes the Chief Priests and scribes had brought against Him. When he learned that Jesus was from Galilee, he turned Him over to Herod (whose jurisdiction was Galilee) who happened to be in Jerusalem at that time. And Herod and Pilate, although they had had enmity between them up to that time, became friends with each other that day.

Herod was glad for the opportunity to see Jesus and was hoping Jesus would perform a miracle for him. Herod questioned Jesus at length, but Jesus did not answer him. So Herod and his soldiers treated Jesus with contempt, mocking Him, and dressing Him in a *"gorgeous robe sent Him back to Pilate." (23:11)*

Pilate called together the people who were accusing Jesus of inciting a rebellion. He told them that he had found no wrongdoing in Jesus and that he wanted to punish Him and then release Him. But the people kept calling out, saying, *"Crucify, crucify Him!" (23:21)* Three times Pilate asked them what Jesus had done to deserve death, but the people were insistent that He be crucified and that Barabbas be released (as it was the custom to release a prisoner at the Feast of Passover). Pilate, finally giving in to their demands, released Barabbas and ordered that Jesus be crucified.

As Jesus was being led to the place of crucifixion, the soldiers *". . .laid hold of one Simon of Cyrene, coming in from the country, and placed on him the cross to carry behind Jesus."* Following Jesus along the way were many people, among them, *". . .women who were mourning and lamenting Him."* But Jesus said to the women, *"Daughters of Jerusalem, stop weeping for Me, but weep for yourselves and for your children. . ." (23:26-28)*

Jesus was crucified at the place called "The Skull" with a criminal on either side of Him. And regarding those who were carrying out Pilate's command, Jesus said, *"Father, forgive them, for they do not know what they are doing." (23:34)*

The soldiers gambled for Jesus' garments and others were sneering at Him, saying, *"He saved others; let Him save Himself if this is the Christ of God, His chosen One."* The soldiers also mocked Jesus saying, *"If You are the King of the Jews, save Yourself."* And they put a sign above His head, on the cross, *"THIS IS THE KING OF THE JEWS." (23:35-38)*

While one of the two criminals being crucified with Jesus was insulting Him, the other one asked for Jesus' mercy, saying, *"'Jesus, remember me when You come into Your kingdom!' And He said to him, 'Truly, I say to you, today you shall be with Me in Paradise.'"* (23:42-43)

After six hours, darkness fell over all the land until the ninth hour and the veil of the temple was torn in two. *"And Jesus, crying out with a loud voice, said, 'Father, into Your hands I commend My spirit.'"* (23:46) When the centurion who was standing nearby saw what had happened, *". . .he began praising God, saying, 'Certainly this man was innocent.'"* (23:47)

A member of the Jewish Council, a man named Joseph from Arimathea, *". . .a good and righteous man,"* obtained permission from Pilate to take the body of Jesus. He then wrapped Jesus' body in a linen cloth,

> *". . .and laid Him in a tomb cut into the rock, where no one had ever lain. And it was the preparation day, and the Sabbath was about to begin. Now the women who had come with Him out of Galilee followed after, and saw the tomb and how His body was laid. And they returned and prepared spices and perfumes. And on the Sabbath, they rested according to the commandment [given to Moses by God Himself]."* (23:50-56)

On the first day of the week (three days after Jesus' death), several of the women (Mary Magdalene and Joanna and Mary the Mother of James and other women) returned to the tomb in order to put spices on Jesus' body. But *". . .they found the stone rolled away from the tomb. . . [and] did not find the body of the Lord Jesus."* Instead two men in *"dazzling apparel"* were there who advised them, *"Why do you seek the living One among the dead? He is not here, but He has risen. Remember how He spoke to you while He was still in Galilee, saying that the Son of Man must be delivered into the hands of sinful men, and be crucified, and the third day rise again."* (24:5-7) The women told all they had seen and heard to the apostles.

> *"But Peter arose and ran to the tomb; stooping and looking in, he saw the linen wrappings only; and he went away to his home, marveling at that which had happened."* (24:12)

"And behold, two of them [Jesus' disciples] *were going that very day to a village named Emmaus, which was about seven miles from Jerusalem. And they were conversing with each other about all these things which had taken place. And it came about that while they were conversing and discussing, Jesus Himself approached, and began traveling with them. But their eyes were prevented from recognizing Him. And He said to them, 'What are these words that you are exchanging with one another as you are walking?' And they stood still, looking sad. And one of them, named Cleopas, answered and said to Him, 'Are you the only one visiting Jerusalem and unaware of the things which have happened here in these days?' And He said to them, 'What things?' And they said to Him, 'The things about Jesus the Nazarene, who was a prophet mighty in deed and word in the sight of God and all the people, and how the chief priests and our rulers delivered Him up to the sentence of death, and crucified Him. . . And He said to them, 'O foolish men and slow of heart to believe in all that the prophets have spoken! Was it not necessary for the Christ to suffer these things and to enter into His glory?' And beginning with Moses and with all the prophets, He explained to them the things concerning Himself in all the Scriptures. And they approached the village where they were going, and He acted as though He would go farther. And they urged Him, saying, 'Stay with us, for it is getting toward evening, and the day is now nearly over.' And He went in to stay with them. And it came about that when He had reclined at the table with them, He took the bread and blessed it, and breaking it, He began giving it to them. And their eyes were opened and they recognized Him; and He vanished from their sight."* (24:13-31)

211.

"The two left that very hour and returned to Jerusalem and told the eleven apostles, 'The Lord has really risen'. . .and they began to relate their experience on the road and how He was recognized by them in the breaking of the bread." (24:34-35)

And while they were talking, Jesus appeared in their midst. Because the gathered apostles and those who were with them were frightened, Jesus showed them His hands and feet – where the nails had been driven through His flesh, and He ate with them. Jesus then *". . .opened their minds to understand the scriptures and He said to them, 'Thus it is written that the Christ should suffer and rise again from the dead the third day; and that repentance for forgiveness of sins should be proclaimed in His name to all the nations, beginning from Jerusalem. . .'" (24:45-47)*

Some days later, Jesus led His apostles and disciples out of the city as far as Bethany, *". . .and He lifted up His hands and blessed them. And it came about that while He was blessing them, He parted from them. And they returned to Jerusalem with great joy and were continually in the temple, praising God." (24:50-53)*

THE GOSPEL ACCORDING TO JOHN

John was a son of Zebedee the fisherman (and brother to James the Elder).

Jesus named John and James "Sons of Thunder" (Boanerges). During John's discipleship he was a close companion to Peter. John was the "beloved disciple", one of probably only two disciples who did not die by martyrdom.

It is believed that this Gospel was written last, since John seems to have a knowledge of the other three gospels (Matthew, Mark and Luke – the synoptic gospels), and possibly was written about 80 – 90 A.D.

John's Gospel reflects the mature thinking of someone who had meditated deeply on the meaning of the happenings surrounding Jesus.

It is believed that John also wrote the Book of Revelation, during the later years of his life, while a prisoner on the Island of Patmos.

In this Gospel John answers the question, *"who is Jesus Christ?"* He begins with words which correlate to the opening of the book of Genesis: *"In the beginning was the Word* [Logos] *and the Word was with God, and the Word was God. He was in the beginning with God. All things came into being by Him, and apart from Him nothing came into being that has come into being. In Him was life, and the life was the light of men. And the light shines in the darkness, and the darkness did not comprehend it." (1:1-5)*

John quotes Jesus as having used the phrase, "I am" in many different contexts. It is here we are clearly given to understand that Jesus is the Son of God; that Jesus <u>IS</u> God; and that He is the way to our salvation.

The many "I am" phrases found in John's gospel help us recall that God identified Himself to Moses as "I am who I am." John's use of "I am" to identify our Savior Jesus Christ is another connection between God our Father and Jesus Christ, the Son of God – both persons of the trinity – both fully God.

The Gospel of John is also the Gospel of the Holy Spirit, since it is only John who tells us about the coming of the Holy Spirit. And so, the Gospel of the "I am" is also the Gospel of the Church of Christ – the Gospel of the Holy Spirit, the Paraclete who would come only after Jesus departed from our view.

In this Gospel, Jesus' ministry lasted two to three years (possibly even four) and included numerous trips to Jerusalem.

The phrase "Kingdom of God" is replaced with "eternal life" in this gospel.

From this gospel we learn more about Jesus' life of ministry as he chooses his disciples: Andrew and his brother Simon (later to be known as Cephas or Peter) and Philip are from Bethsaida. Philip then found Nathanael and told him, *"We have found Him of whom Moses in the law and also the Prophets wrote, Jesus of Nazareth, the son of Joseph."* *(1:44-45)* Nathanael's initial reaction was to say, *"Can any good thing come out of Nazareth?"* When Jesus later met Nathanael, his first comment was to wryly say, *"Behold, an Israelite indeed in whom there is no guile!" (1:46-47)* When Nathanael inquired of Jesus what he meant by that, Jesus said to him, *"'Before Philip called you, I saw you under the fig tree.' And Nathanael answered Him, 'Rabbi, You are the Son of God; You are the King of Israel.'" (1:48-49)*

John relates the miracle at the Wedding in Cana which is where, at the request of His mother Mary, Jesus performed His first recorded miracle by turning water into wine. *(2:1-10)*

Through John we can see Jesus in the temple, chasing out those who were selling cattle, sheep and doves. He said, *"Stop making My Father's house a house of merchandise." (2:16)*

Jesus meets with Nicodemus, a Pharisee and a Jewish leader. Jesus tells Nicodemus that before he can get into God's kingdom, he must be born of water and the Spirit. *(3:1-6)* Later, when the Pharisees are concerned about Jesus and are lobbying against him, Nicodemus supports Jesus. Near the end of John's gospel we learn that after Jesus' death, Nicodemus brought about a hundred pounds of spices (aloe and myrrh) to put with Jesus' body in the tomb.

Jesus meets a Samaritan woman at a well near the field which Jacob had given to his son Joseph, centuries before. Jesus speaks to the woman about water that gives eternal life (meaning Himself). *(4:4-30)*

On His travels to Galilee, while passing through Cana, Jesus heals the son of a royal official, after the man begs Jesus to save the boy. Jesus assures the man that, because of his faith, the boy will live. *(4:46-53)*

Jesus heals a sick man near the sheep gate in Jerusalem where there was a pool with five porticoes (which in Hebrew is called *"Bethesda"*). Now the Jewish leaders want to kill Jesus for two reasons: He has broken the law of the Sabbath (healing someone on the Sabbath) and He has said that God is His Father. *(5:1-18)*

Jesus feeds 5,000 people near Lake Galilee (also known as Tiberias), with five loaves of bread and two fishes. Later, His disciples get into a boat and start across for Capernaum. When the wind comes up making the water rough, Jesus comes to them, walking on the water. *(6:1-13)*

Jesus talks about the bread that never spoils:

> *"Do not work for the food which perishes, but for the food which endures to eternal life, which the Son of Man shall give to you, for on Him the Father, even God, has set His seal." (6:27)*

This reference to bread ties the Old Testament manna (which the Israelites were given during their exodus out of Egypt) to Jesus being mankind's salvation from eternal death.

In telling people to work for food that gives eternal life, Jesus also said:

> "'. . .I am the bread of life: he who comes to Me shall not hunger, and he who believes in Me shall never thirst. But I said to you, that you have seen Me, and yet do not believe. All that the Father gives Me shall come to Me, and the one who comes to Me I will certainly not cast out. For I have come down from heaven, not to do My own will, but the will of Him who sent Me. And this is the will of Him who sent Me, that of all that He has given Me I lose nothing, but raise it up on the last day. For this is the will of My Father, that everyone who beholds the Son and believes in Him, may have eternal life; and I Myself will raise him up on the last day.'" But some of those who heard him were full of doubt and were complaining. "Jesus answered and said to them, 'Do not grumble among yourselves. No one can come to Me, unless the Father who sent Me draws him; and I will raise him up on the last day. . .Truly, truly, I say to you, he who believes has eternal life. I am the bread of life. Your fathers ate the manna in the wilderness, and they died. This is the bread which comes down out of heaven, so that one may eat of it and not die. I am the living bread that came down out of heaven; if anyone eats of this bread, he shall live forever; and the bread also which I shall give for the life of the world is My flesh."(6:35-58)

One morning when Jesus was teaching in the temple, the scribes and Pharisees, hoping to trip Him up, brought to Him an adulterous woman and reminded Him that, according to Moses, she should be stoned. Jesus quietly and calmly, without looking up from writing something on the ground, said, *"He who is without sin among you, let him be the first to throw a stone at her."* One by one, beginning with the older scribes and Pharisees, they all departed, leaving Jesus alone with the woman. He asked her, *"'Woman, where are they? Did no one condemn you?' And she said, 'No one, Lord.' And Jesus said, 'Neither do I condemn you; go your way. From now on sin no more.'" (8:1-11)*

More and more the leaders of the Jewish people were becoming suspicious of Jesus, questioning where He got His authority to preach as He did, and to heal people, even on the Sabbath. When speaking to the common people, Jesus told them, *"I am the light for the world; he who follows Me shall not walk in the darkness, but shall have the light of life." (8:12)* He also told them, *"If you abide in My word, then you are truly disciples of Mine; and you shall know the truth, and the truth shall make you free." (8:32)*

In Chapter 10, Jesus uses a figure of speech to explain His relationship to those who would follow Him.

> *"Truly, truly, I say to you, he who does not enter by the door into the fold of the sheep, but climbs up some other way, he is a thief and a robber. But he who enters by the door is a shepherd of the sheep. To him the doorkeeper opens, and the sheep hear his voice, and he calls his own sheep by name, and leads them out. When he puts forth all his own, he goes before them and the sheep follow him because they know his voice. . .Truly, truly, I say to you, I am the door of the sheep. . .I am the door; if anyone enters through Me, he shall be saved, and shall go in and out, and find pasture. . .I am the good shepherd; the good shepherd lays down His life for his sheep. . .I am the good shepherd; and I know My own and My own know Me, even as the Father knows Me and I know the Father; and I lay down My life for the sheep. And I have other sheep, which are not of this fold; I must bring them also, and they shall hear My voice; and they shall become one flock with one shepherd. For this reason the Father loves Me, because I lay down My life that I may take it up again. . ." (10:1-17)*

There were those who were affronted by Jesus' teachings and they asked Him,

> *"'If you are the Christ, tell us plainly. And Jesus answered them, 'I told you, and you do not believe; the works that I do in my Father's name, these bear witness of Me. But you do not believe, because you are not of My sheep. My sheep hear My voice and I know them, and they follow Me; and I give eternal life to them, and they shall never perish. And no one shall snatch them out of My hand. My Father, who has given them to Me, is greater than all; and no one is able to snatch them out of the Father's hand. I and the Father are one.'" (10:24-30)*

Those who were doubting Jesus took up stones in an attempt to kill Him, but He eluded their grasp and went away beyond the Jordan River.

And while He was away, His good friend Lazarus became ill. And his sisters, Mary and Martha, sent for Jesus to come and restore Lazarus to good health. But Jesus delayed His coming to their aid for several days, and when He did arrive at their village of Bethany, He was told by Martha that Lazarus had died several days earlier. *"Jesus wept."* *(11:35)*

Jesus then ordered that the stone sealing the entrance to the tomb where Lazarus was be removed. Jesus then cried out loudly for Lazarus to come forth.

> *"He who had died came forth, bound hand and foot with wrappings; and his face was wrapped around with a cloth. Jesus said to them, 'Unbind him, and let him go.'" (11:44)*

And although many of those who witnessed this believed in Jesus, others went to the Pharisees to tell what Jesus had done. And the chief priests and Pharisees, *"convened a council. . .[saying] 'If we let Him go on like this, all men will believe in Him, and the Romans* [under whose rule they were] *will come and take away both our place and our nation.. . .So from that day on they planned together to kill Him."* (11:47-53)

Because Jesus knew **that the Pharisees and the high priests** were plotting against Him, He withdrew from there, *". . .into a City called Ephraim; and there He stayed with the disciples." (11:54)*

Six days before Passover, Jesus again went to Bethany to the home of Lazarus and his two sisters, Mary and Martha. When Mary anointed the feet of Jesus with a costly perfume, Judas Iscariot expressed concern, saying that money wasted on perfume could have been better spent on poor people. But Judas' real reason for saying this was that he was a thief and had pilfered from the money box in the past. Jesus answered Judas' objections by stating that Mary had anointed Him in preparation for the day of His burial. Jesus then added, *"For the poor you always have with you, but you do not always have Me." (12:7-8)*

Crowds of people came to Lazarus' home, not just to see and hear Jesus but also to see Lazarus, *". . .whom He had raised from the dead." (12:9)* And the chief priests took council and planned to not only murder Jesus but Lazarus, as well.

The next day Jesus departed for Jerusalem and crowds of people took palm branches and put them on the roadway, as Jesus, mounted on a young donkey, passed by them.

Among those who had followed Jesus into Jerusalem were *"certain Greeks"* who were going there for the Feast of the Passover. They told the disciple Philip that they wanted to meet Jesus.

> *"Jesus answered [and said to the crowd around Him]. . . 'The hour has come for the Son of Man to be glorified. Truly, truly, I say to you, unless a grain of wheat falls onto the earth and dies, it remains by itself alone; but if it dies, it bears much fruit. He who loves his life loses it; and he who hates his life in the world shall keep it to life eternal.*
>
> *"If anyone serves Me, let him follow Me; and where I am there shall My servant also be; if anyone serves Me, the Father will honor him. Now My soul has become troubled; and what shall I say, 'Father save Me from this hour?' But for this purpose I came to this hour. Father, glorify Thy name.' There came therefore a voice out of heaven: 'I have both glorified it, and will glorify it again!'. . .and Jesus. . .said, 'This voice has not come for My sake, but for your sakes. Now judgment is upon this world; now the rulers of this world shall be cast out. And I, if I be lifted up from the earth* [in resurrection from death] *will draw all men to Myself.'. . .[after speaking these things] He departed and hid Himself from them." (12:20-36)*

Before the Feast of the Passover, Jesus, *". . .knowing that His hour had come that He should depart out of this world to the Father" (13:1)* had a last supper with His apostles. During that meal, Jesus *". . .rose from supper. . .and washed His disciples' feet."* When Peter protested having Jesus humble Himself to wash his feet, Jesus said to Peter, *" 'If I do not wash you, you have no part with Me.' Simon Peter said to him, 'Lord, not my feet only but also my hands and my head.' "* *(13:8-9)*

After washing their feet, Jesus again reclined at the table and said to them, *"Do you know what I have done to you? You call Me Teacher and Lord; and you are right, for so I am. If I then, the Lord and the Teacher, washed your feet, you also ought to wash one another's feet. . .[serve each other, assist each other, help each other]."* *(13:13-14)*

Jesus then predicted that one among those gathered there was about to betray Him. His disciples wondered amongst themselves to whom Jesus was referring, and so Jesus said, *"That is the one for whom I dip the morsel and give it to him.' So when He had dipped the morsel, He took and gave it to Judas, the son of Simon Iscariot. . .* [and said to him] *'What you do, do quickly.' "* Judas then left the gathering. Jesus said to the eleven remaining, *"Now is the Son of Man glorified and God is glorified in Him. . .A new commandment I give to you, that you love one another, even as I have loved you, that you also love one another. By this all men will know that you are My disciples, if you have love for one another."(13:26-35)*

Peter asked Jesus where He was going – and asked if he could also go. Jesus answered, *"Will you lay down your life for Me? Truly, truly, I say to you, a cock shall not crow, until you deny Me three times."* *(13:37-38)*

Jesus then offers comfort to His disciples, as He tells them,

"Let not your hearts be troubled; believe in God, believe also in Me. In My father's house are many dwelling places; if it were not so, I would have told you; for I go to prepare a place for you. . .I will come again, and receive you to Myself; that where I am, there you may be also.. .I am the way and the truth and the life; no one comes to the Father, but through Me. . . .Believe Me that I am in the Father and the Father in Me. . .And whatever you ask in My name, that will I do, that the Father may be glorified in the Son. If you ask Me anything in My name, I will do it. If you love Me, you will keep My commandments." (14:1-15)

Then Jesus told His disciples about the Holy Spirit by saying that He would not leave His followers like orphans, but rather that, *". . .The Helper, The Holy Spirit, whom The Father will send in My name, He will teach you all things, and bring to you remembrance all that I said to you." (14:26)*

In Chapter 15, John tells us that Jesus likens Himself to a vine and His followers to the branches of the vine.

"I am the true vine, and My Father is the vinedresser. . .I am the vine, you are the branches; he who abides in Me, and I in him, he bears much fruit; for apart from Me you can do nothing. . .This is My commandment, that you love one another, just as I have loved you. Greater love has no one than this, that one lay down his life for his friends. . .I have called you friends. . .you did not choose Me, but I chose you, and appointed you, that you should go and bear fruit. . ." (15:1-16)

"When the Helper [the Holy Spirit] comes whom I will send to you from the Father, that is the Spirit of Truth, who proceeds from the Father, He will bear witness of Me, and you will bear witness also, because you have been with Me from the beginning." (15:26-27)

". . .But I tell you the truth, it is to your advantage that I go away; for if I do not go away, the Helper shall not come to you; but if I go, I will send Him to you. . .But when He, the Spirit of Truth, comes, He will guide you into all the truth;. . .He shall glorify Me; for He shall take of Mine, and shall disclose it to you." (16:7-14)

Speaking of His impending suffering and death, Jesus told His disciples,

"A little while, and you will no longer behold Me; and again a little while, and you will see Me. . .Therefore, you too now have sorrow; but I will see you again and your heart will rejoice, and no one takes your joy away from you. . .[but] an hour is coming and has already come, for you to be scattered, each to his own home, and to leave Me alone; and yet I am not alone, because the Father is with Me." (16:16-32)

**And Jesus prayed to His Father that the Father would glorify Him
and give eternal life to his followers.**

> *". . .Father, I desire that they also, whom Thou has given Me, be
> with Me where I am, in order that they may behold My glory, which
> Thou hast given Me; for Thou didst love Me before the foundation
> of the world. O righteous Father, although the world has not
> known Thee, yet I have known Thee; and these have known that
> Thou didst send Me; and I have made Thy name known to them, and
> will make it known; that the love wherewith Thou didst love Me may
> be in them and I in them." (17:24-26)*

Jesus and His disciples (minus Judas who was meeting with those
who were seeking to kill Jesus) then went, *". . .over the ravine of the
Kidron"* and to a garden. Judas and *". . .the Roman cohort and officers
from the chief priests and the Pharisees came there with lanterns and
torches and weapons." (18:1-3)*

Jesus asked them, *"Whom do you seek?"* And when they answered,
"Jesus the Nazarene," He said, "I am He." (18:4-5)

Simon Peter, in an effort to defend Jesus, took out his sword and,
*"struck the high priest's slave, and cut off his right ear, and the slave's
name was Malchus."* But Jesus told Peter to put away his sword,
saying, *". . .the cup which the Father has given Me, shall I not drink
it?" (18:10-11)*

**In Luke's Gospel, we are told that, even as he was
being arrested, Jesus touched the slave's ear and
healed him.** *(Luke 22:50-51)*

**Jesus was then brought before Annas, the father-in-law of the high
priest Caiaphas.** Caiaphas had earlier advised the Jews, *"that it was
expedient for one man to die on behalf of the people." (18:13-14)*
Annas, having questioned Jesus, then had Him bound and sent to
Caiaphas.

Peter, who had followed Jesus, was at a distance in the court yard.
And when challenged as to whether he was a disciple of Jesus, Peter
denied knowing or having anything to do with Jesus three different
times, *". . .and immediately a cock crowed." (18:27)*

Early in the morning, Jesus was taken from Caiaphas to Pilate in the Praetorium. Pilate demanded that those gathered there tell him of what they were accusing Jesus. They answered, *"If this Man were not an evildoer, we would not have delivered Him up to you." (18:29-30)*

Pilate then summoned Jesus to him and asked Him, *"'Are You the King of the Jews?' Jesus answered, 'Are you saying this on your own initiative, or did others tell you about Me?'"* Pilate then said to Jesus, *"'So You are a king?' Jesus answered, 'You say correctly that I am a king. For this I have been born, and for this I have come into the world, to bear witness to the truth. Everyone who is of the truth hears My voice.'" (18:33-37)*

Finding no guilt in Jesus, Pilate again asked the crowd if they wished to have Jesus released to them, but the crowd cried out, *"Not this Man but Barabbas* [who was a robber]." (18:40)

Pilate then had Jesus scourged and the Roman soldiers, *"wove a crowd of thorns and put it on His head"* and put a purple robe (signifying royalty) on Him. They ridiculed Him and beat Him in the face. When He was thus brought out before the crowd, the chief priests and the officers cried out, *"'Crucify, crucify.' Pilate said to them, 'Take Him yourselves, and crucify Him; for I find no guilt in Him.' The Jews answered him, 'We have a law, and by that law He ought to die because He made Himself out to be the Son of God.'" (19:1-7)*

Pilate then asked Jesus where He was from, but Jesus gave no answer. Pilate then told Jesus he had the power to release Him or to have Him crucified. Jesus responded, *"You would have no authority over Me, unless it had been given you from above. . ." (19:11)*

After hearing this, Pilate continued to make efforts to release Jesus but the Jews who were gathered cried out, saying to Pilate, *"If you release this Man, you are no friend of Caesar; everyone who makes himself out to be a king opposes Caesar." (19:12)*

Pilate then delivered Jesus up to be crucified. Jesus was made to carry His own cross to the *"Place of a Skull, which is called in Hebrew, Golgotha." (19:17)*

"There they crucified Him, and with Him two other men, one on either side and Jesus in between. And Pilate wrote an inscription also, and put it on the cross. And it was written, 'JESUS THE NAZARENE, THE KING OF THE JEWS.'. . .written in Hebrew, Latin, and in Greek." (19:18-20)

The soldiers took Jesus' outer garments and divided them so that each soldier had a part, but they gambled for His tunic, which was seamless. And in so doing, fulfilled the scripture *(Psalm 22:18)* which reads, *"They divided My outer garments among them, and for my clothing they cast lots." (19:24)*

". . .Standing by the cross of Jesus [were] His mother, His Mother's sister, Mary, the wife of Cleopas, and Mary Magdalene. When Jesus therefore saw His mother, and the disciple [John] whom He loved standing nearby, He said to His mother, 'Woman, behold your son!' Then he said to the disciple, 'Behold your mother!' And from that hour the disciple took her into his own household." (19:25-27)

Then Jesus, *". . .Knowing that all things had already been accomplished, in order that the scriptures might be fulfilled, said, 'I am thirsty.'"* So a sponge filled with sour wine was put on a branch and lifted to Jesus' mouth. He then said, *"'It is finished!' And He bowed His head, and gave up His spirit." (19:28-30)*

Because the hour of the beginning of the Sabbath was nearly there, the soldiers, in order to hasten the deaths of the two men who were crucified with Jesus, broke the men's legs. But seeing that Jesus was already dead, they did not break His legs, but rather, *". . .pierced His side with a spear, and immediately there came out blood and water." (19:33-34)*

Then Joseph of Arimathea, being a secret disciple of Jesus, asked Pilate for permission to take Jesus' body for burial. *"And Nicodemus came also. . .bringing a mixture of myrrh and aloes, about a hundred pounds weight." (19:38-39)* And they wrapped Jesus' body in a linen wrapping, along with the spices, and placed Him in a new tomb in a garden near where He had been crucified.

After the Sabbath, on the first day of the week, Mary Magdalene
went to Jesus' tomb. She saw the stone had been rolled away and upon
entering the tomb saw that Jesus' body was no longer there. She ran
from the tomb and encountered Simon Peter and another disciple and
told them that Jesus' body had been taken away. The two men ran to
the tomb and Peter went in and found the linen cloths which had been
wrapped around Jesus' body. Still not understanding that Jesus must
rise from the dead, as He had told them, they returned to their homes.
But Mary Magdalene remained and looking into the tomb, she saw *". .
.two angels in white sitting, one at the head, and one at the feet, where
the body of Jesus had been lying." (20:12)* The angels asked her why
she was crying and she said to them that someone had taken away her
Lord, *"And I do not know where they have laid Him." (20:13)*

**When Mary Magdalene turned to leave the tomb, she saw a man
she thought must be the gardener** (not knowing it was Jesus). When
Jesus called her name, she said to Him, *"Rabboni (which means,
Teacher)." (20:16)* Jesus said to her, *"Stop clinging to Me, for I have
not yet ascended to the Father; but go to My brethren, and say to them,
'I ascend to My Father and your Father, and My God and your God.'
Mary Magdalene came, announcing to the disciples, 'I have seen the
Lord,' and that He had said these things to her."(20:18)*

**That evening, when the disciples were gathered together, in secret,
for fear of their lives** from the people who had planned and carried out
Jesus' crucifixion, *". . .Jesus came and stood in their midst, and said to
them, 'Peace be with you.'" (20:19)*

Jesus then showed His disciples, *"both His hands and His side. .
.[and] said to them again, 'Peace be with you. . .' And when He had
said this, He breathed on them and said to them, 'Receive the Holy
Spirit. If you forgive the sins of any, their sins have been forgiven them;
if you retain the sins of any, they have been retained.'" (20:20-23)*

**However, Thomas, one of Jesus' disciples, was not among this
group.** (His Greek name was Thomas and his Hebrew name was
Didymus.) At some point after Jesus had left this gathering, Thomas
rejoined them. They told Thomas that they had seen the Lord alive, but
Thomas did not believe this, and said that, in order to believe, he would
have to be able to put his, *". . .finger into the place of the nails and. .
.[his] hand into His side. . .'" (20:24-25)*

Eight days later, when the disciples (including Thomas) were again gathered together behind closed doors,

> Jesus suddenly, *". . .stood in their midst, and said, 'Peace be with you.' Then He said to Thomas, 'Reach here your finger, and see My hands; and reach here your hand, and put it into My side; and be not unbelieving, but believing.' Thomas answered. . .'My Lord and My God!' Jesus said to him, 'Because you have seen Me, have you believed? Blessed are they who did not see and yet believed.'"* (20:26-29)

> *"Many other signs therefore Jesus also performed in the presence of the disciples, which are not written in this book; but these have been written that you may believe that Jesus is the Christ, the Son of God; and that believing you may have life in His name."* (20:30-31)

Some time later (John does not tell us how long), **at the Sea of Tiberias,** Simon Peter, Thomas, Nathanael, James and John, the sons of Zebedee and two other unnamed disciples, had decided to go fishing. They had fished all night and caught nothing. At daybreak, Jesus was seen standing on the beach, although the disciples did not immediately recognize Him. When Jesus said to them, *"'Children, you do not have any fish, do you?' They answered Him, 'No.'"* (21:3-5) Jesus then told them to cast their net on the right side of the boat and when they did so, their catch of fish was so great they were not able to haul it in.

"And so when they got out upon the land, they saw a charcoal fire already laid, and fish placed on it, and bread. Jesus said to them, 'Bring some of the fish which you have now caught.' Simon Peter went up and drew the net to land, full of large fish, a hundred and fifty-three, and although there were so many, the net was not torn." (21:9-11) This was the third time Jesus had appeared to His disciples after being raised from the dead.

After breakfast Jesus asked Simon Peter, three times, if he loved Him. Each time Simon Peter responded, *"Yes Lord; You know that I love You."* And with each declaration of love, Jesus said to him, *"Tend My lambs. . .Shepherd My sheep. . .Tend My sheep.'" (21:15-17)*

Then Jesus said to Simon Peter, *"Truly, truly, I say to you, when you were younger, you used to gird yourself, and walk wherever you wished; but when you grow old, you will stretch out your hands, and someone else will gird you and bring you where you do not wish to go."* By this, Jesus was indicating the kind of death Simon Peter would suffer. Jesus then said to Peter, *"Follow Me."* Peter asked Jesus what would become of John, and Jesus responded, *"If I want him to remain until I come, what is that to you? You follow Me!" (21:18-22)*

John (about whom Jesus was speaking) then ends his gospel by saying that he bears witness to – and writes – all these things in truth. *"And there are also many other things which Jesus did, which if they were written in detail, I suppose that even the world itself would not contain the books which were written." (21:24-25)*

This ends the summary of all four Gospels.

By reading the Gospels (not just summaries such as these) one can more fully gain an understanding of **our Lord and Savior Jesus Christ** and His desire to be in our lives.

THE ACTS OF THE APOSTLES

Luke is believed to be the author of Acts which was probably written about A.D. 61.

Acts is composed as a letter written by Luke to Theophilus (who was probably a Gentile convert to Christianity) to give him a greater knowledge of Christian origins and to explain how it came about that the Gospel ("good news") which began with the promise of the restoration of the kingdom to Israel, ends with the Gentile church in Rome.

Acts begins after Jesus' resurrection and ends with Paul's imprisonment in Rome where it is believed that he was martyred. Acts describes approximately the first 30 years of the Christian church's history and expansion from Jerusalem to Rome.

There appear to be two themes in Acts: first, the rejection of the Gospel by the Jews and the reception of the Gospel by the Gentiles; second, the treatment of the early church by local and Roman officials.

Acts is a very active, ongoing description of the formation of the baby Christian church and so, is essential to an understanding of the roots of Christianity.

While Acts is mostly about Paul, it details the apostleship of both Peter and Paul and records the development and growth of Christ's church.   This book emphasizes the activity of the Holy Spirit and might have been more aptly named the Acts of the Holy Spirit.

Acts is our best guide to understanding the work of the Holy Spirit through the Church and in the world.

Acts gives us a profound understanding of the nature and mission of the Church.

Jesus announced that He would found the Church and His followers (disciples) who later formed the Church, were required to wait and pray in Jerusalem until they were empowered to be witnesses unto Christ.

Thus, Pentecost - 40 days after Easter (the seventh Sunday after Easter) - commemorates the descent of the Holy Spirit upon the disciples (and is also called Whitsunday) - **is the day of the Church's being anointed with Power** for her mission.

This anointing of the disciples parallels the experience of Jesus, himself. At His baptism, thirty years after his birth by John the Baptist in the River Jordan, Jesus was anointed by the Holy Spirit for His Messianic mission.

Acts opens with Jesus presenting Himself alive to his disciples a number of times over a period of 40 days, following His resurrection.

Jesus instructs His disciples on things pertaining to the kingdom of God. He tells them not to leave Jerusalem, but to wait for what the Father has promised, *"'which', he said, 'you heard of from Me; for John baptized with water, but you shall be baptized with the Holy Spirit not many days from now.... you shall receive power when the Holy Spirit has come upon you; and you shall be My witnesses both in Jerusalem, and in all Judea and Samaria, and even to the remotest part of the earth.'"* *(1:8)*

At the end of His 40 days on earth following His resurrection, Jesus ascended into heaven.

The Ascension of Jesus (and the foretelling of the Second Coming of Jesus) took place as Jesus was lifted up into heaven and disappeared from the sight of His apostles, as is written about by Mark and Luke in their gospels.

Shortly afterwards, the 11 apostles, along with Mary, the Mother of Jesus, Jesus' brothers, a number of unnamed women and many other persons – about 120 in all – are gathered again in the upper room. Peter talks about Judas having betrayed Jesus (as foretold in Holy Scripture), and they discuss two candidates to fill Judas' spot (as the 12th apostle). The two candidates are Joseph (aka Barsabbas) and Matthias. They draw lots and Matthias becomes the 12th apostle.

Pentecost: 40 days after Jesus' ascension into heaven, His apostles were again gathered together in one place. The Holy Spirit came upon them like a *"violent, rushing wind,"* filling the whole house and appearing to them as tongues of fire resting on each of them. They were all filled with the Holy Spirit and *"began to speak with other tongues, as the Spirit was giving them utterance."* (2:1-4).

Those who heard the apostles, heard them in their own language. Peter gave a speech in which he quoted the prophet Joel, *"And it shall be that everyone who calls on the name of the Lord shall be saved."* (2:21)

And those who heard Peter asked what they should do. Peter said to them, *"Repent and let each of you be baptized in the name of Jesus Christ for the forgiveness of your sins; and you shall receive the gift of the Holy Spirit."* *(2:38)* That day three thousand persons were baptized.

Many signs and wonders began taking place through the apostles and people began joining them, selling their property and sharing with all. They took *"meals together with gladness and sincerity of heart, praising God. . ."* *(2:46-47)*

Peter begins performing the first of many miracles by healing a lame beggar, *"In the name of Jesus Christ the Nazarene. . ." (3:1-6)*

Because they were teaching the people about Jesus and His resurrection from the dead, Peter and John were arrested by the priests, the Captain of the Temple Guard and the Sadducees.

Peter and John were put in jail until the next day. The rulers, elders and scribes gathered in Jerusalem and asked Peter where he got the power to do what he had been doing (miracles). Peter, filled with the Holy Spirit, addressed them saying,

> *". . .let it be known to you and to all the people of Israel, that by the name of Jesus Christ the Nazarene, whom you crucified, whom God raised from the dead – by this name this man* [the lame man] *stands here before you in good health."* He went on, referring to Jesus, *"He is the stone which was rejected by you, the builders, but which became the very cornerstone. And there is salvation in no one else; for there is no other name under heaven that has been given among men, by which we must be saved." (4:10-12)*

Not being able to deny that a miracle had taken place - and hearing and seeing the confidence of Peter and John, who were uneducated and untrained men - greatly concerned the Jewish rulers and they worried that the message of Jesus' apostles would spread. These rulers ordered Peter and John not to speak or teach in the name of Jesus. But Peter and John replied that they could not stop speaking, *"what we have seen and heard." (4:20)*

After being threatened again, Peter and John returned to their group of disciples and told them what had happened. They all prayed together, lifting their voices to God, and while they prayed the place where they were gathered was shaken and they were all filled with the Holy Spirit and they began to, *"speak the word of God with boldness."* *(4:31)*

It was shortly thereafter that a Cyprian who was a Levite named Joseph (renamed Barnabas by the apostles – "Barnabas" means "son of encouragement") came and gave all the money he had received from the sale of his tract of land to the apostles. *(4:37)*

Acts contrasts Barnabas giving freely of all that he had with the story of a couple named Ananias and Sapphira who sold a piece of property and, while holding back a portion of the proceeds, came to the apostles, giving them the remainder, lying and leading the apostles to believe it was the entire sum. When Peter accused Ananias of lying to the Holy Spirit, Ananias fell down and died. Shortly after, Sapphira came in and she also lied to Peter about the sale price of the land. When Peter told her she had lied, along with her husband who was now dead, she too, lay down and died. *(5:1-10)*

The apostles continued to perform miracles and sick people were carried into the street so that when Peter passed by his shadow might fall on them and heal them.

The high priest and his associates, the Sadducees, were increasingly concerned and jealous of the apostles and put them in a public jail. But during the night an angel of the Lord opened the gates of the jail and took them out, saying, *"Go your way, stand and speak to the people of the temple the whole message of this Life."* *(5:19-20)*

So at daybreak, the apostles entered the temple and began teaching. Not knowing this latest development, the high priest, the Sadducees, the Council and the Senate of the sons of Israel gathered for the purpose of bringing the apostles before them for questioning. When they were told the apostles were in the temple, teaching, they were shocked, since the guard reported that the prison house was still securely locked and guards were still standing at the doors.

The apostles were again brought before the Council (without violence, since the Council was now afraid of the people who were following the apostles). The Council reminded the apostles that they had been told not to teach in the name of Jesus, but Peter responded,

> *"We must obey God rather than men. The God of our fathers raised Jesus, whom you had put to death by hanging Him on a cross. He is the one whom God exalted to His right hand as a Prince and a Savior, to grant repentance to Israel, and forgiveness of sins." (5:29-31)*

The Council was angered by this and intended to slay the apostles, when a Pharisee named Gamaliel, a teacher of the Jewish law, spoke to the Council and reminded them that others had risen up within Israel, *". . .claiming to be somebody. . ." (5:36)* and those who followed simply dispersed and it came to nothing. Gamaliel reasoned that, if these men (the apostles) were following a plan made by men, they, too, would be overthrown, *". . .but if it is of God, you will not be able to overthrow them, or else you may even be found fighting against God." (5:38-39)*

The council took Gamaliel's advice, flogged the apostles, ordered them to speak no more in the name of Jesus, and then released them. The apostles rejoiced that they had been considered worthy to suffer shame for Jesus' name.

As the followers of Jesus were increasing in number, a conflict arose between the Hellenistic (Greek) Jews and the native Hebrew Jews regarding that Hellenistic widows were being overlooked in the daily service of food (since caring for widows and children was something they were now routinely doing). The 12 apostles then asked that seven men be selected to take charge of this function, so that the apostles could devote themselves to prayer and ministry of the Word.

Among the seven chosen was *"Stephen, a man full of faith and of the Holy Spirit. . . and Stephen, full of grace and power, was performing great wonders and signs among the people." (6:5-12)* And because Stephen had attracted attention, the elders and the scribes had him dragged away and brought before the council.

False witnesses accused Stephen of speaking against the holy place and the Law (referring to Stephen having told people that Jesus said He would destroy this place and change the customs which Moses gave to his people). Stephen was asked if this was so, and as he spoke, his face shone like the face of an angel. He summarized the Jewish history for the council, beginning with God appearing to Abraham, going on to talk about Joseph in Egypt and all the Jews in Egyptian captivity, Moses leading God's people out of slavery in Egypt, David, Solomon, and so on. Stephen ended his speech by saying, *"Which one of the prophets did your* [fore]*fathers not persecute? And they killed those who had previously announced the coming of the Righteous One, whose betrayers and murderers you have now become. . ." (7:52)*

The council was very angered by this and as Stephen said, *"Behold, I see the heavens opened up and the Son of Man standing at the right hand of God,"* they drove him out of the city and began stoning him, after laying their robes at the feet of a young man named Saul. As they proceeded to stone Stephen to death, Stephen called upon the Lord, saying, *"Lord Jesus, receive my spirit. Lord do not hold this sin against them!"* He then died. *(7:56-60)*

"And Saul [later known as Paul] *was in hearty agreement with putting him [Stephen] to death."* It was then that persecution of the Christians began in earnest and *"Saul began ravaging the church. . . dragging off men and women"* and putting them in prison. *(8:1-3)* However, the disciples and apostles continued going about their business of preaching about Jesus.

As an example, Philip went down to the city of Samaria and was healing people and casting out demons and many people were being baptized. Even a magician named Simon became a believer and was baptized.

And when the apostles who were in Jerusalem heard that Samaria had received the word of God, they sent Peter and John who went to Samaria and prayed that the people would receive the Holy Spirit, since the Holy Spirit had not *". . .fallen upon any of them; they had simply been baptized in the name of the Lord Jesus." (8:14)*

When Peter and John began laying their hands on people in Samaria, the Samarians began receiving the Holy Spirit. Simon, seeing this, offered the apostles money so that he, too, would receive the Holy Spirit, but Peter told him that money had nothing to do with the receiving of the Holy Spirit.

Peter, John and Philip were on their way back to Jerusalem when an angel of the Lord spoke to Philip, directing him to go south to Gaza. He did so, and encountered an Ethiopian eunuch sitting in his chariot reading the prophet Isaiah. The Ethiopian asked Philip to explain the reading. Philip preached Jesus to the Ethiopian who then asked to be baptized, saying, *"I believe that Jesus Christ is the Son of God."* After Philip baptized the Ethiopian, Philip was snatched away by the Spirit of the Lord. *(8:25-39)*

"Now Saul, still breathing threats and murder against the disciples of the Lord," (9:1) had set out for Damascus (in Syria) but along the way, was stopped and blinded by a light from heaven. As he fell to the ground, he heard, *"Saul, Saul, why are you persecuting me?"* When Saul asked who it is that is speaking, he was told, *"I am Jesus, whom you are persecuting." (9:4-5)*

Jesus then told Saul to rise and go to Damascus and wait to be told what he must do. Saul did as he was told and waited three days without sight or food or drink. The Lord then sent a disciple named Ananias to minister to Saul. The Lord told Ananias that Saul was His chosen instrument. After Ananias laid his hands on Saul, Saul's sight was restored and he was filled with the Holy Spirit. *(9:17)*

After a few days with the disciples at Damascus, Saul began to proclaim Jesus in the synagogues saying, *"He is the Son of God." (9:20)* The Jewish leaders plotted to do away with Saul, but he escaped when his disciples lowered him outside the city wall in a basket.

Saul went to Jerusalem, but the other disciples were, understandably, afraid of him. Barnabas, however, convinced them that Saul had seen Jesus and was now one of them. And so Saul began to boldly speak out in the name of the Lord.

Meanwhile, Peter was continuing to heal the sick and brought a good woman named Tabitha back to life.

Then a Centurion named Cornelius saw, in a vision, an angel of God who sent him to find Peter. Peter, in the meantime, also had a vision in which he learned that God's word is meant for all peoples, not just for Jews. So when Peter met Cornelius, he understood that God is not one to show partiality, but rather that, in every nation, the man who fears Him and does what is right, is welcome. It was then that Jesus' apostles and disciples realized that they were to make God's Word – Jesus Christ – available to all people everywhere.

Barnabas was then sent to find Saul who was in Tarsus. He brought Saul back to Antioch, and for a year they met with the church and it was here the followers of Jesus became known as "Christians."

About that time, Herod the King laid hands on some people who belonged to the church. He put James, the brother of John, to death by the sword. When he saw that this pleased the Jews, he proceeded to arrest Peter (it was near Passover time) and he directed four squads of soldiers to guard Peter. But that night, while Peter was sleeping between two soldiers and was bound by chains, an angel of the Lord appeared to him and a light shone in the ceiling and the angel told Peter to get up quietly. Peter did what he was told, but didn't quite know if what he was seeing was real or a vision.

Peter's chains had all fallen off of him, and so Peter and the angel passed the guards and left the prison. Peter knew that the angel of the Lord had rescued him. He went to the house of Mary, the mother of John who was also called Mark, where many Christians were gathered in prayer. They were overjoyed to see Peter!

But back in the prison, the soldiers were very disturbed to find Peter gone. When Herod learned of Peter's escape, he became so upset he had the guards executed. Soon after that, Herod was struck by an angel of God, eaten by worms and died.

By now, Saul, now known as Paul, was filled with the Holy Spirit and was spreading the Word of God.

Paul's First Missionary Journey: At Antioch (Syria) there were prophets and teachers: Barnabas and Simeon (also called Niger), Lucius and Manaen (who had been brought up with Herod) and Saul. The Holy Spirit said, *"Set apart for me Barnabas and Saul for the work to which I have called them." (13:2)* And so they fasted and prayed and went down to Seleucia and set sail for Cyprus (John Mark was also with them).

Paul and his companions set out by sea for Perga in Pamphylia and John returned to Jerusalem. (Later Paul was critical of John for not having continued with them.) Paul went to Antioch and on the Sabbath was invited to preach in the synagogue. He gave a brief historical overview of the Jewish people, starting with the exile from Egypt, wandering in the desert for 40 years, Samuel, Saul, David, Jesus, John the Baptist, Jesus' death and resurrection, and forgiveness of sins through Jesus.

By the next Sabbath nearly the whole city gathered to hear Paul preach the Word of God. The Jewish leaders became jealous of Paul's popularity and began instigating a persecution against Paul. They drove Paul and Barnabas out of their district.

Paul and Barnabas went to Iconium and entered the synagogue there and *"spoke in such a manner"* that many believed, both Jews and Greeks. But the city was divided regarding Christianity, and an attempt was made to stone Paul and Barnabas. They fled to the cities of Lycaonia (an ancient region situated north of the Taurus mountains in modern-day Turkey), Lystra and Derbe and continued to preach. *(14:1-6)*

At Lystra, Paul healed a man crippled from birth. And those that saw this began treating Paul and Barnabas as if they were gods. At this, Paul and Barnabas became very upset and adjured the crowd, saying they were only men and were preaching the gospel in order that the people would turn from their vain ways to the living God who made all things.

But Jews from Antioch (from where they had just recently fled) won over the crowd so that they stoned Paul and, believing him to be dead, dragged him out of the city. But as the apostles stood around him, Paul arose and reentered the city. The next day he and Barnabas went to Derbe, then to Lystra and Iconium and to Antioch, saying to the other apostles, *"Through many tribulations we must enter the Kingdom of God."* *(14:22)*

They then passed through Pisidia and came to Pamphylia, Perga and Attalia. From there they sailed for Antioch (in Syria) where they gathered the church members together and reported all that God had done with them and how He *"had opened a door of faith to the Gentiles."* *(14:27)*

The question of the importance of circumcision then came up and there was much dissention and talk. It was determined that Paul and Barnabas should go to Jerusalem regarding this issue.

On their way, they passed through Phoenicia and Samaria, telling their brethren about the conversion of the Gentiles. But, when they reached Jerusalem there was much debate about circumcision. Paul made a public argument regarding this issue, in which he said it was no longer necessary to be circumcised in order to be God's people, but rather that people are, *"saved through the grace of the Lord Jesus. . ."* *(15:11)*

It was then decided that Paul and Barnabas, Barsabbas (formerly named Judas) **and Silas** were to go to Antioch to tell the Christians there about the necessity to abstain from things sacrificed to idols and things strangled and from fornication. Paul and Barnabas stayed in Antioch, teaching and preaching the Word of God. *(15:22)*

Paul's Second Missionary Journey: Paul asked Barnabas to go with him on a second journey to the same cities they had visited before. Barnabas wanted to bring John (called Mark) along, but Paul didn't want him along, since, during the first trip, he had left them in Pamphylia. They had so sharp a disagreement about this matter that Barnabas took Mark and left for Cyprus. *(15:39)*

Paul then chose Silas to accompany him and they traveled through Syria and Cilicia, strengthening the churches. They went to Derbe and Lystra (where they met Timothy), Phrygian and Galatian regions, Mysia, Bithynia and Troas, where Paul had a vision in which he was told to go to Macedonia (Greece).

So they put out to sea from Troas and ran a straight course to Samothrace and then to Neapolis and then to Philippi. It was there they converted a woman named Lydia and her household. *(16:14-15)*

At one point, they were followed by a certain slave girl who was possessed by a spirit of divination and who was fortune-telling for her masters. After being followed for several days, Paul became annoyed, and commanded, *"In the name of Jesus Christ"* that the spirit which had inhabited her come out. And it did. *(16:18)* But the girl's masters were so upset at the loss of their fortune-teller, they had Paul and Silas beaten with rods and thrown in jail, where their feet were locked in stocks.

Paul and Silas prayed and sang hymns to God, and at midnight there was a great earthquake and all the prison doors were opened and everyone's chains unfastened. The jailer became so distraught he tried to kill himself, but Paul told him, *"Do yourself no harm, for we are all here."* (Meaning that they hadn't even tried to escape.) The jailer asked what he had to do to be saved and they told him, *"Believe in the Lord Jesus, and you shall be saved, you and your household." (16:28-31)*

The jailer took Paul and Silas to his home, washed their wounds and immediately he and his household were baptized. The jailer fed them and then rejoiced greatly. The next day the chief magistrate wanted to release Paul and Silas but Paul didn't want to leave without a trial. The chief magistrate, however, convinced them to leave and so they went to the house of Lydia.

When they left the house of Lydia, they traveled through Amphipolis and Apollonia and came to Thessalonica, to a Jewish synagogue. Paul went there for three Sabbaths to reason with them from the scriptures. When some people joined Paul and Silas, the Jews became jealous and formed a mob. The Christians sent Paul and Silas away by night to Berea, where they also went into the synagogue to talk about Jesus. But the Jews of Thessalonica came after Paul, so the brethren sent Paul to go as far as the sea, while Silas and Timothy remained behind.

Paul went to Athens to wait for Silas and Timothy, and while there, he became bothered by all the idols in the city. He was in the synagogues, reasoning with the Jews and the God-fearing Gentiles as well as some Epicurean (happiness-seeking) and Stoic (self-control) philosophers.

In the midst of the Areopagus (a rocky hill northwest of the Acropolis in Athens where the Greek council met), Paul gave a sermon about the altar bearing the inscription, *"TO AN UNKNOWN GOD."(17:23)* Paul used this Greek altar inscription to illustrate to the people that God is near to each of us, and *". . .in Him we live and move and exist."* And that we ought not to think of God as an image carved in stone but that God is declaring that men everywhere should repent, because *". . .He has fixed a day in which He will judge the world in righteousness through a Man [Jesus Christ] whom He has appointed, having furnished proof to all men by raising Him from the dead." (17:31)*

Although some in the crowd sneered at Paul, others in the crowd believed. Paul then left Athens and went to Corinth. He found a Jewish couple – Aquila and Priscilla (who had left Rome at the command of Claudius who had expelled all the Jews from Rome).

Paul stayed with Aquila and Priscilla, because they were of the same trade as he – being tent-makers. Paul was reasoning in the synagogue every Sabbath and trying to persuade Jews and Greeks. And when Timothy and Silas came down from Macedonia, Paul began to devote himself completely to the Word.

When the Jews resisted, Paul stated that he would go instead to the Gentiles. He then went to Titus Justus' house and stayed a year and a half, teaching and preaching.   The Jews, however, rose up against Paul and brought him before the judgment seat, but Gallio refused to be a judge in the matter and drove Paul's accusers away.

Paul then set out by sea for Syria (Aquila and Priscilla went with him) and they came to Ephesus (a city located on the western coast of Turkey), where he entered the synagogue to reason with the Jews. They asked him to stay, but he set sail from Ephesus, landed at Caesarea, greeted the church there, and then went down to Antioch.

Paul spent some time at Antioch and then went through the Galatian region and Phrygia. At that time, a Jew named Apollos began speaking out in the synagogue concerning Jesus, but Priscilla and Aquila took him aside and explained the way of God more accurately.

Paul passed through the upper country, returned to Ephesus and found some disciples who didn't know of the Holy Spirit, but only knew of John the Baptist. Paul laid his hands on them and the Holy Spirit came on them. He entered the synagogue and spoke out boldly and when some spoke evil of The Way (as Christianity had first been known), he withdrew from them and took away the disciples. For two years, Paul reasoned daily in the school of Tyrannus and God performed extraordinary miracles through him, so that even his handkerchiefs or aprons were used to cure the sick and dispel evil spirits. And the name of the Lord Jesus was magnified and many who practiced magic began burning their books in the sight of all.

Paul purposed to go to Jerusalem, after passing through Macedonia and Achaia, saying that after he had done so, he would go to Rome. He then sent Timothy and Erastus to Macedonia and he stayed in Asia (Ephesus) for a while.

While in Ephesus, a disturbance arose in which Demetrius the silversmith was losing customers (his business was making silver shrines of the goddess Artemis). He and others began complaining, because Paul was turning people away from man-made idols. People were close to rioting and were crying out, *"Great is Artemis of the Ephesians!" (19: 28, 34)* The town clerk quieted them down by saying that the dispute was between Demetrius and the craftsmen against whomever they had a complaint and that it would be settled in the lawful assembly.

After the uproar ceased, Paul exhorted the disciples who were to stay in Ephesus and he departed for Macedonia and came to Greece where he spent three months.

When a plot to kill Paul became known to him, he set sail for Syria, determined to return through Macedonia. A number of disciples went ahead of him and were waiting at Troas. They sailed from Philippi, came to Troas and stayed there seven days.

While in Troas, Paul was with an assembly of people on the third floor when a young man named Eutychus fell asleep on the window sill and fell out. It was thought that he was dead. Paul went down and embraced him and said, *"Do not be troubled, for his life is still in him. . .and they took away the boy alive, and were greatly comforted." (20:9-12)*

The disciples who had gone ahead, set sail for Assos where they met Paul and went to Mitylene and from there to Chios, then to Samos and then Miletus. Paul had decided to sail past Ephesus so that he could be in Jerusalem on the day of Pentecost.

While at Miletus, Paul called together the elders of the church of Ephesus and reminded them of the length of time he had spent with them on behalf of the Lord Jesus Christ.

> He admonished them to, *"Be on guard for yourselves and for all the flock, among which the Holy Spirit has made you overseers, to shepherd the church of God which He purchased with His own blood." (20:28)*

Paul told them they would never see him again and amidst their sorrowful embraces, he left by ship for Jerusalem.

From Miletus, they ran to Cos and Rhodes and to Patara and then boarded another ship for Phoenicia. They landed at Tyre. Paul looked up the disciples there and stayed seven days. They told him (through the Spirit) not to go to Jerusalem.

Paul and his company departed and sailed to Ptolemais where they stayed for a day. They then left for Caesarea and stayed with Philip the evangelist. While there, a prophet named Agabus came down from Judea and demonstrated to Paul what his fate would be in Jerusalem. He said the Jews would bind Paul's hands and feet and deliver him into the hands of the Gentiles. Paul would not be dissuaded from going to Jerusalem and responded by saying, *"The will of the Lord be done."* *(21:14)*

In a few days, Paul and his group went to Jerusalem where the brethren received them gladly and they shared information about their ministries.

After seven days, the Jews from Asia, seeing Paul in the temple, began stirring up the people. They laid hands on Paul and accused him of preaching against the Jewish people and the Law and the temple. They also accused him of defiling the holy temple. They then dragged him out of the temple and were going to kill him. A commander of a Roman cohort was alerted and stopped the beating. He ordered Paul bound with two chains and began questioning him. Paul told him that he was a Jew of Tarsus in Cilicia and asked for permission to speak to the people. The commander gave Paul permission to do so.

Paul asked the people to hear his defense and he addressed them in Hebrew. He told them he was a Jew born in Tarsus of Cilicia, but brought up in Jerusalem and educated under Gamaliel (a great Jewish teacher). He admitted that he had earlier persecuted those persons committed to The Way, putting followers to death or into prison. He said he had started off for Damascus to bring followers of Jesus back to Jerusalem for punishment. He then related that while on the road to Damascus, a bright light from heaven flashed around him and he heard a voice saying, *"Saul, Saul, why are you persecuting me?"* *(22:7)* And the voice identified itself as Jesus the Nazarene. Paul related that Jesus directed him to go to Damascus where he would be told what to do. Paul related how he came to be helped by Ananias after having lost his sight for a time, and how he then came to know that he was to be a witness for Jesus Christ.

Paul then told how, when he returned to Jerusalem and the temple, Jesus had appeared to him and told him to leave Jerusalem because the people wouldn't accept Paul's testimony about Him.

With this, the assembly raised their voices and declared that Paul shouldn't be allowed to live and the Roman Commander ordered Paul to be scourged. When the beating was nearly to begin, Paul asked a centurion if it was lawful to scourge a man who was a Roman citizen and uncondemned.

The fact that Paul was a Roman citizen (having been born in the city of Tarsus, in the Roman province of Cilicia) was an issue for the Roman cohort and they were afraid, since it was against Rome's rule to abuse a Roman citizen. The Roman commander released Paul and ordered the chief priests and Jewish Council (the Sanhedrin) to assemble to hear Paul.

Paul declared that he had lived his life with a good conscience, that he was a Pharisee and now was on trial for the hope and resurrection of the dead. A heated argument then broke out between the Pharisees and the Sadducees, for the Pharisees believed in angels and spirits and the resurrection, but the Sadducees didn't believe in any of those things.

In order to protect him, Paul was taken away by force. That night, the Lord stood at Paul's side and said, *"Take courage, for as you have solemnly witnessed to my cause at Jerusalem, so you must witness at Rome, also." (23:11)* The next day the Jews conspired to kill Paul, but Paul's nephew, having heard about the plot, came to the barracks where Paul was being held in order to warn him.

Paul sent the young man to Claudius Lysias, the Roman Commander, to tell him of this plan. The Commander then had Paul moved to Caesarea (under guard by 200 spearmen and 70 horsemen) to Felix, the Governor.

The Governor decided to give Paul a hearing when his accusers got to Caesarea. Five days later the high priest, Ananias and an attorney named Tertullus, brought charges against Paul. They referred to Paul as a, *"real pest and a fellow who stirs up dissension among all the Jews of the world and a ringleader of the sect of the Nazarenes." (24:5)*

Paul, in answer, responded that,

> ". . .according to The Way which they call a sect, I do serve the
> God of our fathers. . . having a hope in God. . . that there shall
> certainly be a resurrection of both the righteous and the wicked. . .
> for the resurrection of the dead I am on trial before you today. . ."
> (24:14-21)

Felix (the Governor) and his wife Drusilla (a Jewess) arrived and heard
Paul speak of his faith in Christ Jesus. Felix became frightened and
kept Paul in prison for two years. (24:25-27)

Felix was then succeeded by Porcius Festus, who, after three days,
went to Jerusalem. The chief priests and leading men of the Jews
brought charges against Paul and they were hoping he would be brought
to Jerusalem so they could ambush him and kill him on the way. But
Festus told the people who wanted to harm Paul that he (Festus) was
returning to Caesarea and if they wanted to question Paul, they could go
there with him.

When Festus returned to Caesarea, he ordered Paul brought before
him. The Jews who had come down from Jerusalem stood around Paul,
making many serious charges which they could not prove.

**Festus asked Paul if he was willing to go to Jerusalem and stand
trial** on the charges. Paul replied that he appealed to Caesar and Festus
then answered that he would go to Caesar.

After a few days, King Agrippa and Bernice came to Caesarea and
paid their respects to Festus who told them about Paul who had been
kept a prisoner by Felix.

Festus explained that the Jews were accusing Paul of crimes but that
the main disagreement was about their own religion and about, *"a
certain dead man, Jesus, whom Paul asserted to be alive."* (25:19)
Agrippa wanted to see and hear Paul and so Festus arranged for Paul to
be brought before him. King Agrippa told Paul he was permitted to
speak for himself and so Paul did. He explained that he had lived as a
Pharisee and was now, *"standing trial for the hope of the promise made
by God to our fathers, the promise to which our twelve tribes hope to
attain. . . and for this hope, O King, I am being accused by Jews."*
(26:6-7)

Paul went on to explain that, as a Pharisee, he had done many things hostile to the name of Jesus of Nazareth. He had locked up many of the saints and had been in favor of them being put to death. He had forced them to blaspheme and pursued them even to foreign cities. He told King Agrippa about his encounter with Jesus on the road to Damascus and how Jesus had appointed Paul as a minister and witness to the Gentiles.

Paul related to them that Jesus had said to him,

> *"I am Jesus whom you are persecuting. But arise and stand on your feet; for this purpose I have appeared to you, to appoint you a minister and a witness not only to the things which you have seen, but also to the things in which I will appear to you; delivering you from the Jewish people and from the Gentiles, to whom I am sending you, to open their eyes so they may turn from darkness to light and from the dominion of Satan to God, in order that they may receive forgiveness of sins and an inheritance among those who have been sanctified by faith in Me* [Jesus].*"* *(26:15-18)*

Paul continued, saying that what he had been testifying to was just what the prophets and Moses had said was going to take place (Christ's suffering and resurrection from the dead).

Paul then said to Agrippa,

> *"Do you believe the prophets? I know that you do."* And Agrippa replied, *"'In a short time you will persuade me to become a Christian.' And Paul said, 'I would to God, that whether in a short or long time, not only you, but also all who hear me this day, might become such as I am, except for these chains.'"* *(26:27-29)*

Agrippa then told Festus that Paul had done nothing wrong and would have been set free if he had not appealed to Caesar.

Paul was then sent to Rome by boat with other prisoners, under the control of a centurion named Julius.

They embarked in an Adramyttian ship accompanied by Aristarchus, a Macedonian of Thessalonica. The next day they put in at Sidon and Julius treated Paul with consideration and allowed him to go to his friends and receive care.

From there they sailed under the shelter of Cyprus because the winds were contrary; then along the coast of Cilicia and Pamphylia and they landed at Myra in Lycia. There they changed to an Alexandrian ship sailing for Italy and after difficult sailing because of the wind, they arrived off Cnidus and sailed under the shelter of Crete, off Salmone and with difficulty they came to a place called Fair Havens near the City of Lasea.

The voyage now became dangerous (it was the fall of the year) and Paul admonished them that the cargo, the ship and their lives were in danger. But the centurion was more persuaded by the pilot and the captain than by Paul. And, because the harbor wasn't suitable for wintering, they put out to sea in hopes of reaching Phoenix, a harbor of Crete, where they could spend the winter. They sailed along Crete, close inshore.

Then a violent wind called Euraquilo rushed down, and it drove the ship along. They ran under the shelter of a small island called Clauda (off the southwest coast of Crete) and were barely able to get the ship under control. They let down the sea anchor and so let themselves be driven along.

The next day the ship was violently storm-tossed and so they began jettisoning cargo. Next they threw the ship's tackle overboard. For days they couldn't see the sun or the stars and began losing hope of being saved.

Paul stood up in their midst and told them if they had followed his advice and not set sail from Crete, they wouldn't have incurred the damage and loss. He then urged them to keep up their courage and assured them no lives would be lost, but only the ship.

Paul told them that an Angel of God had stood before him and told him he would stand before Caesar and that God would save him and all who sailed with him. Paul then told them the ship must run aground on a certain island.

After 14 days, they were being driven about in the Adriatic Sea and when the sailors took soundings, they could tell they were coming to shallower waters. They cast four anchors into the sea and wished for daybreak. Some of the sailors tried to escape by letting down the ship's boat, but Paul told the centurion and soldiers that unless all the men stayed in the ship, no one could be saved. So the soldiers cut the ship's boat free and let it fall away.

As day began to break, Paul urged them all to eat some food for strength, and told them that not a hair on any of their heads would perish. Paul then took bread, gave thanks to God in the presence of all, broke it and began to eat. The 276 persons aboard were encouraged and also ate. After eating, they lightened the ship by throwing the wheat into the sea.

When day came, although they couldn't see land, they could see a bay and a beach and they determined to drive the ship onto it if they could. They cast off the anchors and loosened the ropes of the rudders and hoisting the foresail to the wind, they headed for the beach.

They struck a reef where two seas met, and ran the vessel aground. The prow stuck fast and the stern began to be broken up by the force of the waves.

The soldiers planned to kill the prisoners so that none of them could escape, but the centurion, who was determined to bring Paul safely through, stopped them. He commanded those who could swim to jump overboard first and get to land and the rest followed, some on planks and others on various things from the ship. Thus, they all were brought safely to land.

The island they landed on was Malta. The natives showed them kindness and kindled a fire because of the cold. Paul had gathered a bundle of sticks and when he laid them on the fire, a viper came out because of the heat and fastened onto Paul's hand. The natives thought this meant Paul was a murderer and they believed he would die from the snake's bite. But Paul shook off the viper and suffered no harm.

When nothing bad happened to Paul, the natives decided he must be a god. In a nearby neighborhood the leading man of the island, Publius, welcomed them and entertained them three days.

It came about that Publius' father was very ill with fever and dysentery. Paul went in to see him and after he prayed, Paul laid his hands on the man and healed him. Then many more people came to Paul and were getting cured.

> **It is believed that nearly the entire island population of Malta became Christians** because of Paul's three month stay there and his words and work amongst them.

At the end of three months, they set sail on an Alexandrian ship which had twin brothers for its figurehead. They put in at Syracuse and stayed three days. Then they sailed to Rheguim and to Puteoli. There they stayed for seven days, thus they came to Rome.

The brethren came to meet Paul and his group and when Paul saw them, he took courage and thanked God. When they entered Rome, Paul was allowed to stay by himself with the soldier who was guarding him.

After three days Paul called together those who were the leading men of the Jews and told him what had happened to him regarding why he was a prisoner. They told him they wished to hear from him regarding his views about this sect (The Way – Christianity) because it was being spoken against everywhere. *(28:23)*

They set a day for Paul where they came in large numbers. And he explained to them and testified about the Kingdom of God and tried to persuade them regarding Jesus, from both the Law of Moses and from the prophets. Some were persuaded, but others were not. Paul stayed for two full years in his own rented quarters and *"was welcoming all who came to him, preaching the Kingdom of God and teaching concerning the Lord Jesus Christ with all openness unhindered." (28:30-31)*

> **This is the end of the summary of Acts. No one knows what happened to Paul** after this point. It is believed he was martyred in Rome, as was Peter.

✝

INTRODUCTION TO THE EPISTLES

Now begins the books of the Bible known as Epistles - or letters.

Most of the Epistles, as titled, are attributed to Paul, although, in some cases, it is not known if he was, in fact, the author.

Paul is a most interesting and controversial figure. He was an intelligent and well-educated Pharisee from Tarsus. As a young man, he had initially joined others in attempts to silence and destroy followers of Jesus who were beginning to spread Christ's teachings after His death and resurrection. As related in Acts of the Apostles, Paul (then known as Saul) stood by as a disciple named Stephen was stoned to death.

Following Paul's encounter with Jesus on the road to Damascus, he became a fervent Christian and devoted the rest of his life to the spreading of the word of Jesus, as can be seen in the Acts of the Apostles.

Many of Paul's letters were directed to the new Christian communities established throughout Asia Minor (today's Turkey).

Some of Paul's teachings seem to be male chauvinistic in nature and have been hotly debated through the centuries. Although there is no way of knowing, Paul's writings about the role of women may seem harsher than he intended, since we might assume that his viewpoint may have been colored by the times in which he lived (e.g., the First Epistle of Paul to Timothy).

THE EPISTLE OF PAUL TO THE ROMANS

Paul's letter to the church – or group of believers - in Rome – was probably written sometime between 53 – 58 A.D.

This letter was written on Paul's third missionary journey. Since he spent three months in Greece and he recommends Phoebe the Deaconess, from Cenchrea (eastern seaport of Corinth, Greece), who probably carried this letter to Rome, it seems likely that Corinth, Greece is where it was written.

Romans is a letter of instructions, touching on central truths of the gospel which Paul felt was needed by those followers of "The Way" in Rome.

Romans deals with the importance of righteousness in man's relationship with God.

Romans is considered Paul's finest letter. It is the inspired, systematic theology of the Christian Faith.

If Paul did write this letter from Corinth – a city which was steeped in depravity – he was seeing firsthand the ills of mankind which he describes in 1:18-32.

> *"And just as they did not see fit to acknowledge God any longer, God gave them over to a depraved mind to do those things which are not proper, and being filled with all unrighteousness, wickedness, greed, evil, full of envy, murder, strife, deceit, malice. They are gossips, slanderers, haters of God, insolent, arrogant, boastful, inventors of evil, disobedient to parents, without understanding, untrustworthy, unloving, unmerciful. . .they not only do the same, but also give hearty approval to those who practice them." (1:28-32)*

Paul talks about circumcision – an essential Jewish rite which had been in place for centuries as a means of dedication to the One Lord God. Paul says that physical circumcision is no longer necessary to be pleasing to God, but that loving and obeying God is circumcision enough.

Paul talks about the name "Jew" since it seemed to some that non-Jews (Gentiles) were not to be considered worthy to be God's chosen people. Paul says that although Jews were God's chosen people, all people who come to God through Jesus Christ are God's chosen people.

Paul touches briefly on faith vs. works:

> *"But now apart from the law the righteousness of God has been manifested, being witnessed by the Law and the Prophets, even the righteousness of God through faith in Jesus Christ for all those who believe; for there is no distinction; for all have sinned and fall short of the glory of God, being justified as a gift by His grace through the redemption which is in Christ Jesus; who God displayed publicly as a propitiation in His blood through faith. This was to demonstrate His righteousness, because in the forbearance of God He passed over the sins previously committed; for the demonstration, I say, of His righteousness at the present time, that He might be just and the justifier of the one who has faith in Jesus. Where then is boasting? It is excluded. By what kind of law? Of works? No, but by a law of faith. For we maintain that a man is justified by faith apart from works of the law." (3:21-28)*

Paul says, *"For the wages of sin is death, but the free gift of God is eternal life in Christ Jesus, our Lord." (6:23)*

Paul states,

> *"If God is for us, who is against us?. . .who shall separate us from the love of Christ? Shall tribulation, or distress, or persecution, or famine, or nakedness, or peril or sword?. . . For I am convinced that neither death, nor life, nor angels, nor principalities, nor things present nor things to come, nor powers, nor height, nor depth, nor any other created thing, shall be able to separate us from the love of God, which is in Christ Jesus our Lord."(8:31-39)*

In 10:9,

> *". . . if you confess with your mouth Jesus as Lord, and believe in your heart that God raised Him from the dead, you shall be saved."*

And in 10:13,

"For whoever will call upon the Name of the Lord will be saved."

In 12:6-15, Paul has this to say about each person's gifts:

"And since we have gifts that differ according to the grace given to us, let each exercise them accordingly:. . . if service, in his serving; or he who teaches, in his teaching; or he who exhorts, in his exhortation; he who gives, with liberality; he who leads, with diligence; he who shows mercy, with cheerfulness. . . Be devoted to one another in brotherly love; give preference to one another in honor. . . Bless those who persecute you; bless and curse not. . . Rejoice with those who rejoice; weep with those who weep."

✝

THE FIRST EPISTLE OF PAUL TO THE CORINTHIANS

Paul probably wrote his first letter to the people of Corinth, Greece, on his second missionary journey. This letter is believed to have been written in 55 A.D., from Ephesus, a city in Turkey, where Paul spent about 18 months living with Aquila and Priscilla (who were tentmakers like himself) and ministering in the Synagogue.

Corinth was a morally depraved, but wealthy city. It was a strategic hub of commerce, located on the isthmus connecting Greece and Peloponnese.

Today's Corinth is located about 50 miles west of Athens, Greece.

Regarding our bodies, Paul states,

"Do you not know that your bodies are members of Christ?. . . Flee immorality. Every other sin that a man commits is outside the body, but the immoral man sins against his own body. Or do you not know that your body is a temple of the Holy Spirit . . . For you have been bought with a price: Therefore, glorify God in your body." (6:15-20)

Paul refers to the ancient Greek games (now the Olympics) as a metaphor and model for Christian living. *"And everyone who competes in the games exercises self-control in all things. They then do it to receive a perishable wreath, but we an imperishable." (9:25)*

Regarding the excellence of love, Paul wrote:

"If I speak with the tongues of men and of angels, but do not have love, I have become a noisy gong or a clanging cymbal. And if I have the gift of prophecy, and know all mysteries and all knowledge, and if I have all faith, so as to remove mountains, but do not have love, I am nothing. And if I give all my possessions to feed the poor, and if I deliver my body to be burned, but do not have love, it profits me nothing." (13:1-3)

"Love is patient, love is kind, and is not jealous; love does not brag and is not arrogant, does not act unbecomingly; it does not seek its own, is not provoked, does not take into account a wrong suffered, does not rejoice in unrighteousness, but rejoices with the truth; bears all things, believes all things, hopes all things, endures all things. Love never fails; but if there are gifts of prophecy, they will be done away; if there are tongues, they will cease; if there is knowledge, it will be done away. For we know in part and we prophesy in part; but when the perfect comes, the partial will be done away." (13:4-10)

"When I was a child, I used to speak as a child, think as a child, reason as a child; when I became a man, I did away with childish things. For now we see in a mirror, dimly, but then face to face; now I know in part, but then I shall know fully just as I also have been fully known." (13:11-12)

And now abide faith, hope, love, these three, but the greatest of these is love." (13:13)

In writing about Christ's resurrection, Paul said:

"Behold, I tell you a mystery; we shall not all sleep, but we shall all be changed in a moment, in the twinkling of an eye, at the last trumpet; for the trumpet will sound, and the dead will be raised imperishable, and we shall be changed." (15:51-52)

"Therefore, my beloved brethren, be steadfast, immovable, always abounding in the work of the Lord, knowing that your toil is not in vain in the Lord."(15:58)

✝

THE SECOND EPISTLE OF PAUL TO THE CORINTHIANS

Paul's second letter to the people in Corinth. Written on Paul's third missionary journey – probably written at Philippi in Macedonia about A.D. 57.

This letter is the most personal of all of Paul's epistles. Here we learn more about this "man in Christ." Paul talks about his weaknesses, his trials and tribulations, his *"thorn in the flesh,"* but doesn't tell us what he means by this. In this letter, we see Paul sometimes in great joy and sometimes in deep despair. We see that even the Great Apostle had disappointments. This letter is an ultimatum - calling for total and unconditional surrender to the authority of Christ.

Paul presents the gospel more clearly, pressures the Corinthians to make their promised contributions to the church in Jerusalem and defends his Apostolic ministry and authority.

"Therefore we do not lose heart, but though our outer man is decaying, yet our inner man is being renewed day by day. For momentary, light affliction is producing for us an external weight of glory far beyond all comparison. . ." (4:16-17)

"For we know that if the earthly tent which is our house is torn down, we have a building from God, a house not made with hands, eternal in the heavens. For indeed in this house we groan, longing to be clothed with our dwelling from heaven." (5:1-2)

"For we must all appear before the judgment seat of Christ, that each one may be recompensed for his deeds in the body, according to what he has done, whether good or bad." (5:10)

"Therefore, if any man is in Christ, he is a new creature; the old things passed away; behold, new things have come." (5:17)

"He [God the Father] *made Him* [Jesus the Christ] *who knew no sin to be sin on our behalf, that we might become the righteousness of God in Him." (5:21)*

In defending his apostleship, Paul tells us,

"Five times I received from the Jews thirty-nine lashes. Three times I was beaten with rods, once I was stoned, three times I was shipwrecked, a night and a day I have spent in the deep. I have been on frequent journeys, in dangers from rivers, dangers from robbers, dangers from my countrymen, dangers from the Gentiles, dangers in the city, dangers in the wilderness, dangers on the sea, dangers among false brethren. I have been in labor and hardship, through many sleepless nights, in hunger and thirst, often without food, in cold and exposure. Apart from such external things, there is the daily pressure upon me of concern for all the churches. Who is weak without my being weak? Who is led into sin without my intense concern?" (11:24-29)

"And because of the surpassing greatness of the revelations [given to Paul by Jesus], *for this reason, to keep me from exalting myself, there was given to me a thorn in the flesh, a messenger of Satan to buffet me – to keep me from exalting myself! Concerning this I entreated the Lord three times that it might depart from me. And He has said to me, 'My grace is sufficient for you, for power is perfected in weakness.'. . ."* (12:7-9)

✝

THE EPISTLE OF PAUL TO THE GALATIANS

Paul's letter to the people living in Galatia.

On Paul's third missionary journey from Tarsus to Antioch, he made an arch north to Galatia. He probably wrote this letter from Ephesus or Macedonia around 56 A.D.

This letter served to revolutionize Martin Luther's thinking and played a strategic part in the Reformation (centuries after the letter was written!), namely, that man is not justified by works, but rather by faith.

During Paul's time, Galatia was a Roman province in central Asia Minor (today's Turkey).

In this letter, Paul reiterates Christ's new covenant as being centered in love and faith in Jesus - rather than the Mosaic Law which deemed that circumcision was necessary for salvation.

"For you are all sons of God through faith in Christ Jesus." (3:26) "For in Christ Jesus neither circumcision nor uncircumcision means anything, but faith working through love." (5:6) "For the whole law is fulfilled. . . in the statement, 'YOU SHALL LOVE YOUR NEIGHBOR AS YOURSELF.'" (5:14)

"Now the deeds of the flesh are evident, which are: immorality, impurity, sensuality, idolatry, sorcery, enmities, strife, jealousy, outbursts of anger, disputes, dissensions, factions, envying, drunkenness, carousing, and things like these, of which I forewarn you just as I forewarned you that those who practice such things shall not inherit the kingdom of God." (5:19-21)

But the fruit of the Spirit is love, joy, peace, patience, kindness, goodness, faithfulness, gentleness, self-control, against such things there is no law. Now those who belong to Christ Jesus have crucified the flesh with its passions and desires." (5:22-24)

THE EPISTLE OF PAUL TO THE EPHESIANS

Written by Paul in prison in Rome, about 62 A.D.

This letter gives a panoramic view of God's redemptive purpose. Paul talks about the Body of Christ and how each of us is part of the whole.

The dominant theme of Ephesians is the church as the body of Christ, by which is meant that Christ functions in the world through the church, just as our human personalities function through our physical bodies.

Ephesus was an ancient Greek city in Turkey (Asia Minor).

"Blessed be the God and Father of our Lord Jesus Christ who has blessed us with every spiritual blessing in the heavenly places in Christ. . ." (1:3)

"In Him we have redemption through His blood, the forgiveness of our trespasses, according to the riches of His grace which He lavished upon us. . ." (1:7-8)

". . . having also believed, you were sealed in Him with the Holy Spirit of promise. . ." (1:13)

"And you were dead in your trespasses and sins in which you formerly walked. . ." (2:1)

". . .But God being rich in mercy because of His great love with which He loved us, even when we were dead in our transgressions, made us alive together with Christ (by grace you have been saved). . ." (2:4-5)

". . .For by grace you have been saved through faith; and that not of yourselves, it is the gift of God; . . ." (2:8)

✝

THE EPISTLE OF PAUL TO THE PHILIPPIANS

Paul's letter, probably written from prison in Rome or Ephesus, to the people living in Philippi, is a very "readable" letter – not at all difficult to follow!

This is the most personal of Paul's writings. Here the dominant note is joy! Paul is radiant, amid the storm and strife of life. This letter speaks of social interest regarding others as being more important than oneself.

Philippi was a city in eastern Macedonia and was famous as the gateway to Europe – a miniature Rome. It became the birthplace of European Christianity, following the conversion of Lydia the slave girl and the jailor *(Acts 16)*.

"If therefore there is any encouragement in Christ, if there is any consolation of love, if there is any fellowship of the spirit, if any affection and compassion, make my joy complete by being of the same mind, maintaining the same love, united in spirit, intent on one purpose. Do nothing from selfishness or empty conceit, but with humility of mind let each of you regard one another as more important than himself; do not merely look out for your own personal interests, but also for the interests of others. Have this attitude in yourselves which was also in Christ Jesus. . ." (2:1-5)

"And [Jesus] being found in appearance as a man, He humbled Himself by becoming obedient to the point of death, even death on a cross. Therefore also God highly exalted Him, and bestowed on Him the name which is above every name, that at the name of Jesus every knee should bow, of those who are in heaven, and on earth, and under the earth, and that every tongue should confess that Jesus Christ is Lord to the glory of God the Father." (2:8-11)

". . . work out your salvation with fear and trembling; for it is God who is at work in you. . .Do all things without grumbling. . . that you may prove yourselves to be blameless and innocent children of God above reproach in the midst of a crooked and perverse generation, among whom you appear as lights in the world." (2:12-15)

"Rejoice in the Lord always; again I say rejoice!. . .Be anxious for nothing, but in everything by prayer and supplication with thanksgiving let your requests be made known to God. And the peace of God which surpasses all comprehension, shall guard your hearts and your minds in Christ Jesus. Finally, brethren, whatever is true, whatever is honorable, whatever is right, whatever is pure, whatever is lovely, whatever is of good repute, if there is any excellence and if anything worthy of praise, let your mind dwell on these things." (4:4-8)

✝

THE EPISTLE OF PAUL TO THE COLOSSIANS

Written by Paul from prison. Luke is with him. Paul ends this letter with personal messages to various colleagues.

This letter is an exhortation on how to act. Some Christians were mixing Jewish practices and beliefs and were diluting the true Christian faith. Any teaching which detracts from the centrality of Christ, under the pretense of leading men to maturity and perfection, is a perversion of the faith.

Colossae was an ancient city located in Phrygia in Turkey (Asia Minor) and was populated by people of Greek and Hebrew origin.

". . .We have not ceased to pray for you and to ask that you may be filled with the knowledge of His will in all spiritual wisdom and understanding. . .for He delivered us from the dominion of darkness, and transferred us to the kingdom of His beloved Son, in whom we have redemption, the forgiveness of sins. And He is the image of the invisible God, the first-born of all creation." (1:9-15)

"If then you have been raised up with Christ, keep seeking the things above, where Christ is, seated at the right hand of God. Set your mind on the things above, not on the things that are on earth. For you have died and your life is hidden with Christ in God. When Christ, who is our life, is revealed, then you also will be revealed with Him in glory. . .And so, as those who have been chosen of God, holy and beloved, put on a heart of compassion, kindness, humility, gentleness and patience; bearing with one another and forgiving each other. . .and beyond all these things put on love, which is the perfect bond of unity." (3:1-4, 12-14)

"And whatever you do in word or deed, do all in the name of the Lord Jesus, giving thanks through Him to God the Father." (3:17)
"Devote yourselves to prayer, keeping alert in it with an attitude of thanksgiving. . ." (4:2)

THE FIRST EPISTLE OF PAUL TO THE THESSALONIANS

Thessalonica was the capital of Greek Macedonia and was the second European church. In this letter, Paul lays bare his soul, comparing himself to a tender mother, a firm father and a homeless orphan.

This letter was written by Paul about 50 A.D. In it, he deals with Christ's Second Coming and the role of dead believers in that advent.

The modern city of Thessaloniki now sits atop the ancient (unexcavated) city of Thessalonica.

"For you yourselves know, brethren, that our coming to you was not in vain, but after we had already suffered and been mistreated in Philippi. . .we had the boldness in our God to speak to you the gospel of God amid much opposition. . . ." (2:1-2)

"But we proved to be gentle among you, as a nursing mother tenderly cares for her own children. Having thus a fond affection for you, we were well-pleased to import to you not only the gospel of God but also our own lives, because you had become very dear to us. . .just as you know how we were exhorting and encouraging and imploring each one of you as a father would his own children, so that you may walk in a manner worthy of the God who calls you into His own kingdom and glory." (2:7-8, 11-12)

"Rejoice always; pray without ceasing; in everything give thanks; for this is God's will for you in Christ Jesus. Do not quench the Spirit; do not despise prophetic utterances. But examine everything carefully; hold fast to that which is good; abstain from every form of evil. Now may the God of peace Himself sanctify you entirely; and may your spirit and soul and body be preserved complete, without blame at the coming of our Lord Jesus Christ." (5:16-23)

✝

THE SECOND EPISTLE OF PAUL TO THE THESSALONIANS

In this letter, Paul talks about the "lawless one" (the antichrist?).

Paul implores the Church at Thessalonica to remain faithful, to give thanks to God and to look forward to the Second Coming of Jesus.

"Let no one in any way deceive you, for it will not come [the coming of our Lord Jesus Christ] *unless the apostasy comes first, and the man of lawlessness is revealed, the son of destruction, who opposes and exalts himself above every so-called god or object of worship, so that he takes his seat in the temple of God, displaying himself as being God." (2:3-4)*

"For the mystery of lawlessness is already at work. . .And then that lawless one will be revealed whom the Lord will slay with the breath of His mouth and bring to an end by the appearance of His coming, that is, the one whose coming is in accord with the activity of Satan, with all power and signs and false wonders. . .And for this reason God will send upon them a deluding influence so that they might believe what is false, in order that they all may be judged who did not believe the truth, but took pleasure in wickedness. . ." (2:7-12)

"Finally, brethren, pray for us that the word of the Lord may spread rapidly and be glorified. . .and that we may be delivered from perverse and evil men; for not all have faith. But the Lord is faithful, and He will strengthen and protect you from the evil one." (3:1-3)

THE FIRST EPISTLE OF PAUL TO TIMOTHY

Paul's first letter to Timothy was written between 61 and 63 A.D. Although biblical scholars agree that Paul may not have written this letter, it has long been attributed to him.

It appears that Paul is writing a very personal letter to his son Timothy, instructing him on how to be a good leader to members of the church.

This letter – and Paul's letter to Titus – were written by Paul during travel and missionary work between Paul's two Roman imprisonments.

In this letter, Paul specifically addresses how men and women are to comport themselves and it is here that we see what could be described as Paul's male chauvinism, colored by the times in which he lived.

"It is a trustworthy statement deserving full acceptance, that Christ Jesus came into the world to save sinners, among whom I am foremost of all. And yet for this reason I found mercy, in order that in me as the foremost, Jesus Christ might demonstrate His perfect patience, as an example for those who would believe in Him for eternal life." (1:15-16)

". . .I urge that entreaties and prayers, petitions and thanksgivings, be made on behalf of all men, for kings and all who are in authority, order that we may lead a tranquil and quiet life in all godliness and dignity. This is good and acceptable in the sight of God our Savior., who desires all men to be saved and to come to the knowledge of the truth." (2:1-4)

"Likewise, I want women to adore themselves with proper clothing, modestly and discreetly, not with braided hair and gold or pearls or costly garments; but rather by means of good works, as befits women making a claim to godliness. Let a woman quietly receive instruction with entire submissiveness. But I do not allow a woman to teach or exercise authority over a man, but to remain quiet. . . with self-restraint." (2:9-15)

"But the Spirit explicitly says that in later times some will fall away from the faith, paying attention to deceitful spirits and doctrines of demons. . .for everything created by God is good, and nothing is to be rejected, if it is received with gratitude; for it is sanctified by means of the word of God and prayer." (4:1-5)

"Do not sharply rebuke an older man, but rather appeal to him as a father, to the younger men as brothers, the older women as mothers, and the younger women as sisters, in all purity. Honor widows who ae widows indeed. . .Now she who is a widow indeed, and who has been left alone has fixed her hope on God, and continues in entreaties and prayers night and day. But she who gives herself to wanton pleasure is dead even while she lives." (5:1-6)

"Let all who are under the yoke as slaves regard their own masters as worthy of all honor so that the name of God and our doctrine may not be spoken against. . .godliness actually is a means of great gain. . .For we have brought nothing into the world, so we cannot take anything out of it either." (6:1-7)

"For the love of money is a root of all sorts of evil, and some by longing for it have wandered away from the faith, and pierced themselves with many a pang." (6:10)

"Fight the good fight of faith. Take hold of the eternal life to which you were called. . ." (6:12)

"Instruct those who are rich in this present world not to be conceited or to fix their hope on the uncertainty of riches, but on God, who richly supplies us with all things to enjoy. Instruct them to do good, to be rich in good works, to be generous and ready to share, storing up for themselves the treasure of a good foundation for the future, so that they may take hold of that which is life indeed." (6:17-19)

THE SECOND EPISTLE OF PAUL TO TIMOTHY

> **This letter constitutes the last writings of Paul** before his death. As with the First Epistle of Paul to Timothy, although this letter has been attributed to Paul, biblical scholars agree that he probably did not write this letter.
>
> **Paul was in a Roman prison** and it is believed that he was suddenly martyred between A.D. 65 and 68.

Timothy and Titus are charged to:

*"Guard through the Holy Spirit who dwells in us,
the treasure which has been entrusted to you." (1:14)*

Knowing that his life is soon to end, Paul writes to his son, Timothy:

"For I am already being poured out as a drink offering, and the time of my departure has come. I have fought the good fight, I have finished the course, I have kept the faith; in the future there is laid up for me the crown of righteousness, which the Lord, the righteous Judge, will award to me on that day; and not only to me, but also to all who have loved His appearing." (4:6-8)

✝

THE EPISTLE OF PAUL TO TITUS

Titus was a Greek Christian and a companion of Paul's.

In his letter to Titus, Paul talks about grace (unmerited favor), which is seen as the great doctrine of salvation and is linked with good works.

As with the letters to Timothy, biblical scholars agree that Paul probably did not write this letter.

"He [God] saved us, not on the basis of deeds which we have done in righteousness, but according to His mercy, by the washing of regeneration and renewing by the Holy Spirit, whom He poured out upon us richly through Jesus Christ our Savior, that being justified by His grace we might be made heirs according to the hope of eternal life." (3:5-7)

✝

THE EPISTLE OF PAUL TO PHILEMON

Paul's letter to Philemon (a friend) was written in prison. It is a highly personal plea on behalf of Philemon's slave, Onesimus who had run away.

"For perhaps he [Onesimus]was for this reason parted from you for a while, that you should have him back forever, no longer as a slave, but more than a slave, a beloved brother, especially to me, but how much more to you, both in the flesh and in the Lord." (1:15-16)

✝

THE EPISTLE OF PAUL TO THE HEBREWS

Hebrews' author is unknown, but it has a Pauline flavor, suggesting that whoever wrote it had been instructed and influenced by the Apostle Paul.

This letter is meant to strengthen Jewish Christians in their new faith.

Because this letter doesn't mention the destruction of the temple in Jerusalem, (70 A.D.), it is thought that it was written either before 68 A.D. or after 80 A.D.

There are two main ideas in Hebrews:

The first is expressed in the word "consider." Jesus is to be considered as the "Apostle and High Priest of our confession," and to be considered as the One who endured, as the ultimate example of the faith life. He is shown to be superior over angels, Moses, Aaron, Melchizedek and the Levitical system. In other words, He IS the Messiah. As the Priest of God and as the supreme sacrifice acceptable to God, Christ guarantees to every believer an entrance into the very presence of God, and an immediate hearing of petitions and requests.

The second idea in Hebrews is in the word "exhortation" (urging, encouraging). The whole purpose of this letter seems to be to inform, encourage and support the discouraged Jewish Christians through innumerable examples of Christ, as well as those who had successfully lived by faith.

In Hebrews, the superiority of Christ is argued, point by point, against the claims of Judaism. It is a strong message about faith. The priesthood of Christ is the most important concept to be grasped here. It is designed to encourage – to exhort.

"Take care, brethren, lest there should be in any one of you an evil, unbelieving heart, in falling away from the living God. But encourage one another day after day, as long as it is still called 'Today,' lest any one of you be hardened by the deceitfulness of sin." (3:12-13)

"For we have become partakers of Christ, if we hold fast the beginning of our assurance firm until the end. . ." (3:14)

"For the word of God is living and active and sharper than any two-edged sword and piercing as far as the division of soul and spirit. . .and there is no creature hidden from His sight, but all things are open and laid bare. . .For we do not have a high priest who cannot sympathize with our weaknesses, but one who has been tempted in all things as we are, yet without sin"(4:12-15)

"Let us therefore draw near with confidence to the throne of grace, that we may receive mercy and may find grace to help in time of need. . ."(4:16)

". . . He [Jesus Christ] is able to save forever those who draw near to God through Him, since He always lives to make intercession for them."(7:25)

"And inasmuch as it is appointed for men to die once and after this comes judgment, so Christ also, having been offered once to bear the sins of many, shall appear a second time for salvation without reference to sin, to those who eagerly await Him." (9:27-28)

In Chapter 10, pointed reference is made to the law which formed the covenant that God had made with Moses and the Israelites and contrasts it with God's new covenant through Jesus Christ:

"For the law, since it has only a shadow of the good things to come. . . can never by the same sacrifices year by year. . make perfect those who draw near. . .For it is impossible for the blood of bulls and goats to take away sins. . .then He [Jesus Christ] said, 'Behold, I have come to do Thy [God's] will. He takes away the first [covenant] in order to establish the second [covenant]. By this will we have been sanctified through the offering of the body of Jesus Christ once for all. . . but He, having offered one sacrifice for sins for all time, sat down at the right hand of God, waiting from that time onward until His enemies be made a footstool for His feet. . .And the Holy Spirit also bears witness to us, saying, 'This is the covenant that I will make with them after those days,' says the Lord: 'I will put My laws upon their heart, and upon their mind I will write them. . .And their sins and their lawless deeds I will remember no more.'" (10:1-17)

". . .and let us consider how to stimulate one another to love and good deeds. . . encouraging one another. . .For if we go on sinning willfully after receiving the knowledge of the truth, there no longer remains a sacrifice for sins, but a certain terrifying expectation of judgment, and the fury of a fire which will consume the adversaries. Anyone who has set aside the Law of Moses dies without mercy on the testimony of two or three witnesses. How much severer punishment do you think he will deserve who has trampled under foot the Son of God and has regarded as unclean the blood of the covenant by which he was sanctified, and has insulted the Spirit of grace?. . .It is a terrifying thing to fall into the hands of the living God." (10:24-31)

This letter goes on to talk about the importance of faith:

"Now faith is the assurance of things hoped for, the conviction of things not seen. For by it, the men of old gained approval. By faith we understand that the worlds were prepared by the word of God, so that what is seen was not made out of things which are visible. By faith Abel offered to God a better sacrifice than Cain. . .By faith Enoch was taken up so that he should not see death. . .And without faith, it is impossible to please Him, for he who comes to God must believe that He is, and that He is a rewarder of those who seek Him."(11:1-6)

Paul cites Noah's faith in following God's warning by building an ark; Abraham's faith by sojourning away from his home to receive an inheritance (and becoming the father of nations); Sarah's faith that God would give her the ability to become a mother. Paul continues offering examples of faith on the part of the Israelites such as Isaac, Jacob, Joseph, Moses, Gideon, Barak, Samson, Jephthah, David, Samuel and the prophets.

". . . who by faith conquered kingdoms, performed acts of righteousness, obtained promises, shut the mouths of lions, quenched the power of fire, escaped the edge of the sword, from weakness were made strong, became mighty in war, put foreign armies to flight. . . They were stoned, they were sawn in two, they were tempted, they were put to death with the sword; they went about in sheepskins, in goatskins, being destitute, afflicted, ill-treated. . .And all these, having gained approval through their faith, did not receive what was promised, because God had provided something better for us. . ." (11:33-40)

The importance of discipline:

"Therefore, since we have so great a cloud of witnesses surrounding us, let us also lay aside every encumbrance, and the sin which so easily entangles us, and let us run with endurance the race that is set before us, fixing our eyes on Jesus, the author and perfecter of faith, who for the joy set before Him endured the cross, despising the shame, and has sat down at the right hand of the throne of God." (12:1-2)

"You have not yet resisted to the point of shedding blood in your striving against sin;. . .for those whom the Lord loves He disciplines. . . It is for discipline that you endure. . .for what son is there whom his father does not discipline?. . .we had earthly fathers to discipline us, and we respected them; shall we not much rather be subject to the Father of spirits, and live?. . ." (12:4-9)

This letter then talks about love:

". . .Do not neglect to show hospitality to strangers, for by this some have entertained angels without knowing it. . .Let marriage be held in honor among all, and let the marriage bed be undefiled; for fornicators and adulterers God will judge. Let your character be free of the love of money, being content with what you have; for He Himself has said, 'I will never desert you, nor will I ever forsake you'; so that we confidently say, 'the Lord is my helper, I will not be afraid. . .'. . .Jesus Christ is the same yesterday and today, yes and forever. . . For here we do not have a lasting city, but we are seeking the city which is to come. . . And do not neglect doing good and sharing; for with such sacrifices God is pleased. . . Now the God of peace, who brought up from the dead the great Shepherd of the sheep through the blood of the eternal covenant, even Jesus our Lord, equip you in every good thing to do His will, working in us that which is pleasing in His sight through Jesus Christ, to whom be the glory forever and ever. Amen." (13:1-21)

THE EPISTLE OF JAMES

> **The traditional view** is that James is the brother of Jesus.
>
> **It is believed that this Epistle was written in the middle 40s** or early 60s (just before James' death).
>
> **James talks about the power** (for good or evil) of the tongue.
>
> **This epistle deals with good works** and talks about "faith" and "works," both being necessary for salvation.

"Consider it all joy, my brethren, when you encounter various trials, knowing that the testing of your faith produces endurance. And let endurance have its perfect result, that you may be perfect and complete, lacking in nothing. But if any of you lacks wisdom, let him ask of God, Who gives to all men generously and without reproach, and it will be given to him. But let him ask in faith without any doubting, for the one who doubts is like the surf of the sea driven and tossed by the wind." (1:2-6)

"What use is it, my brethren, if a man says he has faith, but he has no works? Can that faith save him? If a brother or sister is without clothing and in need of daily food, and one of you says to them, 'Go in peace, be warmed and be filled,' and yet you do not give them what is necessary for their body, what use is that? Even so faith, if it has no works, is dead, being by itself. . ." (2:14-16)

"For just as the body without the spirit is dead, so also faith without works is dead." (2:26)

"Is anyone among you suffering? Let him pray. Is anyone cheerful? Let him sing praises. Is anyone among you sick? Let him call for the elders of the church, and let them pray over him, anointing him with oil in the name of the Lord; and the prayer offered in faith will restore the one who is sick, and the Lord will raise him up, and if he has committed sins, they will be forgiven him. Therefore, confess your sins to one another, and pray for one another, so that you may be healed. The effective prayer of a righteous man can accomplish much." (5:13-16)

"My brethren, if any among you strays from the truth, and one turns him back, let him know that he who turns a sinner from the error of his way will save his soul from death and will cover a multitude of sins." (5:19-20)

✝

THE FIRST EPISTLE OF PETER

A truly beautiful and easy to read letter!

Written at a time of severe Christian persecution.

Probably written in Rome (referred to as Babylon) shortly before the martyrdom of Peter and Paul and probably in 63 or 64 A.D.

Peter wrote to the Christians in the five provinces of Asia Minor, both Jewish and Gentile.

The pre-Pentecost Peter shifted from loyalty to Christ to treacherous self-interest. *"Not the cross!"* had been his advice to his Lord.

But Pentecost and the Holy Spirit brought about a radical change in Peter. And now, at the time of these letters, Peter had already endured beatings and had faced death at Herod's hands. He now comes forward to encourage and strengthen his brethren in Asia to face the impending Calvary which he could see coming upon them.

"Blessed be the God and Father of our Lord Jesus Christ who according to His great mercy has caused us to be born again to a living hope through the resurrection of Jesus Christ from the dead." (1:3)

". . . for you have been born again not of seed which is perishable but imperishable, that is, through the living and abiding word of God." (1:23)

"For Christ also died for sins once for all, the just for the unjust, in order that He might bring us to God, having been put to death in the flesh, but made alive in the spirit." (3:18)

THE SECOND EPISTLE OF PETER

Written by Peter probably in Rome about 66 A.D., also at a time of severe Christian persecution.

Peter's second letter warns against false teachers (Gnostic heresy). He urges a growth in Christian virtues and staying prepared for Christ's coming . .

Peter rails against antinomianism, the heresy that a Christian does not have to be moral.

Simon Peter states that he was an eyewitness of the transfiguration of Christ:

> *"For we did not follow cleverly devised tales when we made known to you the power and coming of our Lord Jesus Christ, but we were eyewitnesses of His majesty, for when He received honor and glory from God the Father, such an utterance as this was made to Him by the Majestic Glory, 'This is My beloved Son with whom I am well-pleased' - and we ourselves heard this utterance made from heaven when we were with Him on the holy mountain." (1: 16-18)*

Peter warns of false prophets:

> *"But false prophets also arose among the people, just as there will also be false teachers among you, who will secretly introduce destructive heresies, even denying the Master who bought them, bringing swift destruction upon themselves" (2:1)*

> *". . .in the last days mockers will come with their mocking, following after their own lusts, and saying, 'Where is the promise of His coming?. . .For when they maintain this, it escapes their notice that by the word of God the heavens existed long ago and the earth was formed out of water. . .But the present heavens and earth by His word are being reserved for fire, kept for the day of judgment and destruction of ungodly men. But do not let this one fact escape your notice, beloved, that with the Lord one day is as a thousand years, and a thousand years as one day." (3:3-8)*

287.

THE FIRST EPISTLE OF JOHN

Known as the "apostle of love," the word "intense" might best describe John.

This epistle was probably written about 90 A.D.

All three of John's epistles were written from the city of Ephesus.

John was the brother of James and son of Zebedee (the fisherman), and was sometimes also identified as John the Elder.

John's family was a fairly well-to-do, upper class family, for they had servants and John's mother helped with the financial support of Christ.

John had been thoroughly trained in the Jewish religion at home. He was a stern man, intolerant of heresy.

John introduces the Incarnate Word:

"What was from the beginning, what we have heard, what we have seen with our eyes, what we beheld and our hands handled, concerning the Word of Life – and the life was manifested, and we have seen and bear witness and proclaim to you the eternal life, which was with the Father and was manifested to us – what we have seen and heard we proclaim to you also, that you also may have fellowship with us; and indeed our fellowship is with the Father, and with His Son Jesus Christ." (1:1-3)

"And this is the message we have heard from Him and announce to you, that God is light and in Him there is no darkness at all." (1:5)

"If we say that we have no sin, we are deceiving ourselves, and the truth is not in us. If we confess our sins, He is faithful and righteous to forgive us our sins and to cleanse us from all unrighteousness. If we say we have not sinned, we make Him a liar, and His word is not in us." (1:8-10)

"My little children, I am writing these things to you that you may not sin. And if anyone sins, we have an Advocate with the Father, Jesus Christ the righteous; and He Himself is the propitiation for our sins; and not for ours only, but also for those of the whole world. And by this we know that we have come to know Him, if we keep His commandments." (2:1-3)

"The one who says, 'I have come to know Him' and does not keep His commandments, is a liar, and the truth is not in him; but whoever keeps His word, in him the love of God has truly been perfected. By this we know that we are in Him: the one who says he abides in Him ought himself to walk in the same manner as He walked." (2:4-6)

"Do not love the world, nor the things in the world. If anyone loves the world, the love of the Father is not in him. For all that is in the world, the lust of the flesh and the lust of the eyes and the boastful pride of life, is not from the Father, but is from the world. And the world is passing away, and also its lusts; but the one who does the will of God abides forever." (2:15 -17)

"Beloved, let us love one another, for love is from God; and everyone who loves is born of God and knows God. The one who does not love, does not know God, for God is love." (4:7-8)

"Whoever believes that Jesus is the Christ is born of God; and whoever loves the Father loves the child born of Him." (5-1)

". . .And the witness is this, that God has given us eternal life, and this life is in His Son. He who has the Son has the life; he who does not have the Son of God does not have the life." (5:11-12)

✝

THE SECOND EPISTLE OF JOHN

> **The tenderness of this letter** stamps it as a personal communication.
>
> **This letter reiterates** that those who do not acknowledge Jesus Christ as the Son of God are the antichrists.

"For many deceivers have gone out into the world, those who do not acknowledge Jesus Christ as coming in the flesh. This is the deceiver and the antichrist." (1:7)

THE THIRD EPISTLE OF JOHN

> **This letter was written to Gaius** who was from Derbe (an ancient city in today's Turkey) and who was a traveling companion of Paul. He had hosted Paul when Paul was in Corinth.

The theme of this epistle is:

"Beloved, do not imitate what is evil, but what is good. The one who does good is of God; the one who does evil has not seen God." (1:11)

THE EPISTLE OF JUDE

Jude is believed to be a brother of Jesus.

This letter was written in the latter half of the first century and warns against the heresy of Gnosticism (a belief that physical matter is evil and only the spirit is good). The derivation of the word is this: gnostic = knowledge. Agnostic, therefore, is the opposite of knowledge and means, "cannot or does not know."

Gnosticism gave rise to two results: 1) Antinomianism -- the belief that one is not obliged to obey the moral law, and 2) the belief that abuse of the body promotes spirituality. Both beliefs are opposed by scripture.

"For certain persons have crept in unnoticed, those who were long beforehand marked out for this condemnation, ungodly persons who turn the grace of our God into licentiousness and deny our only Maser and Lord, Jesus Christ." (1:4)

"And angels who did not keep their own domain, but abandoned their proper abode, He has kept in eternal bonds under darkness for the judgment of the great day." (1:6)

"But you, beloved, ought to remember the words that were spoken beforehand by the apostles of our Lord Jesus Christ. . .keep yourselves in the love of God, waiting anxiously for the mercy of our Lord Jesus Christ to eternal life. And have mercy on some, who are doubting; save others, snatching them out of the fire; and on some have mercy with fear, hating even the garment polluted by the flesh. Now to Him who is able to keep you from stumbling, and to make you stand in the presence of His glory blameless with great joy, to the only God our Savior, through Jesus Christ our Lord, be glory, majesty, dominion and authority, before all time and now and forever. Amen." (1:17-25)

THE REVELATION TO JOHN
(THE APOCALYPSE)

Revelation (the Apocalypse) is a book of prophesy.

Revelation was, at least in theory, written by the apostle John (positive proof is not available) in approximately the years 81 – 96 A.D. It was during this time period that John was exiled to the Island of Patmos.

The Book of Revelation begins with a letter written to each of the seven churches in the Roman Province of Asia Minor (Ephesus, Smyrna, Pergamum, Thyatira, Sardis, Philadelphia and Laodicea).

Following the letter to the seven churches, Revelation focuses on the second coming of Christ and the definitive establishment of God's Kingdom at the end of all time.

Although Revelation is difficult to comprehend, a writing technique of the day was to convey messages through metaphors or allegories. Much of the language, wordage and ways of referring to Jesus Christ ("Logos" or "The Lamb") are unique to John the Apostle. The term, "The Lamb of God" is also used by John in both Revelation and in his gospel, John 1:29.

Revelation particularly emphasizes the repeated and increasingly violent world-wide attempts, led by Satan, to oppose and prevent the execution of the declared intention of Christ to establish His kingly rule on earth.

Revelation makes clear that this conflict is certain to end in the complete overthrow of Satan and his evil forces, resulting in the establishment of the everlasting kingdom of Christ. This age-long conflict terminates in the final judgment at the "Great White Throne," the appearance of the new Jerusalem and the beginning of eternity.

While the central meaning of Revelation is not clear, there are four schools of thought:

1. **The Spiritual Scheme of Interpretation**: believes this book's purpose is to teach fundamental spiritual principles.

2. **The Preterist Scheme of Interpretation**: believes the book relates to events which took place in the Roman Empire during the author's time (first century).

3. **The Historicist Scheme of Interpretation**: believes this book sets forth particular events in world history which relate to the welfare of the church from the first century down to modern times.

4. **The Futurist Scheme of Interpretation**: insists that the visions of this book will be fulfilled toward the end – and at the end – of this age, and immediately preceding, accompanying and following the Second Advent of our Lord and Savior.

No matter which school of thought one follows, it is clear that Revelation is a book of predictive prophesy and that at least some of John's visions aren't meant to be taken literally.

John lived in the first century, a time of great persecution of Christians and the Christian churches. It may well be that the 2nd Scheme – the Preterist Scheme of Interpretation – is, at least, for part of the Book of Revelation, the most accurate interpretation.

NOTE: The following are excerpts from Revelation and do not include the bulk of John's prophesies.

"The Revelation of Jesus Christ, which God gave Him to show to His bondservants, the things which must shortly take place; and He sent and communicated it by His angel to His bond-servant, John. . .Blessed is he who reads and those who hear the words of the prophecy, and heed the things which are written in it; for the time is near. John to the seven churches that are in Asia: Grace to you and peace, from Him who is and who was and who is to come. . .and from Jesus Christ, the faithful witness, the first-born of the dead, and the ruler of the kings of the earth. To Him who loves us, and released us from our sins by His blood. . .Behold, He is coming with the Clouds and every eye will see Him, even those who pierced Him; and all the tribes of the earth will mourn over Him. Even so. Amen. 'I am the Alpha and the Omega,' says the Lord God, 'who is and who was and who is to come, the Almighty.'" (1:1-8)

John then states: *"I, John, your brother and fellow partaker in the tribulation and kingdom and perseverance which are in Jesus, was on the island called Patmos. . .I was in the Spirit on the Lord's day, and I heard behind me a loud voice like the sound of a trumpet, saying, 'Write in a book what you see, and send it to the seven churches. . .'" (1:9-11)*

In part, these are the messages to the seven churches in the Roman Province of Asia Minor:

"Message to Ephesus. . .
I know your deeds and your toil and perseverance, and that you cannot endure evil men. . .but I have this against you, that you have left your first love. Remember therefore from where you have fallen, and repent and do the deeds you did at first. . .To him who overcomes, I will grant to eat of the tree of life, which is in the Paradise of God." (2:1-7)

"Message to Smyrna. . .
I know your tribulation and your poverty. . .Do not fear what you are about to suffer. Behold, the devil is about to cast some of you into prison, that you may be tested. . .Be faithful until death, and I will give you the crown of life. . ."(2:8-10)

"Message to Pergamum. . .

I know where you dwell, where Satan's throne is;. . .I have a few things against you, because you have there some who hold the teaching of Balaam. . .to commit acts of immorality. . .Repent, therefore, or else I am coming against you quickly. . .To him who overcomes, to him I will give some of the hidden manna. . .and a new name. . ." (2:12-17)

"Message to Thyatira. . .

I know your deeds and your love and faith and service and perseverance. . .But I have this against you, that you tolerate the woman Jezebel. . .and she teaches and leads My bond-servants astray, so that they commit acts of immorality. . .And he who overcomes, and he who keeps My deeds until the end, to him I will give authority over the nations. . .He who has an ear, let him hear what the Spirit says to the churches." (2:18-29)

"Message to Sardis. . .

I know your deeds. . .Wake up and strengthen the things that remain, which were about to die; for I have not found your deeds completed in the sight of My God. . .you have a few people in Sardis who have not soiled their garments; and they will walk with Me in white; for they are worthy. He who overcomes shall thus be clothed in white garments, and I will not erase his name from the book of life, and I will confess his name before My Father and before His angels. He who has an ear, let him hear what the Spirit says to the churches.'"
(3:1-6)

"Message to Philadelphia. . .

I know your deeds. Behold, I have put before you an open door which no one can shut, because you have. . .kept My word and have not denied My name. . .Because you have kept the word of My perseverance, I also will keep you from the hour of testing, that hour which is about to come upon the whole world, to test those who dwell upon the earth. . .He who overcomes, I will make him a pillar in the temple of my God, and he will not go out from it anymore; and I will write upon him the name of My God and the name of the city of My God, the new Jerusalem, which comes down out of heaven from My god and My new name. . ." (3:1-13)

"Message to Laodicea. . .
I know your deeds, that you are neither cold nor hot; I would that
you were cold or hot. So because you are lukewarm, and neither
hot nor cold, I will spit you out of my mouth. . Those whom I love, I
reprove and discipline; be zealous therefore and repent. Behold, I
stand at the door and knock; if anyone hears My voice and opens
the door, I will come in to him, and will dine with him, and he with
Me. He who overcomes, I will grant to him to sit down with Me on
My throne, as I also overcame and sat down with My Father on His
throne."
(3:14-22)

Following the words which John's heavenly visitor gave him to write
to the seven churches, John wrote, *". . .I looked, and behold, a door*
standing open in heaven. . .Immediately I was in the spirit; and behold,
a throne was standing in heaven, and One sitting on the throne. . ."
(4:1-4)

John then describes many scenes shown to him: the end of the world,
the eventual overthrow of Satan and the judgment of all mankind.

"And I saw a great white throne and Him who sat upon it, from
whose presence earth and heaven fled away, and no place was
found for them. And I saw the dead, the great and the small,
standing before the throne, and books were opened; and another
book was opened, which is the book of life; and the dead were
judged from the things which were written in the books according to
their deeds. . .And the sea gave up the dead which were in it, and
death and Hades gave up the dead which were in them; and they
were judged, every one of them according to their deeds. And death
and Hades were thrown into the lake of fire. This is the second
death, the lake of fire. And if anyone's name was not found written
in the book of life, he was thrown into the lake of fire." (20:11-15)

John describes his vision of heaven –

"And I saw a new heaven and a new earth; for the first heaven and the first earth passed away, and there is no longer any sea. And I saw the holy city, new Jerusalem, coming down out of heaven from God, made ready as a bride adorned for her husband. And I heard a loud voice from the throne saying, 'Behold the tabernacle of God is among men, and He shall dwell among them; they shall be His people, and God Himself shall be among them, and He shall wipe every tear from their eyes; and there shall no longer be any death; there shall no longer be any mourning or crying, or pain; for the first things have passed away.' And He who sits on the throne said, 'Behold, I am making all things new.' And He said, 'Write, for these words are faithful and true.' And He said to me, 'It is done. I am the Alpha and the Omega, the beginning and the end. I will give to the one who thirsts from the spring of the water of life without cost. He who overcomes shall inherit these things, and I will be his God and he will be My son.'"(21:1-7)

John ends his revelation by saying :

"And he showed me a river of the water of life, clear as crystal, coming from the throne of God and of the Lamb, in the middle of its street. And on either side of the river was the tree of life, bearing twelve kinds of fruit, yielding its fruit every month; and the leaves of the tree were for the healing of the nations. And there shall no longer be any curse; and the throne of God and of the Lamb shall be in it, and His bond-servants shall serve Him; and they shall see His face, and His name shall be on their foreheads. And there shall no longer be any night; and they shall not have need of the light of a lamp nor the light of the sun, because the Lord God shall illumine them; and they shall reign forever and ever." (22: 1-5)

"Behold, I am coming quickly, and My reward is with Me, to render to every man according to what he has done. I am the Alpha and the Omega, the first and the last, the beginning and the end. . .I, Jesus, have sent My angel to testify to you these things for the churches. I am the root and the offspring of David; the bright morning star." (22:13-16)

"And the Spirit and the bride say, 'Come'. And let the one who hears say, 'Come.' And let the one who is thirsty come; let the one who wishes take the water of life without cost. I testify to everyone who hears the words of the prophesy of this book: if anyone adds to them, God shall add to him the plagues which are written in the book; and if anyone takes away from the words of the book of this prophesy, God shall take away his part from the tree of life and from the holy city, which are written in this book. He who testifies to these things says, 'Yes, I am coming quickly.' Amen. Come, Lord Jesus. The grace of the Lord Jesus be with all. Amen." (22: 17-21)

May this bible study summary –
and any other reading of the Word of God,
given to us in the Bible –
serve as a blessing for you -
strengthening and enlightening you
and bringing you closer
to our Savior and Lord, Jesus Christ.
Amen

RESOURCES

Efird, James M.
These Things are Written: An Introduction to the Religious Ideas of the Bible. John Knox Press. 1977.

Green, Michael
Who is This Jesus? Oliver Nelson Books, a division of Thomas Nelson, Inc., Publishers. 1990.

Heston, Charlton
Charlton Heston presents The Bible.
GT Publishing Corporation and Agememnon Films, 16 East 40th Street, New York, NY 10016. 1997.

Kerr, William F.
Kregel Bible Handbook: A full-color guide to every book of the bible. International Publishing, San Dimas, CA. 2000.

McBirnie, William Steuart, Ph.D.
The Search for the Twelve Apostles. 1973.

Metzger, Bruce M.
Breaking the Code – Understanding the Book of Revelation. Abingdon Press. 1993.

Reader's Digest Association, Inc.
After Jesus: The Triumph of Christianity. Pleasantville, New York/Montreal. 1992.

Reader's Digest Association, Inc.
The Bible Through the Ages. Pleasantville, NY/Montreal. 1996.

Roberts, Jenny
The Bible Then & Now. Chartwell Books, Inc., a division of Book Sales Inc., 114 Northfield Avenue, Edison, New Jersey 08837. 2001.

Roetzel, Calvin J.
The Letters of Paul: Conversations in Context. Second Edition. John Knox Press, Atlanta, GA 30365. 1975 and 1982.

The Thorncrown Journal.
> *Who were the Romans?* The Thorncrown Journal, a publication of Thorncrown Chapel. http://www.thorncrown journal.com/time of christ/romans.html 5/28/2013.

Thomas Nelson, Inc.
> *The Open Bible.* Based on the KJV New American Standard Bible) 1978.

Thomas Nelson Publishers.
> *The Promise. Contemporary English Version. God's Word in Your Words.* 1995.

Library of Congress © 2016 Patricia J. Setter
ISBN-13: 978-1533217912
Title I.D.: 6267592

CPSIA information can be obtained
at www.ICGtesting.com
Printed in the USA
BVOW10s1808070816

458242BV00010B/121/P